Verbivoracious Press

Festschrift Volume One

Christine

BROOKE-ROSE

Forthcoming reprint titles:

A Grammar of Metaphor
The Languages of Love
The Sycamore Tree
Dear Deceit
The Middlemen
Go When You See The Green Man Walking

by Christine Brooke-Rose

Forthcoming titles:

The Letters of Christine Brooke-Rose
Poems & Other Paraphernalia

edited by G. N. Forester & M. J. Nicholls

The Logαλφαgeis of kLeubʰː /laːʃ/; /lʌv/

by Chretine Broke-Prose

other Verbivoracious titles @

www.verbivoraciouspress.org

Verbivoracious Press

Festschrift Volume One

edited by G. N. Forester & M. J. Nicholls

Christine

BROOKE-ROSE

*have you ever tried to do
something very difficult
for a very long time,
unnoticed?*

Verbivoracious Press

Glentrees, 13 Mt Sinai Lane, Singapore

First published in Great Britain & Singapore

by Verbivoracious Press

www.verbivoraciouspress.org

ISBN: **978-981-07-9407-1**

Printed and bound in Great Britain & Singapore

Contents

Contents

Contents

Acknowledgements

Essays, articles, short stories, and poetry written by Christine Brooke-Rose are gratefully reproduced with the kind permission of the Estate and accessed via the Christine Brooke-Rose Archive in the Harry Ransom Center, University of Texas at Austin, made possible by the generosity of Frances Winkler, who spent many hours carefully perusing the Archive, and to whom we are forever grateful.

Gold was first published by The Hand and Flower Press, Aldington, 1954.

"Illiterations" and "Ill Wit and Good Humour" also appear in *Stories, theories, and things*, Cambridge, Cambridge University Press, 1991. Both essays are based on reworking the original "Ill Wit and Good Humour: Women's Comedy and the Canon", *Comparative Criticism: Volume 10, Comedy, Irony, Parody*, edited by E. S. Schaffer, Cambridge, Cambridge University Press, 1989.

"Troglodyte" and "On Terms" originally appeared in the collection of short stories *Go When You See The Green Man Walking*, London, M. Joseph, 1970.

"Ganging Up" and "Le Pop" originally appeared in the British magazine *The Spectator*, 1976.

Once Upon a Time first published in *Truth*, 1956.

Aubade and *Heaven's Hospital* were first published in the *The Transatlantic Review*, No. 13 (Summer 1963).

"A Conversation with Christine Brooke-Rose", Maria del Sapio Garbero, first appeared in *British Postmodern Fiction*, edited by Theo D'haen and Hans Bertens, Amsterdam—Atlanta, Rodopi, 1993, and is gratefully reproduced with the kind permission of the publishers.

Preface

Editors

A festschrift, as defined by Merriam-Webster online, is "a volume of writings by different authors presented as a tribute or memorial especially to a scholar." The writer fêted in the Verbivoracious flagship festschrift was a scholar who also happened to be one of the most innovative writers of the 20th century (and certainly for the first decade of the 21st century). This collection contains essays, homages, and stories inspired by the work of Christine Brooke-Rose, arranged in the publication order of her books, commencing with the poem *Gold* (reprinted for the first time here), and concluding with *Life, End of.* The writers featured are an eclectic mix[1] of critics, storytellers, ardent readers, academics, pasticheurs, homageurs, and people coerced to read the works of Christine Brooke-Rose for the sole purpose of contributing to this festschrift. Those not yet acquainted with her work should find sufficient entry points to her varying, often complex, sometimes cryptic, always playful, methods. Unswerving converts to her constraints will find many rapturous moments in the numerous flawlessly executed fictions included.

---

1   As a result of which, readers will note a variety of citation styles, syntax, spellings etc, reflecting the linguistic diversity and backgrounds of the contributors.

Foreword: A Farewell to Tess' Perfect Gardens

Jean-Michel Rabaté

On March 21st 2012, the English novelist Christine Brooke-Rose passed away in Cabrières d'Avignon. The cause of death was a degenerative disease of the nervous system, which had left her blind and paralyzed for the last years of her life. Ever the wry observer and playful novelist, she had documented unflinchingly—as long as she could—the progression of her increasingly crippling disease in her last novel, *Life, End of* (2006). This farewell to life and its diminished pleasures is devoid of sentimentality. What matters to the ailing woman is the difficulty of relating to "other people," soon called O. P. for short, all those who cannot imagine the hurdles that every day activities bring to an ailing body. However, true friends remained, as well as the small but crucial comforts provided by music, news and culture on the radio.

Christine Brooke-Rose had written her own obituary in advance with this moving memoir about old age. Born January 16th 1923 in Geneva in a trilingual family to an English father and a Swiss-American mother, she moved at a young age to Brussels and then to London. During the war, her knowledge of German helped as she worked at Bletchley Park, deciphering coded German army messages for Enigma. There she met her first husband, but the marriage soon dissolved. Immediately after, she went to Oxford, specializing in Old English at Somerville College where she earned a B. A. in 1949. Then she married the distinguished Polish poet Jerzy Peterkiewicz, who died in 2007. Her first novels were set in London where they lived: *The Languages of Love* (1957), *The Sycamore Tree* (1958) and *The Dear Deceit* (1960). She would also regularly publish critical works, beginning with the acclaimed *A Grammar of Metaphor* (1958).

A kidney operation that proved almost fatal, and strains in her marriage, led her to move to Paris and take more risks in her writing, soon identifying with the French *nouveau roman*. For a while she was compared to Alain Robbe-Grillet whom she had translated and promoted. Her novels became more and more experimental with *Out* (1964), *Such* (1966) and *Between* (1968). *Between*, for instance, was written with a constraint: the omission of the verb "to be." In fact, more than the *nouveau roman*, her true affiliation would have been with the international Oulipo group, but she had arrived at the same rules and practices independently and did not like the idea of belonging to a school. She had only praise for Georges Perec, who had written a whole novel without using the letter "e", she admired Italo Calvino, another member of the international group, and felt proud that they had wanted to include her in their association.

Her constraints either were missed or failed to appeal to readers or critics. In *Invisible Author*, she complains bitterly that she has been doing difficult things all along without anyone noticing them. In fact, the difficulties that she chose to overcome were devices allowing her to progress. She could never have written an autobiography, as she did with the spectacular *Remake* (1996), had she not found it more interesting to write about her life without using the first person. She is called either "Tess" as a young woman or the "old lady" for the later years. It is impressive to see how smoothly and effortlessly the narrative flows. Yet as soon as critics discovered those devices, they gave her the unenviable label of being an "experimental" writer. Whatever the term may mean, Christine never repeated a technique from one book to the next. Her constraints were ad hoc inventions; thus she wrote a novel without any indicative tenses, mostly in the future or conditional (*Amalgamemnon*, 1984). She composed a story musically, as a series of dialogues (with some monologues as well) between ten homeless persons, each speaking a different variety of Cockney, and sharing various shelters in *Next* (1998). This new lingo was ushering, according to her, an "Estuarian" English located around London that we will use twenty years from now. Yet, when I pointed out that this was not far from what Joyce had accomplished with *Finnegans Wake*, she would assert clearly that she had never been influenced by him and above all did not like him.

The major shift in Christine's career had occurred when she moved to Paris and started teaching at a truly "experimental" university (that was its official name), Paris-VIII at Vincennes. Having been invited to join the English faculty by Hélène Cixous, it was there that from 1969 to 1988 she taught English literature, narratology and literary theory to the leftist students of this unique university. In those heady days, theory and narrative crossed lines constantly. What she lost in visibility, she gained in productivity. She was oblivious to the complicated internecine wars between political factions and institutional struggles. She never guessed that the colleagues of her initial department in English literature saw as a betrayal the fact that she had joined the larger Anglo-American studies department, whereas she had accepted their promptings in order to teach where there were more students.

This is where I first met her, in a crowded and smoky graduate seminar at Vincennes, as it was still located near the notorious woods East of Paris. We soon discovered a common fascination for the poetry of Ezra Pound. Her *ZBC of Ezra Pound* was published in 1971, a plucky book in which she used her knowledge of Anglo-Saxon poetry to analyze the Cantos in her inimitable lively manner. At the time, she was working on her most "scientific" approach to poetry, the 1976 *Structural Analysis of Pound's Usura Canto: Jakobson's Method Extended and Applied to Free Verse*, sections of which I heard her teach in her seminar. Throughout the seventies, I was fortunate to have Christine's help as I was completing my dissertation on James Joyce, Ezra Pound and Hermann Broch, quite a ponderous thing since at the time we were required to write at least one thousand pages. In our interactions, her pedagogical qualities shone; she would annotate copiously my Pound chapters, add detailed comments that would run to pages, even though she was in fact not officially on my committee.

It was thanks to Christine that I was introduced to Pound's daughter, Mary de Rachewiltz, who remained her friend throughout. In the Summer of 1982 or 1983, I visited Christine who was staying with Mary. I was then preparing a book on Pound. I went all the way to Tirol, reaching the castle of Brunnenburg where her room was reserved. During an elaborate dinner in which both Boris de Rachewiltz and Olga Rudge were present, the conversation waxed nostalgic, touching on delicate political sentiments; someone said that the days of Mussolini were not so bad after all, since there was more order in the streets of Italy and no unemployment . . . To derail this unpleasant turn in the conversation, all of a sudden Christine asked me pointedly: "Jean-Michel, where was it that you published that piece of yours on Pound's fascism and ideology?" I had to blurt out that it was in a small review called *Marxist-Leninist Papers* . . . A hush of consternation followed. Someone spilled gravy on my trousers. I had to go to the bathroom to clean them—when I came back, the conversation had rolled on to innocuous matters and Christine gave me an arch smile.

At the time, French students considered Christine a gifted and innovative theoretician of literature and would read avidly her essays on the fantastic, on Henry James and on experimental fiction, but did not know her fiction. Her novels, regularly published by Carcanet in England (her *Omnibus* with *Out, Such, Between* and *Thru,* reissued in 2006, is a compact and enduring introduction to her mature work) were not read or translated in France. French critics, whom she knew, were often put off by her first-hand knowledge of literature, philosophy and politics, and her hatred of cant. I had arranged a meeting with French poet Denis Roche, a bold avant-gardist author connected with the *tout Paris* of small magazines and big presses. Denis Roche had translated Pound's *Pisan Cantos,* although he did not know much English. I could not prevent Christine from quoting to him his most funny howlers. Then she explained how much she loved the work of another Roche, Maurice Roche, with whom she had confused him at first. Denis Roche, who would have been in a position to help her to be better known in France, refused to have anything to do with her. Thus, her true following remained in England and in the United States. It took another decade before younger scholars coming from all over the world started writing dissertations about her. Today, those who can fly to Texas are allowed to access her extensive archive kept at the Harry Ransom Center of the University of Texas at Austin.

The scope of her books broadened and included astute remarks about international politics and culture. In *Textermination* (1991), a yearly convention recalling the Modern Language Association conference includes recognizable characters from Jane Austen, Flaubert, Tolstoy and Rushdie who "pray for being," by invoking the Reader, their Almighty God: the reader can indeed decide whether they will live or die by reading them or not. The construction splices together different texts, times, and values in a universal meeting point that would be fiction. Literature and criticism need each other, she argues in this witty *tour de force*. She refused to abandon her fierce and uncompromising critical intelligence in efforts to be creative and spontaneous.

Christine Brooke-Rose retired from teaching in 1988 to settle in the Lubéron, first in Les Maquignons, in a superb country-house with a swimming pool, then when she could not drive any longer, in the small village of Cabrières d'Avignon. At first, she was part of the small group of British literary expatriates based in the village of Ménèrbes, where she would dine with Kingsley Amis and his friends. There had been a brief third marriage to a cousin, Claude Brooke, with whom she started writing novels with scientific themes. *Xorandor* from 1986 and *Subscript* from 1999 develop these concerns. Meanwhile, her life as an invalid was haunted by the voices of the past, including that of her deceased sister who continued to send her daily messages.

I was privy to one of these postmortem transmissions. I had come to visit her for the day, and she was thinking of adding a last chapter to *Life, End of*. This sounded like a good idea, except that she was blind and unable to move much from her reclining chair. She also thought that her day nurse had hidden her notepad. But it was there lying on a desk nearby. I looked for a blank page. There were a few illegible jottings on the first page, I turned it. The second page was blank. I put it in her hand and gave her a pen. She had no sooner taken the pad than she said: "I can't write. It's all covered with writing." I pored over the surface, there was nothing to discern. I urged her to write without fear. Then, to my surprise, following the invisible words with her finger, Christine started reading a letter that took up the whole sheet. It was a rambling letter full of sarcasm and reproach, and she said it was written by her sister, who had been dead for ten years. Again, I said that I could see nothing. I objected: Wasn't she blind? How could she see the words? In a last-ditch effort to convince me, she stated: "I could not have invented this. This is not my style at all. It's my sister's hand and her unique way of writing. I could never invent that . . ." Nonplussed, I turned the page, and gave her a new blank sheet. This time, as she was to write, she stopped and described a baroque drawing with a lush landscape and yellow tiger, like an Indian woodcut. As we went through the pad, each page was either decorated with vividly colored pictures or covered with texts, always other people's writings. What was amazing was the fact that Christine could read them as if they had been printed in her brain. She was always a writer to the end, even when her exhausted neurons made her hallucinate memories of old letters and glimpsed images.

It was as if her plight had been scripted in advance by her superb ghost story 'The Foot', an early text from the sixties, in which a voice haunts a young woman who has lost her foot in an accident. The voice of the phantom limb attempts to inflict pain sadistically while being aware that it will be erased in the end when the woman begins to write about her haunting.[1] Indeed, pain Christine had known, and yet, somehow, had overcome it. Writing would continue there, in spite of the blindness and the paralysis. Christine had had time to prepare for death, which she accepted stoically, finding comfort in language games and puns in several languages. Whenever she expressed that she was tempted to put an end to her dire condition and I should assist her, we were saved by mutual laughter at the thought that I was her literary "executor"—each time, I had to add: "Remember, only *literary* . . ." Thus, in *Life, End of,* a little American girl who visits her (it was my daughter Sofia) happens to be trilingual: she is called "Rosetta" because of the famous stone. Christine had the time, an infinite time to reminisce about her past, and let all the echoes from universal litera-

---

1 See the beautiful analysis of this story by Karen Lawrence in *Techniques for Living: Fiction and Theory in the work of Christine Brooke-Rose*, Columbus, Ohio State University Press, 2010, pp. 8-17.

ture come back to her. The Montaigne quote placed as an epigraph to *Invisible Author* illustrates well her attitude: "I want Death to find me retired in the country and planting my cabbages, not worrying about it, even less about my imperfect garden."

Jean-Michel Rabaté

Introduction

Editors

Christine Brooke-Rose was born in Geneva to an English father and Swiss-American mother in 1923. She attended primary school in Belgium and secondary school in England, and worked in London as a clerk before the Second World War, during which she served in the British Women's Auxiliary Air Force at Liverpool and at the Bletchley Park intelligence centre as a translator of intercepted German messages.

Under the post-War scheme of grants for war-time service, she received a scholarship to study her Bachelor of Arts (English), awarded 1949, and Master of Arts (English) awarded 1953, at Oxford, and subsequently pursued doctoral research on medieval poetry at University College, London. Following graduation in 1954 and unable to find a teaching post, she worked as a reviewer (the anonymous expert on Pound for the *Times Literary Supplement*) and journalist in London, publishing poems (her first published poem was *Gold*, in 1954, by the Hand and Flower Press), as well as her first critical work based on her doctoral thesis *A Grammar of Metaphor* (1958). During the illness of her second husband, she wrote her first novel *The Languages of Love* (1957), meeting with critical success, and produced three more light satires, *The Sycamore Tree* (1958), *The Dear* Deceit (1960), and *The Middlemen* (1961), earning herself a place amongst the "formidable trio" including Muriel Spark and Iris Murdoch. Dissatisfied with the realist mode and already aware of literary developments in France, the long and painful recuperation from losing a kidney provided the opportunity to write in less conventional directions.

With the publication of *Out* (1964) and its inversion of ethnic politics, as well as the speakerless present tense employed so successfully by Robbe-Grillet in his *La jalousie* (1957) and *Dans le labyrinthe* (1959),

Christine Brooke-Rose established herself as a writer of anti-Realist fiction, developing her own ideas further in *Such* (1966), focused on a paranormal experience described using the language of astrophysics as a form of poetical prose, *Between* (1968) excluding the verb *be* and infusing the text with phrases repeated in different languages, just as a frequent traveller is confronted with unknown languages in known situations, and *Thru* (1975), a fiction about narrative and a narrative about fiction, typographically riotous and unapologetically exuberant. *Amalgamemnon* (1984) was written without constative sentences, using only future and conditional tenses, and conflating the imagined voices of several characters in the mind of the protagonist on the evening before the day of a significant event. *Xorandor* (1986) is most often represented as a science fiction novel: the narrative, about the discovery of a silicon-based life-form and its impact on humanity, is related as dialogue by intellectually acute twins Zab and Jip. *Verbivore* (1990) takes up the story years later and introduces the voices of a number of other characters, further complicating the reading with the lack of parentheticals and dialogue tags. *Textermination* (1991), is, in the words of David Seed, who interviewed Brooke-Rose in January 1992 following her visit to Liverpool University, "a comic fantasia on the role of the reader in constructing the character."

Following a period of inactivity, *Remake* (1996) was her first 'bifografy', autobiographical fiction *sans* pronouns; *Next* appeared in 1998 minus the verb *have*, a murder mystery centred on London's homeless, in which the name of each character corresponds to a letter of the Anglo alphabet and with some typographical twisting of the text and development of various dialects (the highlight of the story, if the thematic content is put aside); *Subscript* in 1999 showed the evolution of consciousness and language from prehistoric origins to the later stages of the Pleistocene period, and her final fiction, *Life, End of* (2006), another bifografy, this time focused on the finitude of the body being circumscribed by the infinitude of the mind, and a return to the speakerless narrative, discourse on fiction, and multilingual plays on words.

Her interest in the poetry of Ezra Pound resulted in *A ZBC of Ezra*

Pound (1971) and *A Structural Analysis of Pound's Usura Canto* (1976), the latter considering the nature of negatives. Later critical works amply demonstrate her breadth of reading and willingness to embrace different categories of writing, narrative theory, and analysis, such as *A Rhetoric of the Unreal* (1981) and *Stories, theories, and things* (1991). Lastly, although hints were always given in interviews and essays published in various European and American journals, her *Invisible Author: Last Essays* (2002), provides an invaluable and definitive insight to her development as a literary critic and theorist as well as writer of exploratory fiction.

A number of pieces in the Festschrift deal with the content considerations of Christine Brooke-Rose, held in no less esteem than form, but always subservient to it; some also implement her constraints, a few are mentioned here. The reader preferring to discover these without recourse to a cipher should skip the following until the last paragraph.

Igo Wodan's *Versions* excises the verbs *be* and *have*, uses present tense and modal auxiliaries to describe what may be one or multiple situations from possibly one or multiple different non-gendered perspectives, in an anti-mimetic, metadiegetic first-person narrative wholly devoid of parentheticals. Readers familiar with Gabriel Josipovici's work will note a similarity of style.

Nadine Mainard's *Le Diner* extrapolates a missing scene from *The Languages of Love* using the progressive present tense, similarly lacking the verb *be* except in dialogue. In honour of Christine Brooke-Rose's concern with and appreciation for language, its metamorphosis and its Fehl/Entwicklung, Gottfried Gottlieb's *Mein gott!* constrains by substituting the verb *get* for active verbs, and only allowing the auxiliary forms of *be* and *have*.

Christine Brooke-Rose retired to the south of France in 1988, continuing to write fiction and literary criticism. She died on March 21st, 2012. Fittingly, the Festschrift borrows that date for its launch, preempting what is hoped will be a well-deserved revival of interest in her work, from not only readers, but critics and writers as well.

Gold

Christine Brooke-Rose

Note on the Poem

Gold is an attempt to fuse a mediaeval form with a modern subject, not for mere ingenuity, but because this seemed the only way of visualising a scene barely imaginable in the West.

The medieval dream-vision, usually opening with questions about the cause and validity of different types of dreams, could also be combined with the debate-poem, since the "oraculum," in which some important personification, goddess or departed soul utters certain evident truths, was considered to be the most valuable and divinely inspired form of dream.

One of the finest poems in the English language, the fourteenth century *Pearl*, not only combines the dream-vision and the debate-poem to discuss the problem of Salvation at the highest level, but also becomes an elegy of the poet for his lost little daughter, who appears to him in the vision. *Gold* is also an elegy, but for many million souls, still half-alive.

Pearl is unique in combining the native alliterative line (less strict, however, than Old English) with rhyme, which had come from France, also using a complex stanza pattern with a refrain being echoed at the beginning of each next stanza. The revival of this repetitive technique, together with an attempt to emulate its highly metaphoric language, seemed appropriate to express both the magical element of the vision and the helpless continuity of the tragedy seen. The only formal differ-ence is one of length: *Pearl* has 101 stanzas (1,212 lines), *Gold* has 50 (600 lines), a concession to the modern reader's impatience and lack of leis-ure. Archaism in language, however, has been avoided as pointless.

The symbolism of *Pearl* has been much discussed, for the word changes its meaning throughout, but in general it may be said that *Pearl*, the girl in the vision, represents purity and grace (which is often called a pearl), and that the daughter's name may well have been Margaret or Marguerite (=Pearl). She is also referred to as "that flower," "that gem." The opening stanza of *Pearl* is adapted from the lapidaries, on the appearance and symbolic meaning of the pearl. Similarly the opening stanza of *Gold* is about the alchemical process, which is taken as a symbol instead of the pearl: alchemical gold, never attained, and for which base metals (mankind) are tortured and processed for the sake of a false ideal, in the belief that any substance (or "body") is really its opposite if divested of all the elements which make it what it is.

The conjuring up of the Dark Side of the Moon as the scene of the vision is inspired from the book of that name (anon.,[1] Faber & Faber, 1947), the title of which is itself taken from a description by Arthur Koestler. The Requiem Mass at the end of the poem follows the liturgical instructions: black vestments, purple seats, no organ accompaniment, no incense, no kiss of peace and no blessing. The Latin words are from the Introit. The message beginning "Sleepers, behold . . . " (Stanza 43) echoes the opening of the Gospel appointed for that Mass. The apparition referred to in stanza 44 is that of Our Lady of Fatima in 1917, with her extraordinary message to three peasant children who had never heard of Russia.

Christine Brooke-Rose (1954)

---

1 Editors' Note: The original was written by Zoe Zajdlerowa.

I

1.   Gold as god for gravemen's joy,
Transmuted in mask from metals base.
In seasons secret Saturn's alloy
Elides to elixir at endless pace.
Quicksilver qualmed in cryptic ploy,
Putrefied, punished and purged of grace,
Dissolved, distilled in dim carboy,
Out of the Orient's ageless face
Hidden and housed in hermetic space.
From black to blue in burning cold,
Yang to Yin through a yellowing chase
From black to blue and from blue to gold.

2.   Gold means gore in a gust of dreams
Twining the hall towers of night.
Is it insomnia that eye-green gleams
Or alien oracles in orange blight?
Somnolent salves of celestial beams,
Signs and secrets swifter than light,
Messages, marvels with morse-red seams . . .
How do we hear the hells so bright?
From blood, from bile, from bibulous plight?
Dare we divine that in dreams untold,
Treasure by torment is put to flight
With black from blue for blue to gold?

3.   On a golden globe in the glare of June,
I sank to sleep in a stack of hay
Whose waft had woven a white cocoon
Across my consciousness of day.
My spirit slipped from the summer noon,

Meandered like a moth astray:
I dreamt of the dark side of the moon,
Immense, immeasurable and grey.
Extinct eruptions in albs of clay
Like fallen angels fathomless old,
Primordial in penumbra lay
Black and blue and bilious gold.

4.   Golden green the gangrene dry
On the limbs of land and lightlorn rock.
But the frozen flatlands flinched awry
White and weird in the wire-wet shock
Of virgin forests furlong-high
That halted the heaven's hollow knock.
Waterways wider than wielded cry,
Strapped in straitcoats of icy block,
From the furthest flange of this frigid world
Whirled a waif like a weather-cock
In black and blue and brassy gold.

5.   From a golden groove in chrysalis
Vaned this vision with vagrant stare,
Each of her eyes an iron abyss.
A copper crown eclipsed her hair
Of tin and tungsten tinged amiss,
Her linen of lead in lustreless blare,
Her feet and face of verdigris.
Glabrous her gown in gallium flare
Edged with an orpimental glare.
She moved in mute metallic din,
Hailed me with hand as heavy as care,
This lady of lead, this child of tin.

II

6.   Tingling, timorous, I bowed,
Daunted, endangered, dared to speak:
"O lady of lead on the lurid cloud,
So fulgent fair, so fumid bleak,
With silvery, steely strength endowed,
Yet, child of tin, so tired, so weak!
Inhuman, hell-struck, hardened proud,
Are you mortal or moonland freak,
Eyeless, eerie, oldly meek?
The voice of virtue or virus of sin?
Whither you wander, whom you seek,
O lady of lead, o child of tin?"

7.   Tintinnabula tinged my ear,
Dulcet, dim as a distant chime,
Her voice a voyage as if to steer
The stunted stir of a silent mime.
"O sleeping soul," she said, "so dear
To me that I may master time
And space to speak with you so near—
So near and nuptial as newfound rhyme—
Listen, look to the most lethal crime
That ever orgied since the origin
Of old abjection in archangels prime,
In this limbo of lead, this land of tin."

8.   Tinted with terror, trembling I said:
"O visitation reveal your name.
Do you live, or lie with the long-lost dead?
Whisper why and whence you came,
With copper crown and cloak of lead,

In gallium gown that glints of shame,
With ferrous hair enfurling your head,
Verdigris fingers and feet so lame.
Are you acting some infernal game,
Spat from such source of safranin
Flanked in the fold of a fumarole tame?
O lady of lead, o child of tin!"

9.   Like tinder touched her tone could spark:
"Know then my name which is Azoth.
Alpha and Omega is my mark,
Aleph and Thau in the orb of Thoth.
I am all metals menial, dark,
From whom hermetics hatch gold froth.
As sunfed sap seeps up the bark.
As larva leaps to lustrous moth,
So they believe in lunar wrath
That mercury has gold within.
Made of men's madness I wear its cloth,
A lady of lead, a child of tin."

10.   "Tin and tungsten and tutenag
You may well be," I murmured then.
"But why from my world of wonder drag
Me numb to this nigrescent den?
Where dinosaurs have died as crag,
Ocean has ebbed in endless fen,
And heavens on husky hinges sag.
Why break the bonds of where and when
To wail the wizardries of men?
I would not hear of hell so soon
If hell be harms beyond my ken
Done on the dark side of the moon."

III

11.   "The moon," she mused, "is mists away,
Erring the earth's wide orbic span.
You seem uncertain where you stay:
This wilderness is the world of man,
Beyond the Urals to the Yenisei,
From Komi country to Kazakstan,
Where jaws of giants seem to bray
In the eye of some infernal plan
That casts a curse in caustic fan.
From noon till night, from night till noon,
Around these regions runs a ban
Dark as the dark side of the moon.

12.   The moon indeed, is myriad far,
Yet not beyond a yearning leap.
The minds of men have moved ajar
The gates of galaxy and sleep.
She tambourines to a twanged guitar,
She mimes a mermaid in the deep,
A sovereign or a samovar;
Lovers lilt below her keep
And telescopes return her peep;
We watch her wake, we watch her swoon.
But out of imagination's sweep
Dwells the dark side of this moon.

13.   As the moon wears a mask unknown
So cryptic cries this continent.
No soul has seen its every zone
Though millions move across its bent.
No heart has heard its every groan

That decimates a daily Lent
With no more noise than a nutsize stone
Dropped in a desert of sediment.
The latitudes of lost lament
Where murder moves in mute monsoon,
Making its monstrous monument
Of the deadly dark side of the moon."

14.   "Moon-mad you make my mind," said I,
Limp to the lady's leaden tone,
"My mind migrated on a sigh
To meet the moon and you, alone.
You, made of metals to mystify,
Sprung from stratum in sick cyclone!
With alchemy you occupy
My brain quite blurred by a braille half-known
Half apprehended and quickly flown.
Tell me truly and tell me soon,
Why am I lost in this land of bone
Deemed the dark side of the moon."

15.   "The moon as mortuary here
Has its dark side in death alive.
O sleeping soul assuage your fear,
For you alone can long survive
This numb necrosis that none can hear,
At which all witness must connive.
Look at this landscape so severe,
With waterways in wintry gyve
That snaps in spring for a sea-like dive,
With snow and sky the eye's sole feast,
Where few can feed and fewer thrive,
The scaffold styled the Soviet East.

IV

16.   The Soviet East upon two sides
Open to ocean in icy ban.
A continent whose compass grides
From the Tunguskas to the Turkestan.
The rift in which one river strides
Is wider than West Europe's span,
And England eighty times divides
Into this area of arctic man,
Throughout which throbs a thick-set plan,
Deadly, demoniac at least,
From Kamchatka to Kazakstan,
The scaffold styled the Soviet East."

17.   "The Soviet East a scaffold slow,"
I echoed then and ached to see
What frail my fears refused to know.
"I dare not deem how that can be
In miles of the measures you bestow,
Stretching South to the Aral Sea
And East to the edge of Manchukuo.
Half a hemisphere of human fee
Demised to the devil by degree!
An immolation no arch-priest
Of the blackest blasphemy would decree
On such a scale as the Soviet East."

18.   "The Soviet East," she sighed, "is dread.
Let me show you the shadowy why.
I am the soul of the living dead
That toil and travail till they die,
Weary men, women, waifs that tread

In fetters of frost and deformity,
Kept half-crazed on a crust of bread
Till starving scurvy dims their eye
Sealed by the snow, the snow, the sky.
Guards and guarded are unreleased
For fear the facts should further cry
Than the scaffold styled the Soviet East.

19.	"Look East," she echoed, "through this glass
Ground from the grains of dead men's graves."
Into an eyeball arched with brass
I peered, and paled at the penal slaves,
Installed as Satan could scarce surpass
Aslant Siberian's snowy waves,
Called as the kilometres pass
The thousand and thirteenth throng of knaves.
The sights I saw my soul engraves,
Where even the letters of life have ceased.
Nobody breathes but as death behaves
On the scaffold styled the Soviet East.

20.	"The Soviet East," said the spirit now,
"Is over vast to visualise
In one survey of a secret brow.
To Magadan now move your eyes,
Where the light of lives is left like slough,
In transit to the tilth of cries,
Domains the devil would disavow.
Five million freighted in foul demise
To Kolýma's crypts of cold replies.
Five million fated with failing breath
Have sown the sounds that stigmatise:
Kolýma kills, Kolýma means death."

V

21.   "What is Kolýma?" "Kolýma is gold,
Gold as a god for gravemen's joy.
No one knows how much they hold,
These many mines of the great Dalstroy,
These hundred hells of hungry cold,
With denizens daily in death's employ.
The gravel, gulleys, groves enfold
Gold exploited in primitive ploy
From arctic ores that ever destroy
These destitutes, who with dying breath,
Mould the maxim's macabre envoy:
Kolýma kills, Kolýma means death."

22.   "Kolýma kills!" I cried in grief.
"And shall no shadow-selves emerge?
Let life allow my disbelief
That horror from my heart may surge.
Is human hell thus held in fief
To Satan for souls in sinless purge?
Say that for some the stay is brief,
That a few are freed, and hear me urge
That some do not in the snow submerge
To whisper their wasting breath
Their torment in a tolling dirge:
Kolýma kills, Kolýma means death."

23.   "Kolýma is gold," the goddess said,
"And gold means gore in the gusts of time.
Closely kept and crudely bled,
Men from the mines are maimed with rime,
Devoured by vermin, voidly fed,

Limbs loosen as if laked in lime.
Men gouge for gold, men grub for lead,
Infusing its fumes and fatal grime
Until their lungs lather with slime.
These thousands only, with thinning breath,
Ever emerge to enact the rhyme:
Kolýma kills, Kolýma means death.

24.   From Kolýma they come, crippled quite,
To Bukhta baled in bestial train,
Earless, armless from arctic blight,
Some without feet and some insane,
Blind, broken and in barbarous plight:
One youthful year can yield this bane.
Benight the notion that now they might
Be freed to flout their fearful gain!
Sent to a secret sealed terrain,
They are shot, but with shrivelled breath,
Murmur the maxim's mad refrain:
Kolýma kills, Kolýma means death."

25.   Kolýma cripples coded my shriek
Into sobbing, stuttering prayer:
"O Lord, O Lamb of love so meek,
King of the crucified! Oh, tear
The heart of heaven at hell so bleak,
Redeemless, damned in dumb despair.
Does Lucifer lie a lonely freak
At the nexus of this numb nightmare?
Demon of dark so debonaire,
How art thou fallen, O flare of morn!
Are these creatures criminal so to fare?
The age of assassins again is born!"

VI

26.   Borne on the breeze, the lady's voice
Filed ferrous on a frost of zinc:
"These men," she murmured, "have no choice.
It is a sin to speak or think,
To weep, to whisper, to rejoice,
To laugh, to love, to look, to blink.
These men," she murmured, "have no choice:
Between deeds and death there is no link.
'Can you drink the cup that I must drink?'
Once mused a Man murdered in scorn.
These slaves are supplied from sins in ink:
The age of assassin again in born."

27.   "Born in a breath of beatitude,
This world," I wept, "has waxed in sin
Of almost measureless magnitude.
O lady of lead, O child of tin,
Living in lightlorn latitude,
Moving in metallic din,
I envy your aimless attitude.
Your heart is a hearse in harlequin,
Armoured in iron as anodin,
Feeling no fear for these fates forlorn.
What is your tearless task within
This age of assassins that now is born?"

28.   "Born abreast of each decade,"
The lady lined her leaden tone
With a sigh that soft on my senses played,
"Each assassin age is sown
In the heart of the human renegade.

Every soul has the seed unknown
And every age is retrograde.
But the grace of God so great has grown
That the turf of time is trimmed and mown,
The lithe and loath to a level shorn.
Yet in human hearts that hunger alone
The age of assassins again is born.

29.   "Born from this blight of barbarous deeds,"
The sage pursued now more severe,
"I am the soul of these suffering breeds.
I am their essence, their eye, their ear,
Weighted by their wants, their needs,
Sharing every shock and tear,
Bleeding when each blister bleeds;
Not only with these slave souls here,
But with the mass that moves in fear,
Abject, undermined, outworn.
They fashion my form, my fever steer,
In this age of assassins newly born."

30.   "Born from the bone of a basalt thigh
Or sprung from the surf!" I said in wrath,
"What use is your yearning sigh,
Your fluttering like a frenzied moth
Aslant the dazzle of snow and sky?
Though tin and tungsten, your task is froth!"
"Not merely I mourn these men that die,"
Lanced the lady of the leaden cloth,
"I am their essence, I am Azoth,
I suffer Satan's same trepan
For aeons in the orb of Thoth.
I am the mercury of man.

VII

31.　　Mercury molten to matter prime,
Ebbed of elements of earth and air,
Wilted of water and fire with time,
Consumed in sulphur, salt and flare
Arsenic, ammonia in ardent slime,
Mingled in metals menial, bare
Of qualities as quack quicklime!
Admire the method which mortals dare
To think shall thrive in gold so rare
Through seasons of a secret span.
Admire the method which mortals swear
Transmutes the mercury of man.

32.　　Mercurial man is made to be
Querying, quick, in silver quest,
Limber, lithe and lambent free
And in his essence undistressed,
Grown in the grace of God's decree.
Only the uninvited guest,
Sapping his soul with satanic plea,
Can dastardly his soul divest
Of all opponent ardours, lest
They might not mingle as they fan
The aimed imaginary alkahest,
Transmuting the mercury of man.

33.　　Mercury moves the menial tin,
And iron is the orb of Mars.
Saturn sleeps in leaden din
While Venus veers and copper lars.
And microcosmic man within

Himself constrains all earth and stars.
Assassins aim in arctic sin
To hold him in hermetic jars,
And with tormenting trial to parse
Grey gallium to a gilded plan.
A furnace with but frost for bars
Transmutes the mercury of man.

34.   Mercurial man must calcinate,
Putrefy to a pitchy black.
His essence they incarcerate
Until the grime to grey must crack,
Distil, dissolve, to white dilate,
Purified, purged upon the wrack;
Suppurated, must sublimate
To yellowing yeast in yearning lack,
In gore that grovels to green and back
With bastard breath in bilious tan,
And failing to fix, reforms to black,
The transmuted mercury of man.

35.   Mercury maimed and metals base,
Bodies imperfect impaired the more
In winter wide as the world's dark face
Where never opens night's numb door;
Seeps to spring at simpering pace
In dusky daze of dust and hoar;
Simmers to summer of sealèd space,
Torrid, torpid, tainted sore,
Where mirages move in mystic gore,
To autumn an endless impediment.
Ever away as ever before,
The aurum is only orpiment."

VIII

36.   "Orpiment!" said I bemused,
"Yet the gold they grasp is gold indeed,
Though the men that mine it are much abused.
Though hewn in hells from hearts that bleed,
The riches are real and unrefused
By the wintry wold to wordly greed,
Durable, dazzling, undiffused.
You argue alchemy cannot succeed:
Autumn's elixir must ever recede,
Leaving but leather and sediment.
Show me why so sharp you plead
The aurum is only orpiment."

37.   "Orpiment in the ore of dreams,
A treasure of tears, a tinkling bell,
A flower that fades before it beams!"
The vision's voice was a vibrant knell
That clung concordant to crevice gleams.
"Rich and real and ripe to sell,
Gold is gouged from the global seams.
But menial metals that melt, and swell
The giant jar with generic yell,
Do not more than a dream cement.
Amber art for an empty shell,
The aurum is only orpiment.

38.   Orpiment apes eternal life,
Invalid, they vouch, when void of sweat.
This panacea of purge and strife,
This alkahest of old regret,
This equal Eden ever rife,

Through the soul in sempiternal debt
Cleaves with procrastination's knife.
Perfection, paradise is set
In temporal tenders, but not yet.
The ritual still a rudiment
With hecatomb for amulet,
The aurum is only orpiment.

39.   Orpiment ebbs in icy towers
Through seasons secret and Saturnine,
Embroidered with blood in burning flowers,
Tinged with tears like tannic wine.
But the towers tune to tyrant powers:
Like stork-nets in a scattered line,
Their vigil veers, converging lowers
Of bilious beaks like beams that shine.
Blossoms are but carbuncles fine
On the skin of a septic sentiment.
In a season semperly Saturnine
The aurum is only orpiment.

40.   "Orpiment!" I echoed then.
"Oh, heaven pays hell too high a price.
Did the Deity Who died for men
Suffer a senseless sacrifice?
Day after day He dies again
And scarcely has the cock crowed thrice,
The soul has sprouted a sickly wen,
An ulcer in an urn of lice.
What dare I do, and what device
Can minister to molten lead?
And can repeated prayer suffice
As requiem for the living dead?"

IX

41.   "Requiem aeternam eis
Dona, Domine," she prayed.
And all at once from every crevice
Words were wirelessly relayed.
"Lux perpetua luceat eis . . . "
And all at once I was afraid.
All around an arctic daïs
Old eruptions I surveyed,
In jet-black chasubles arrayed,
With aureoles about their head.
Their tones entwined the time like braid,
In requiem for the living dead.

42.   In requiem their ritual kneeled
With incense unentuned, unfanned.
No lilt of lute nor lyre did weld
This massive and monastic band
Essenced of angels unrebelled.
The stars suspended on the land
So low they looked like tapers held
By each acolyte in his hand.
Their voices fused in filing strand,
Their song the purple snow did tread,
Measured as by memorial sand,
In requiem for the living dead.

43.   Ad requiem their ritual came,
But ardent still as ambergold
Embered in evangelic flame,
While calm in canopy condoled.
The child of tin, of changing name,

Singed the air with a seal as old
As sacrifice for a sinner's shame.
She spoke and said: "Sleepers, behold,
And I will tell you a tale retold
By the angels in eternal thread,
The mystery of the marigold
As requiem for the living dead.

44.   In requiem of rubric weird,
Enclasped in cloud across a tree,
As Western the old world veered,
Yet soon this self-same century,
Our Lady of the Light appeared.
To the chary charge of children three
She entrusted tidings now revered
By Heaven and the Holy See:
'Torment and trouble in high degree
Will rise from Russia now,' She said.
'This country consecrate to me
In requiem for the living dead.'

45.   In requiem of rubric rare
She came upon a cloudy fan,
Limned of light and lustrous air,
The Mother of the Son of Man.
Harkening us with Her to share
Such mortal misery as Magadan.
The golden galaxy of prayer
Is Mary's gold and moves the span
Of all the evil earth can plan.
With marvels, missives manifold
Throughout the ages and the orbs it ran,
The mystery of the Marigold.

X

46.   Mary's gold is all mankind,
Her intercession's alkahest
Transmuted from our metal mind
In an eternal, arduous quest."
The child of tin this charm defined.
And all at once at one behest
The Sanctus, Sanctus, Sanctus lined
The looming light, and like a crest
The moon a mammoth host did rest
Above the mountains, a marigold,
Humbling the hills in its halo dressed
From black to blue and from blue to gold.

47.   The marigold in a mouthing cloud
Vanishing from view, and a vintage night
Muzzled among the mountains bowed,
Until returned a tamer light.
No blessing had my breast endowed,
No kiss of peace had passed my sight.
But suddenly they sang aloud,
Each archangelic acolyte:
"Requiescant in pace." White
The snow received in silent fold
The voices of their vibrant rite,
Burning its black from blue to gold.

48.   Mary's gold, immanent through
Interstellar space and time,
A light upon the landscape threw,
On angels in eternal prime.
The child of tin, of changing hue,

With brass and bronze and bismuth chime,
In a waning whirl away she flew,
Smaller and smaller she seemed to mime
A marigold on a moonward climb.
She left me lonely, lost and cold
In a phantom world of frigid clime,
Blackening now from blue and gold.

49.   "Mary's gold a mystic rune,"
I mused and measured the mournful grey
Of this the dark side of the moon,
From tundra teeth in the titanic bray
To swamp and steppe in silent swoon.
The suddenly in swift affray
I swing from sleep. The summer noon
Had shifted to a shimmering play.
Of gory gold in the gleaming hay.
With thrift my thought began to unfold.
Do dreams our daedal dallying spray
From black to blue and from blue to gold?

50.   Gold as god for grave men's joy,
Transmuted in mind from metals base,
In seasons sanctified Satan's alloy
Elides to elixir at endless pace.
Quicksilver souls in styptic ploy
Can alter the ends of the earth with grace
That travels like a truce envoy
Into the Orient's ageless face
Hidden and housed in hermetic space;
Can dissolve, distil the dirge untolled,
The fathomless, frozen, funereal place,
From black to blue and from blue to gold.

AMEN.

The (lack of)di-facile-facere<=>do/schwer/sweer/serius in the Work of Christine Brooke-Rose

G. N. Forester

In 2010, living in Cairo and having arrived at the end of tethered patience, deciding to withdraw from a number of *pro bono* projects undertaken in the environmental services and agricultural sectors—relinquishing the reigning reins to those shouldering responsibility for furthering and developing the work (always an optimistic notion, made laughable by the advent the following year of the Arab Spring)—and to disappear over the shimmering horizon, although answering the occasional call for urgent advice.[1]

Scribbling: e're regarded as something to be eschewed in favour of pursuing filthy lucre, when the latter would present as an option; too many blue moons having waxed and waned since the publication of poetry or short essays on expat life (whether as vagabond or vassal) in bygone daze. But having never ceased to indulge in the secret hope of writing a micklestück such as Frank Herbert's *Dune* (no doubt exacerbated by a desert existence opaquing the illusion), or Aldous Huxley's *Brave New World*, penning a young adult science-fiction novel ineluctably determined as the goal (and not the goat) for that year.

(Flying from Europe back to Egypt during the same period, the onbored entombanement included a strange film about a teenached triangle of girl, boy, and boy, and vampires and werewolves, watched sporadically without the sound, leaving a vague impression of having encountered something similar before. But where? Oh yes, browsing the bookshelves earlier that year in another country, the breast-seller list being topped by a series of books concerning a teenplagued threesome (twothsome?) of girl, boy, and boy, and *vamp-pire* and wearwools (or fearfools?) apparently garnering accolades always shouted in lowest

---

1 The interested *lisibleur* may like to re-visit this paragraph after having read the essay.

common denominators (money maid, number of books soul'd) and rarely about the quality of the prose (structure, vocabulary, innovative form), the latter receiving attention, if at all, for its atrocious construction).

Thus springs foolishness eternal. If this were the iron pyrites standard of current pubications, why, how difficult could it be to (re)produce something better? Target market investigated, John Ray writing studied. And the project shelved almost before commencement. Were people really reading such guff? And with such gusto? Yes, (un)seemingly. Perhaps it would have all been digestible, apart from the vivid contempt displayed for the craft of composition. *Writing 101* websites propounding the sage advice: do not use the passive, defined as any instance of *was* and the present participle (termed *-ing* form by such fonts of pissdom) of the verb. Since when? End sentences with prepositions! Why? (Oh, simply because the writer of the website *content* has *con*flated a *pre*-position with the construction <verb + dependent *proposition*> such as break up, and this should now become the global *ruel*). In short, for no good linguistic reason (but since Oxford Dictionaries suffer this malaise that must surely validate it? Having quite forgotten that English, for all its Latinate character, owes much to Teutonic verbs + dependent prepositions, *klärte ab!*).

Do not use *-ing* forms of verbs, ever! Say again? Delete every instance of the gerund (otherwise known as the means by which nouns and adjectives are constructed from verbs (oh drat, a passive slipped in there), although obviously not known by (slap that passive wrist!) the spouters of such spurious stuff) and participles (apparently equally unknown as the active usage of a verb). *How to Win Readers & Influence Reviewers! Characterise Your Characters! Plot Yourself to Publication! Monetise a Mass-Market Readership!* Well, yes. It's all been done before, nothing new there. The only qualification required seeming to be the ability to string at most two words (with at most two syllables) together, in something vaguely resembling sentence form. Gr8!

The path to fame and fortune is littered with corpses. Ergo, neither the goad nor path to choose. With no real intent to create constraints (at the time of writing the 'high fantasy' narrative, the word 'constraint' had yet to be discovered), the reaction to the spam being distributed in Stückchen numbering millions (in trees-and-ink or bits-and-bytes) was to remove any occurrence of the worst textual offenders (here termed using the accepted jargling, as per the caveat above with respect to constraint):

1. Omniscient author (masquerading as narrator), thus excising both free indirect and narrativised discourse, and associated commentary;
2. Dialogue tags (of any description, since 'said' repeated *ad infinitum* is as redundant as 'exclaimed' following an exclamation mark);
3. Description other than what the camera can see (the camera held by the character and no one else);
4. Narrative 'and then' (actions in the past tense have ended and are thus sequential, hence 'and then' is logically superfluous[2]);
5. There was, there is, there were, there are (existence may or may not be a given, what existence does or does not do is far more interesting);
6. The characters' thoughts indicated via thought attribution tags: he thought (even worse, to himself);
7. Parentheticals, such as: "he said, his heart sinking to his toes";
8. Adverbs/prepositions indicating direction already indicated by the verb: "his heart sinking ~~down~~ to his toes"; and
9. Verbs whose meanings have become so opaque and amorphous that entire paragraphs can be written with the one verb, relying purely on subject or object to provide meaning and context, but lacking any specificity of action.

All of which led to setting as well as the actions of the characters being privileged (oh dear, and breaching genre writing rule #1.1oh2: **Do not Use PassivE/-ING** or whatever it's called form of the verb bcoz I saw it on a blog and if I give the write admanvice I'll of got lots of site [s]hits

---

2 S/he/one walks/walked to the book shop, eating an apple. S/he/one buys/bought a book while singing. S/he/one returns/returned home, tired but happy with the purchase. The 'and then' extraneous.

LOL) by using the present participle, but still in the traditional narrative of past tense, as well as a camera point-of-view focused on what was happening, how it was happening, in the narrative time sense (still past), and providing direct access to the characters' thoughts using italics. Conventional punctuation was not discarded. Content? Ah, content was generated by the actions of the characters and if the camera could not capture the heart sinking to the toes, it was not recorded.

In the world of young adult science fiction, what sort of prose do these constraints produce? Nothing out of the ordinary. In fact, something so ordinary that no reader would even notice (nor has done so) these constraints . . .

Sounding no doubt not unfamiliar to the reader of either the fiction or literary theory and criticism of Christine Brooke-Rose (CB-R):

> Any narrative sentence, even by unpracticed writers and without their conscious knowledge, assumes certain conventions . . . imposes certain "content" choices, which then become constraints.[3]

CB-R has variously attributed her development as an exploratory or alternative fiction writer[4] to the influence of (inclusive but not limited to) Pound, Roche, Beckett, Sarraute and Robbe-Grillet[5] for:

1. her recognition and rejection of:
   a. authorful (awforfool) past tense narrative being overwhelmed by the pontificating, pulpit-pounding, patriarchal paradigmatic au-

---

3 Brooke-Rose, Christine:, *Invisible Author: Last Essays*, Columbus, The Ohio State University Press, 2002, pp. 36-7.

4 "I was simply dissatisfied with what I was doing. I had written four novels, which are really quite traditional, satirical, comic novels. I did experiment with time in one of them, which was written backwards, for instance, so that in each chapter the hero gets younger and younger. But that was still classical irony. They were basically traditional modern novels, if I can use such a phrase, in that the main concern was, like most novels, epistemological, concerned with reality and illusion. But I felt it was too easy. It was great fun, but it wasn't what I wanted." Friedman, Ellen & Fuchs, Miriam, "A Conversation with Christine Brooke-Rose". *The Review of Contemporary Fiction*, Fall 1989, Vol. 9.3.

5 Brooke-Rose, Christine:, *Invisible Author: Last Essays*, pp. 135-40. See also the interview with David Hayman, *Contemporary Literature*, Vol 17, No 1, Winter 1976, pp. 14-5, for a discussion on Pound, Roche, and Beckett.

thor determined to either interpret every last nuance of her/his characters' actions (you, dear reader, being too naive/inattentive/unintelligent to discern intent) or else tub-thump a piece of hard-won universal sagacity without which the world will wither and die on a petard of its own making (you, dear reader, being too naive/inattentive/unintelligent to discover this earth-shattering erudition without an all-seeing, all-knowing, all-trancing guydance). Where the demarcation might have been respected in traditional narrative once upon a time, by the twentieth century, free indirect discourse, as a means of mingling interpolating author with the thoughts of (barely there) characters, has become ubiquitous and obnoxious.[6]

b. narrative past tense because it allows free indirect discourse, the path to author insertion;

c. I-narrative, since the narrator and the author appear as one;

d. content privileged over form;

e. the "... banal verbalised search for identity ... the relatively recent concept [which] has caused so much harm"[7];

f. realist parody which collapses to the thing parodied[8]; and

---

6   Hopefully the irony is not lost, since phaction is riddled with the same bellicose sophistry.

7   Brooke-Rose, Christine:, *Invisible Author: Last Essays*, p. 44.

8   See "Illusions of Parody", *Stories, theories, and things*, Cambridge, Cambridge University Press, 1991, pp. 192-203 for a discussion and response to McHale's analysis of her earlier essay "Metafiction and Surfiction", *A Rhetoric of the Unreal*, Cambridge, Cambridge University Press, 1981, pp. 364-89 in which she examines a select number of works to demonstrate these realist 'parodies' are indistinguishable, to the reader, from that being parodied ie realism. In the later essay, she re-poses the question: "Why, in other words, do we experience in these supposed parodies, so much of the time, a tipping over into the model, which in principle (according to Bakhtin) should happen only with stylization, the two voices in parody being too hostile to each other for this to occur?" and progresses (with a logical explication) to adopt Genette's formulation of the differences between pastiche and parody to ask the same question, and answer it in Genette's terms, "[these texts] are not what they seem, neither interpretations nor parody of interpretation. The very uncertainty in the status of the discourse, in the ontology of the world presented, and, at best (for instance in Gass or Barthelme or later Coover, rather than in early Coover or early Pynchon), the very hidden nature of the sideglance on other discourses, the very secrecy of the inner polemic, gives us illusions of parody that are truer (that is, more chimerical) than Genette perhaps intended in his dispute over nomenclature, when he called parody of genre *une chimere de parodie*." The point being that she accepts a specific use of parody, but finds what is termed "parodies of realism" failing to perform as parody in the terms/senses she uses.

---

  g. parentheticals and dialogue punctuation;

2. her adoption and development of the techniques privileging form to generate content as narrative[9]:

  a. theory: "I do not, when writing, put away the literary theory I have absorbed and used."[10] *Remake* was first written[11] as chronological facts and rewritten with the imposition of constraints derived from theory, such as pronounless narrative: all personages of significance designated either a masculine or feminine variation of Chomsky's John since pronouns must be replaced with proper nouns. Writing as both author aware of theory and theorist aware of creativity, a key characteristic in all her novels, exhilarates and motivates CB-R, even, as in the case of the personal and academic reasons for the incubation of *Thru*, the split between critic/theorist and author results in a jettisoning, a repositioning, a recombination of the theory learned (or earlier, in the case of the four conventional novels, the style adopted).[12] *Xorandor*, originally written "in as mainstream a way as possible, with every narrative cliché in use . . . a classic title *The Alphaguys*"[13] was re-written as pure dialogue (including a computer-language-based patois invented by its two juvenile protagonists) with no attribution, as a commentary on the success (and failure) of language (artificial and received) as a means of communication, as well as the process of producing fiction—a clear example of theory informing form to produce content;

  b. technique: the craft of writing is not simply granted because "we can all hold a pen and cover paper . . . the belief that anyone who

---

9 It must noted here that CB-R was always a story-teller, from the time of *Jo's Club* (archival material) written during her secondary school years, to her last fiction, ably demonstrated in *Go When You See the Green Man Walking* (London, M. Joseph, 1970), a collection of short stories, some of which contain applications of her lipograms, but all clearly engaging narratives.

10 Brooke-Rose, Christine, *Stories, theories, and things*, p. 13.

11 Brooke-Rose, Christine, "Self-Confrontation & The Author", *New Literary History*, Vol. 9, No. 1, Self-Confrontation and Social Vision (Autumn, 1977), pp. 129-36. John is given quite an airing, as is Tess masquerading under the first person pronoun.

12 "A Conversation with Christine Brooke-Rose", Maria del Sapio Garbero, *British Postmodern Fiction*, edited by Theo D'haen and Hans Bertens, Amsterdam—Atlanta, Rodopi, 1993, p. 105.

13 Brooke-Rose, Christine, *Stories, theories, and things*, p. 21

has learnt to write can WRITE is a popular one"[14], but false, since in no other artistic endeavour are the practitioners exempted from completing an apprenticeship, from becoming proficient and demonstrating that proficiency[15], and therefore, "[t]o transgress intelligently, one must know the rule."[16] The purpose of such transgression being, as she notes via Sarraute's inversion of the dichotomy between traditional realist and formalist, to develop new and fresh ways of looking in order to perceive and capture reality[17], in turn part of the process of jolting the reader's awareness, because this is what leads to critical thinking and intelligent discussion, to confronting social, cultural, political issues, by allowing or returning to the mingling of language and philosophy;

c. present tense[18] as the basis for objectified non-narrating narrat-

---

14 *ibid.*, p.25-6.

15 "Indeed, if one sinks very deep to the level of soap operas, their authors seem to know neither line (syntax) nor colour (protean form, transmuted), neither technique (work) nor genius. If technique isn't enough, it is nevertheless essential, and the more one knows the implications of every word one writes, every change of tense or mood or voice (to name only three categories) the more difficult it is to write, because more demanding." *ibid.*, p. 27.

16 *ibid.*, p.26.

17 Brooke-Rose, Christine, *Invisible Author: Last Essays*, p. 178. See also the following essay "Illiterations" for further discussion.

18 The present participle (or progressive, or continuous, or -ing form(!)) is not privileged in CB-R's work (with the exception of *Between*, not intended, but as a result of excising the auxiliary conjugations in this novel, and to a lesser extent in *Life, End of*): she dismisses "[f]or a narrative in the present, [any] grammatical distinction between the punctual and the continuous" (*Contemporary Literature*, Vol 19, #3, 1978, p. 384), although later acknowledges that "the present tense is also the tense of general statements and universal questions . . . the progressive present for simultaneous action" (*Invisible Author: Last Essays*, p. 151), but because her principal concern is to create a speakerless narrative "from inside a character [representing] both reflective and nonreflective consciousness" (*ibid.*, p. 149), achieved either through elimination of pronouns, possessives or using only proper nouns as identification of the character, she is content to use the global form of simple present tense, which she regards as aptly destabilising for repetition (*Contemporary Literature*, Vol 19, #3, 1978, p. 387, footnote 13) and the time of narrated events e.g.: *Tess eats apples* (always and everywhere) and *The head top leans against the bathroom mirror . . .* and was leaning (had been leaning) before, is leaning (has been leaning, having been leaning) now, and will be leaning (will have been leaning) still, until either the next action intervenes, or the reader tacitly accepts the action is completed—contrast this use with theatrical scripts such as Beckett's opening to *Waiting for Godot*:

Estragon, sitting on a low mound, is trying to take off his boot. He pulls at it with

---

ive voice or impersonal/viewpointless (or scientific) fictional text, which CB-R termed the paradoxical use[19]. All her novels are written in the simple present tense, with the exception of *Amalgamemnon*, which makes use of the future and conditional tenses;

d. pronounless narrative: typically narrative is carried by a consciousness, such as a character, via the use of first person perspective (or second person in the case of Calvino's *If On a Winter's Night a Traveller*), or a third person (thus an implied and accepted 'Narrator', somehow external to and separate from the author) perspective. But the paradoxical present tense use to which CB-R refers is where no part of the text identifies the story-teller via author insertion such as dialogue tags, parentheticals, or personal pronouns. Where her earlier exploratory novels all make use of this technique to some extent (personal pronouns are still

---

both hands, panting . . . [until] Vladimir enters . . . advancing with short, stiff strides.

CB-R's present tense narrative, as opposed to the theatrical, mimics most closely the literary speakerless narrative of criticism and history ie the historical Narrative Sentence (NS), impersonal and expressed in third person, which removes both sender and receiver unless morphing into Speech Mode and ceasing to be NS; "It produces the rare impersonal tense of our literary criticism . . . and ultimately derives from science" (*Life, End of*, Manchester, Carcanet, 2006, p. 70). In her discussion of the constraint concerned with deleting all instances of the verb *be*, she delights in the aesthetic impact on her writing: by avoiding *be* in all its uses, she is forced "to find another verb, usually more dynamic, active [the passive construction is less intuitive, although not impossible e.g.: *the girl, known by some person or distinguishing behaviour* and not *the girl who is/was known by* ..], even metaphoric, and this . . . prevent[s] sliding into facility and cliché" (*Invisible Author: Last Essays*, p. 45). She is particularly focused, however, on stray usages of *be* such as apostrophe-s; a concern with the conjugation of point of view, not the conjugation indicating action and time. Further, the omission of the conjugation of point of view is intended to be mimetic, to demonstrate non-existence, since the protagonist is always between states of being somewhere, there, not here, and in the state of not-being, ie without an identity: the protagonist is "permanently translating ideas not her own, permanently waking up in different hotel rooms . . . all the same but in different countries" (*ibid.*, p. 44), which naturally leads to the inclusion of different languages for the same actions. This privileging of movement is achieved, paradoxically, by the NS commencing and moving from a position of being in one place, to finishing at a position of being in another place, but the use of the present participle is incidental to the privileging of story time over narrative time. The action of the protagonist is paradoxically given no story time, although technically corresponding to the present, the tense is the almost aorist (event time external to the protagonist): is/was the action momentary or continuous; when is/was its occurrence?

19 ". . . NS paradoxical because it is impersonal, that is, it is like the traditional historical past-tense NS in which no one speaks, but it is in the present tense which belongs to the personal speech-system" (*ibid.*, p. 158).

used, although much reduced), it is *Remake* that removes *all* instance of identity and grammatical creation/substitution, rendering an autobiography completely separate from its Creator/Originator/ Source. Thus not only *I, me, he, she, it, we, they*, but the possessives and reflexives *my, mine, his, hers, its, theirs, her, him, them, myself, yourself, itself* etc., are absent. She returns to this ultimate of distancing techniques in her final, and arguably most poignant, therefore most aptly applied to maintain her signature humour and resist collapsing under real or imagined (from an empathic or antipathic reader) self-pity, novel *Life, End of*;

e. repetition of set pieces, the efficacy of which she learned through her interest in analysing Pound's poetry, and used to particular effect in *Between, Amalgamemnon*, and *Life, End of* as a means to explore linguistic significance and examine/present complementary and opposing perspectives (the ability to do so attributed to her employment at Bletchley Park) and philosophical debates;

f. comedy: the only way to deal with suffering is to laugh at it.[20] CB-R has used all the literary devices associated with humour in each of her novels to bring comic relief to the serious nature of the themes upon which her work is founded; never used to belittle or bemoan, to diminish or distract, but as a way of coping. Further, for CB-R, language/discourse is *funny*, and, being funny is, for her, as natural as breathing. It was for this reason that of all the French writers, Roche appealed most[21];

g. logical consistency of theme and observation of real-world phenomena: CB-R used the study of her own environment and circumstances as the kernels or seeds from which her innovation in form and content was to germinate. Thus, a thematic cohesion exists across all her works, but the method with which she chose to express her preoccupations is as much dependent on the content of the observation as on the innovative technique itself, res-

---

20 See, in particular, the interview with Maria del Sapio Garbero for an anecdote regarding a scene from *Thru*, but also a conversation in *Between*, between Siegfried and the central female consciousness with respect to language and suffering, p. 358 (*Omnibus* e-book edition).
21 Interview with David Hayman, *Contemporary Literature*, Vol 17, No 1, Winter, 1976, pp. 14-5.

ulting in very different works. Particularly true of *Amalgamemnon*, where first the realisation that media announcements are formulated in terms of conditional statements and that topics are always discussed in terms of what will occur, and not what is happening in the instant of the discussion, generates the constraint of writing in the future tense (and removing all constative statements[22]). Observation informs *Between,* with its lack of the verb *be*, and demonstrates how personality/identity is both a received and autonomous construct, not a single entity, but rather a multiple created out of own experience, external perspective, and internal values and attitudes, thus reflecting CB-R's personal opinion concerning the phenomenon of the "search for identity". *Next*, set in London and focused on homeless people, their circumstances and marginalisation: the text contains no instances of the verb *have*, and not only prevents the characters from possessing either sense of self or physical object or abstract concept, but annihilates any past, any immediacy, and any future, since grammatically *have/had* is required in the construction of perfect tenses. *Xorandor*, deliberately conceptualised with an eye on 'more plot, less play' is concerned with nuclear armament, power production, and waste (with all the institutional polemic from that period faithfully (and satirically)) presented, and is narrated by Zip and Jab, easily recognisable by their paraphrasing of their younger selves and the other characters involved in the story. By the time of the reprisal of the story, in *Verbivore,* now reflecting CB-R's observation of the deluge of dinformation[23] supported by increasing implementation and reliance on technology to replace awareness of time, place and *vis-a-vis* interaction, the number of characters has multiplied. Each speaks but provides no clear ref-

---

22 Lecercle, Jean-Jacques, "Une lecture d'*Amalgamemnon* de Christine Brooke-Rose", Tropismes, L'Errance, 5, Nanterre, Publidix (english version in E.G. Friedman and R. Martin, eds., *Utterly Other Discourse: the Texts of Christine Brooke-Rose*, Dalkey Archive Press, Illinois, 1995, pp. 153-69).

23 At the end of *Xorandor*, CB-R leaves the way open for a return to the story. The conclusion to *Verbivore* dooms communication, the theme she revisits with her plethora of fictional characters in *Textermination.*

erence as to whom has control of the narrative other than through idiosyncrasies of expression consistently replayed during the story; the innovation one step further in *Verbivore* is a return to a technique developed in *Thru* (the puzzle of determining with no textual clues which of the characters is speaking);

h. pungnacious punning, word-tomfoolery, lexical laughs, and general relish in either layering meaning or deconstructing a word to demonstrate the overarching theme of the work, with humour sly and sometimes stinging. Thus, in *Life, End of*, with its concentration on the physical decline of the corpus, Vasco (vascular) and Polly (the head) figure in numerous skits; le me-chant/méchant loup, loop, and lupe (representing the trilingual ability of the bifografical Tess) known as John (stand in for all personages inspiring, whether positively or negatively, the protagonist, including the protagonist/author, during the life related) and first introduced in *Remake*, returns to remind the consciousness telling the story of the filosophical phictions created by me-*mories*. *Amalgamemnon* concentrates its punnilinguistics on the topic of women exploited as resources and women constrained by expectations (social, political, cultural, historical, and physical). *Next*, with its interweaving of dialect and Received Pronunciation, in the mouths of down-and-out but still somewhere and somehow educated characters, provides ample opportunity to highlight double standards and institutionally perpetrated falsehoods through alternative word-spellings, its bleakness rescued from morbidity by unexpected, albeit not as frequent, drollery. Her wordplay distinguishes her earlier four conventional novels *The Languages of Love*, *The Sycamore Tree*, *The Dear Deceit*, *The Middlemen*, demonstrated with both puns and double entendre; each a social satire swinging (at times wildly) between the heavy-handedness of Rabelais and the accurate lance of Swift;

i. relaxing of her main constraint, where it is a character that sustains the narrative, and this is critical to understanding *di-facile* (the lack-of-(easy)do) concerns not the reader, but the writer:

CB-R's constraints are applied to herself, to generate a text delec-*teurable* to the reader (even if that reader would only have been herself) with the expectation that the reader wants to interact with the text, wants to play, and is simply not a vassal in which entombanement is to be poured[24]. Reading, for CB-R, is not a passive activity, since the constraints chosen are intended to generate narrative nouvelle, for the purposes of shaking up the reader, creating a different way of viewing the world. However, while she never abandons the key features of her main constraints: (a) present tense; (b) rejection of dialogue punctuation, parentheticals and authorial comment; and (c) the narrative carried purely by character, she uses proper names, dialogue tags, and repetition to orient and tease the reader. Thus, in *Remake*, although pronounless (and atypical of autobiography for the lack of I-protagonist), who generates the action and events, thoughts and commentary, who is affected by these, is announced via proper nouns; in *Textermination*, the overwhelming number of borrowed characters is balanced on a relatively straightforward text carried by CB-R's invented ones, even allowing the use of a) free indirect discourse, b) author intrusion in the form of a discussion on theory, and c) conventional narrative as lifted from the source novels[25]; and in *Next*, the story is told with the conventional form of realised characters, and the typography, rather than lack of conventional punctuation, indicates who is speaking, what is being heard or read (e.g., media), and what is being thought;[26]

j. realism: for CB-R, all recorded gestures a character makes as described in the narrative are authorial comment and thus es-

---

24 Brooke-Rose, Christine, *Invisible Author: Last Essays*, p. 153.

25 An assortment no reader could possibly expect, unless perhaps, s/he were Steven Moore (see his *The Novel: An Alternative History Vol 1*, 2010, New York, Continuum Books; *Vol 2*, 2013, New York, Bloomsbury), to recognise.

26 After the reception of her novel *Thru*, with the resulting innumerable false readings and interpretations, she "never attempted this kind of experiment again . . . my later novels, whatever their qualities, made a few concessions." *Invisible Author: Last Essays*, p. 107.

chewed[27]; this does not however mean that she is against Realism[28], it is the fact that reality is unreal, thus imitating unreality cannot produce reality. Exploratory fiction is no less unrealistic than is conventional fiction with the latter's pretence of imitation. That readers sympathise with the 'realistic' plight of fictional characters while having no sympathy or empathy for the debased circumstances afflicting much of the world's population[29], mentioned in graphic detail in various guises in each of her novels (but particularly bleak in *Next*), with the exception of *Textermination* and *Subscript*, is morally dubious. She is less interested in the struggle of mainstream writers to depict 'reality' realistically, than to arouse empathy in the mind of the reader at a philosophical and intellectual level for themes being presented and discussed via fiction. Not to say, however, that she considered Realism to be incapable of reinventing itself and emerging invigorated and in a different form[30]—her anti-Realism stance is specific, against the untenable speculations belonging to the formulaic representation of historic 'Realism'.[31]

The table below provides a brief summary of CB-R's novels, main lipograms, and respective content:

Novel	Constraint/Lipogram; content (cursory description)
Out	Speakerless; reversal of ethnic discrimination.
Such	Speakerless; astrophysics terms describing experience.
Between	Removal of verb *be*, repeated phrases in snippets of multiple languages, repetition of scene; life of a translator.
Thru	... *textuality of a text, fictionality of fiction*[32], the impossibility of identifying the narrator's character, typography of text,

---

27 Brooke-Rose, Christine, "Trangressions: An Essay-say on the Novel Novel Novel." *Contemporary Literature*, Vol 19, #3, 1978, p. 384.

28 Brooke-Rose, Christine, *Invisible Author: Last Essays*, p. 41.

29 "A Conversation with Christine Brooke-Rose", Maria del Sapio Garbero, *British Postmodern Fiction*, edited by Theo D'haen and Hans Bertens, Amsterdam—Atlanta, Rodopi, 1993, p. 112, p. 116.

30 Brooke-Rose, Christine, *A Rhetoric of the Unreal*, p. 388.

31 Brooke-Rose, Christine, *Stories, theories, and things*, p. 221-2.

32 Brooke-Rose, Christine, *Invisible Author: Last Essays*, p. 17

Novel	Constraint/Lipogram; content (cursory description)
	directional perspective contrasted to determine orientation (looking at the rear-vision mirror while driving forwards) repeated throughout; story generated by itself.
Amalgamemnon	Future tense, removal of constative sentences[33], repetition, word play (neologues, nonce words), protagonist's situation analogous to both history and the current global financial and resource crisis; musings of the character.
Xorandor	Received dialogue, shifting POV, shifting time; silicon-based alien absorbing nuclear waste/electronic communication.
Verbivore	Received dialogue, shifting POV, shifting time; alien's offspring destroying communication excesses.
Textermination	Metalepsis; characters from a plethora of texts convening to pray to the divine Reader for corporeality.
Remake	bifografy, removal of I-narrator in narrative of the self, pronounless present tense; CB-R life history.
Next	lack of verb *have* (implying characters have no past), multiple unattributed viewpoints, typography to indicate what/who is conveying the text as well as movement from place to place; homelessness, modern living.
Subscript	Sensation-based consciousness expanding to anthropologically similar entity via stages of evolution, graduated introduction of pronouns from *it*, to *they* etc, to possessives *their*; the central consciousness never attains *I*.
Life, End of	Pronounless present tense; lost of control of the body through the onset of various age-related conditions while the consciousness of the brain continues irrespective.

Hindsight is, naturally, always a miraculous thing, and it is particularly doable(facile), after a 'light deconstruction' of the fictions of CB-R, to suggest that the lack-of-facere ie the apparent difficulty of her texts is related to the confrontation of the ill-prepared reader with the new and different, and not an inherent obfuscation of meaning or a willy-nilly

---

33 Defined as having no a yes/no response; a constative utterance can be tested true or false, as opposed to a performative, unable to yield such an outcome. See Austin, J. L., *How To Do Things with Words*, 1975 2nd Ed., edited by J. O. Urmson and Marina Sbisà, Oxford, Oxford University Press.

pastiche of unconventional narrative styles for the purposes of either 'jumping on the bandwagon' or attracting attention. But precisely the thesis of this *essaye*-say conjectures that each of her novels have arisen from a concrete foundation in theory and a desire to explore and test the limits (or create new ones) of language, philosophy, psychology, culture, to delight in observation, cerebration, and communication, and her exclusion from 'the canon' points to an inability to grapple intellectually and emotionally with her form, content, humour, perspective:

> In all my novels . . . I am trying to make the novel once again do what only the novel can do, with words on a page . . . *tant pis* for readers who can't share in this scripting, this fiction was not written for them.[34]

Her work is internally consistent, logical, and although she suffered most with the term 'self-reflexive' applied to *Thru*, which on the same spurious grounds could be thrown at *Life, End of* (the mirror staring back: it sees what? whose reality, whose reflexion, whose deconstructing?), the reflection she invites is from the reader, since:

> . . . my sentences are correct and clear, my wordplay and syntax games are easy . . . the typographic roadblocks are there to wake up the reader, to force him to read in unusual directions, to stop and think . . . to share and partake.[35]

She illuminates a space, a philosophical and literary playground, an Alice's Wonderland, for readers to explore and appreciate, to indulge in the 'pleasure of discovery'. And like all adventurers on all adventures, the expeditions which end with the characters still standing, changed for the better or worse, are those for which each prepared him or herself to rise to the challenges of the journey to the unknown. That is the gift bequeathed us through the (lack of)di-facile-facere<=>do/schwer/ sweer/serius in the work of Christine Brooke-Rose.

---

34 Brooke-Rose, Christine, *Invisible Author: Last Essays*, p. 108.
35 *ibid.*

Illiterations

Christine Brooke-Rose

To be an 'experimental' woman writer is one thing. To write about the situation of 'experimental' women writers is quite another. This will not be a description of specific writers, least of all myself, and their difficulties, but a general, lightly deconstructing speculation on ancient prejudices—and what are prejudices but ill iterations of untenable positions in the face of change? And what can protests against these be but themselves ill iterations?

To be an 'experimental' woman writer

Three words. Three difficulties. *To be a woman:* vast and vastly written up. *To be a woman writer:* narrower but proportionately ditto.

Assuming that most of the problems described by Elaine Showalter (1971)—and many other studies since—for nineteenth-century writers have disappeared, and that the sexes, like classes and races, have on the face of it the same chances, there are nevertheless different types and levels of critical attention, on a sliding-scale that can be subsumed in the general opposition *canonical/non-canonical* (or ephemeral). And as Kermode (1979) has shown, only the canonical is deemed worthy of serious attention. Inside the canon interpretation multiplies wildly, while outside it a text does not exist. I would add, the pressure of the canonic is such that the self-allotted task of interpretation is to transform into qualities elements which, in a non-canonic work, would be considered as serious flaws, and this process of canonization has been more consistently applied to masculine works than to the few feminine entries.

In theory the canonic/non-canonic opposition applies to all writers and thus cuts across the sexual or any other opposition. In practice a canon is very much a masculine notion, a priesthood (not to be polluted), a club, a sacred male preserve; and yet a second matrix, as Norman O. Brown said of clubs and societies (1966). Or a heroic something owned. And not only a male preserve but that of a privileged caste. For women are only one part, however large, of an originally much larger exclusion: that of barbarians and slaves, or, later, other races and the 'lower' classes from peasants to modern workers, who were long considered incapable of any art worth the dignity of attention, indeed of any education towards it or towards anything else, even as late as Hardy's Jude.

Nevertheless male outsiders enter the canon more easily than women do, for reasons much deeper than those of caste. At the individual level, white males of outside origin have long been able to enter a canon, chiefly because of a long (canonic) tradition of the poet as visiting rhapsode, travelling minstrel, outsider. That is how a canon is formed and slowly altered. At the collective level, the canon also absorbs. In *The Secular Scripture* (1975) Northrop Frye speaks of the central 'mythic' tradition of any one culture (in our case the Graeco-Judeo-Christian), which excludes the parallel (popular) or 'secular' art forms, until in moments of exhaustion it has to turn to them for replenishment and renewed vigour (for instance today, SF, comics and so on).

But women's writing does not seem ever to have that role of 'tonic' or outside remedy, nor does it today. On the contrary, it has also turned to popular forms for replenishment, just as male writing has (e.g. Kathy Acker and her 'punk' style, or, for oral traditions, some 'ethnic' writers such as Toni Morrison, Maxine Hong Kingsley, Leslie Marmon Silko and others). Even with the 're-reading' by the feminists of a whole new area of women's literature previously relegated to oblivion (see Kolodny 1975), it is still possible for Nancy K. Miller to write: 'This new mapping of a parallel geography does not, of course, resolve the oxymoron of marginality: how is it that women, a statistical majority in our culture, perform as a "literary subculture?"' (1981, p. 38). And a sub-culture, I would add, *without* the fashionable status and invigorating role described above.

Traditionally then, this notion of a canon, of a central tradition around the central myth, which is essentially male, priestly and castebound, underlies types and levels of critical attention, so that despite the various and increasing waves of emancipation since the nineteenth century, certain relics remain, ill iterations in the unconscious of society.

It is thus one thing for a woman to have only the usual or no difficulties in getting published today, in acquiring a fashionable success or at least getting well-known enough to continue being published, but quite another thing for a woman writer, with equivalent speed and given the usual ups and downs, to enter a canon. One need only mention names like (in order of difficulty) Barbara Pym, Jean Rhys, Christina Stead, Ivy Compton-Burnett, Isak Dinesen, Nathalie Sarraute, who all received the accolade of serious recognition late in life. Or Kate Chopin or Edith Wharton, both dismissed as imitators, who are now being 're-read' and understood long after their death.

Or Gertrude Stein, or Djuna Barnes, who are only now receiving serious critical attention. For of course it is yet a third thing for a woman to be genuinely welcomed and attended to as an 'experimental' writer. This is caught up in a second opposition, that of tradition and innovation. But let us first go back to a more deeply buried concept.

To be a creator

Barely a decade ago, Anthony Burgess wrote an article in the *Observer* ('Grunts from a Sexist Pig,' 21/6/81), in reaction to receiving a Pink Pig Award from the Women in Publishing Group 'for outstanding contributions to sexism.' The article is mildly amusing and even occasionally sensible and fair, until Burgess brings out—in all seriousness—the hoary old chestnut that

> Woman have never been denied professional musical instruction—indeed, they used to be encouraged to have it —but they have not yet produced a Mozart or a Beethoven. I am told by feminists that all this will change some day, when women have learned how to create like *women* composers, a thing men have prevented their doing in the past.

He says this is nonsense and would be denied by composers like Thea Musgrave and the late Dame Ethel Smyth [whom, however, one rarely hears spoken of seriously]. Now Burgess may well be right to poke fun at the notion of composing as *women* composers. But to hear the ancient argument about Mozart and Beethoven (or Michelangelo or Shakespeare) repeated so late in the day is discouraging. He goes on: 'Freud, bewildered, said "What does a woman *want?*"' and insists that this question has not been answered, despite the writings of (here a long list, with amazing omissions, of feminist names from Kate Millett and Simone de Beauvoir all the way back to Mary Wollstonecraft 'and the great Virginia herself').

That such unimaginative assertions can still be made after some twenty years of deconstruction (of Freud among others) and other investigations, would alone justify my title. All this has been much researched and written about. It takes centuries, generations of artists being allowed and expected to practise their art and to show themselves practising it, rather than just looking pretty at a spinet as an asset on the marriage market (composing being for brother Wolfgang), for a Mozart or a Michelangelo or a Shakespeare to emerge. Even today the prejudice against women painters, sculptors and composers runs deeper than that against women writers, for precisely the reasons described by 'the great Virginia herself.'

But where do these judgements come from if not from the canon? Jane Austen is perfect, but of course she is not Shakespeare. Nor for that matter is Thackeray or Trollope. What does it mean? Burgess himself is very careful to welcome the republication by Virago of 'the masterpiece of Dorothy Richardson.' Does he really mean that? Or is it really 'only' a mistresspiece? In which case I would *personally* agree with him but would have the courage to say so: there are secondary works of historical interest in both masculine and feminine writing. And indeed his evaluation is wholly in relation to Joyce (though it is already much to recognize her as 'anticipating' him), and used more to defend himself than to praise her:

In considering [. . .] the masterpiece of Dorothy Richardson I did not say that here we had a great work of women's literature, but rather here we had a great work which anticipated some of the innovations of James Joyce. I should have stressed that this was a work by a woman, but the womanly aspect of the thing didn't seem to me to be important. I believe that the sex of an author is irrelevant because any good writer contains both sexes.

I leave aside the question of whether innovations picked up by a later writer in themselves make a work less (to me) self-indulgent and tedious (or even whether the later writer might not also have been so considered had he not been a man)—since these are questions of literary evaluation which do not belong here. Burgess certainly wants to soften the enemy by calling Richardson's novel a 'masterpiece,' but at once must anger one sect at least by his 'androgynous-great-mind' argument. An impeccable stance on the face of it—and indeed it has been mine in this book, but it is not that of the out-and-out feminist. It goes back to Coleridge, and of course to 'the great Virginia herself' (Woolf 1929, Ch. 6), who however adds:

> Coleridge certainly did not mean, when he said that a great mind is androgynous, that it is a mind that has any special sympathy with women; a mind that takes up their cause or devotes itself to their interpretation.

The androgynous-great-mind stance is what some feminists condemn as 'humanist' rather than 'feminist,' while for others it is the only possible option, providing it is understood properly and not used as a pig-snout mask.

Meanwhile, back to the canon: would anyone now seriously dispute the major status of writers such as Jane Austen, George Eliot, or Emily Dickinson? Probably not. For of course, they are safely dead.

One useful analogy: the nineteenth-century gentleman who would live by the classics (in dead languages), or sometimes study ancient Arabic or Persian or Hebrew, yet show no interest in contemporary equivalents—indeed there couldn't *be* equivalents, oral or written—and would despise any living representative of those cultures as wogs and Jews.

Another useful analogy: the performing arts, where the artists are necessarily alive, but die with their art (or did before the modern media). Thus men did not feel threatened in their real creativity, that is to say, in their desired posterity, and for this reason the performing arts (the living word) have often been considered as vaguely inferior to the creative arts. For although the *work* involved is as great for performing artists, they merely transmit, perform, interpret, the verbal artefact that has been 'created' by the 'real' artist, who alone possesses that mysterious quality called *genius.*[1]

The performing arts require ability, talent, hard work, but genius? No! The contradiction is found already in Plato, who devalues the mere performance and interpretation of the rhapsode in the *Ion,* yet elsewhere devalues writing as against the voice (see 'La Pharmacie de Platon,' Derrida 1972a).

The work/genius opposition goes back at least to Longinus, in what is basically a nature/culture opposition *(On the Sublime,* Ch. 2). The privilege is on genius (nature), with work (culture) as both a curb and a spur.

Genius is the tutelary god or demon that makes the artist. The poet may have his Muse (pre-Hellenic *Montya,* from Indo-European *mon-, men-, mn-* to remember), daughter of Zeus (supreme power) and Mnemosyne (Memory), but she merely presides or inspires, that is, jogs, or, as Beauty, she is both his inspiration and his aim. This notion goes back to an oral tradition, since writing is supposed to kill Memory, but later poets steeped in the classics never seemed to notice the contradiction and went on invoking the Muse, possibly as a dead Letter, and in

---

1 It is not by chance that women were admitted into the performing arts, late but much earlier than in the creative ones (and for that reason were treated as *demi-mondaines,* belonging not to *the* world but to a half-world use by men). Nor is it by chance that even today one can still hear the opinion, unwittingly echoed from the Thirties, and from the same type of man, of the same generation as those who say there have been no women Mozarts, that Jews are brilliant performers and interpreters but not creators.

fact representing the bisexual nature of creativity.

The really mysterious creative force, however, is genius: direct contact with the gods. Plato called it divine madness, Longinus called it ecstasy, the eighteenth-century Genius, the Romantics Imagination but also Genius. And whatever the name it belongs to man.

Gender, genre, genius, genesis: all come from the same Indo-European root *gen* to beget / to be born. Only man begets, woman bears and travails: genius versus work.

Burgess turns this into a back-handed compliment: 'I believe that artistic creativity is a male surrogate for biological activity, and that if women do so well in literature it may be that literature is, as Virginia Woolf said, 'closer to gossip than to art.'

A male surrogate for *bearing?* Or for *begetting?* Both are biological activities. But the metaphors of literary paternity are very curious indeed. On the one hand, 'the text's author is a father, a progenitor, an aesthetic patriarch whose pen is an instrument of generative power like his penis' (Gilbert & Gubar 1979, p. 7). On the other, genius belongs to men in a strangely passive role. He is possessed. He is pregnant. The metaphor for literary works as begotten children and their production as childbirth is older than the pen/penis begetting metaphor. As Elaine Showalter (1981, p. 188) reminds us (quoting Gilbert & Gubar, Nina Auerbach, Tillotson, Ellmann), the eighteenth and nineteenth centuries are full of gestation metaphors, and Joyce echoes them.

In fact they go back to Plato, for whom the speeches of Phaedrus and Lysias are their sons (never of course their daughters), indeed any speech (logos) was a son.

But a quaint, motherless son. For what gets occulted in all this is the woman, just as the real producer, the worker or small farmer, gets occulted by the rise of capitalism.[2]

In the *Symposium* it is Diotima, the only woman allowed into the dia-

---

2 This is only incidental to my argument. Derrida (1972a, pp. 91-5) reminds us that the father is 'also: a *chief,* a *capital,* and a *possession [un bien]. Pater* in Greek means all that' (my translation, his italics). Rabaté (1986, p. 191) takes this up with reference to Pound: 'The questions of generation and usury appear from the start as inextricably confused, for interest is the "offspring," the "son" of money.'

logues but *in absentia,* who has given Socrates the apparently extraordinary revelation that the purpose of love is procreation *in beauty.* For what purpose? For immortality (206e, 207a). And she rapidly moves on (in the account of Socrates) to those who have fecundity *of soul* (men, 209a), who will look for the beautiful object (a boy) and educate him, and at whose contact they will give birth to that with which they have long been pregnant (209c).

Why does Plato put this nonsense into a woman's mouth, via Socrates? Precisely because she is a woman and knows about 'real' childbirth, the literal half of the metaphor, which gives such a solid, physical basis to her figurative sliding, that is, to the meaning Plato wants. The fecund male, though procreating through 'contact' with Beauty (boy or Muse) is already long pregnant, quite independently of this contact. He has been touched with divine madness, with genius. The Muse (or boy), contrary to some feminist analysis, is never a mother in this, but a memory-jogger or an 'ideal.' In practice she is merely a titillating handmaiden, a stage on the Platonic ladder, at most a gorgeous midwife.

Thus in the earliest texts that echo down and influence the European literary tradition, even to modern times (e.g. Pound), men have simply appropriated childbirth as a painless metaphor, a *bearing* over, a mater phor artistic creation. A Muse may or may not preside, but genius begets *and* travails. The woman in this does neither. Indeed when women did start writing, the ancient metaphor was all too easily reversed: her books were produced *instead of* children, as surrogates, in the absence of the all-essential male.

For men have always had it both ways: the begetting *and* the travail (the travail which, as 'work' belongs to culture, but which as bearing and 'labour' belongs to nature); the genius *and* the work (the genius which is itself both passive possession and authoritative production), the penis *and* the womb. Man has in fact appropriated, to represent his relation to truth or God, both aspects of woman's role in relation to man: the being made fecund and the travail. This in addition to begetting. It is his *supplément:* he, as God, begets a work upon himself; he, as poet, is made fecund and labours. But on a safe, metaphoric level: he would never actually die in childbirth.

How perfectly logical, then, in this long tradition, that women should have no role at all in artistic creativity. The double connotation of 'womb' as both birth and death has been split, men appropriating the birth process and leaving its death connotations to the woman. Just as writing is death, the outside *pharmakon*. Obviously then, woman cannot be included in that 'tonic' aspect of 'secular' culture to which the central male tradition now and again turns when exhausted. All she can be is beautiful, and hence not understand beauty.[3]

Can women then, traditionally, never be in that 'masculine' role of creativity, have they ever been supposed to have that privileged, direct contact with the gods, that goes by the name of genius?

The only institutional example seems to be the ancient prophetesses, who might be supposed to be directly inspired from the gods in their oracles. Yet they uttered their 'sibylline' oracles uncomprehendingly in the name of the male gods. They merely transmitted blindly, they were the hidden spokespersons for the gods, and rulers consulted Apollo or Zeus, not his priestess.

Woman cannot have direct access to truth, or to the divine madness of the poet, and *do* something rational with it: *her* divine madness is from the devil, she is a witch, or its modern equivalent, a hysteric.[4]

If as in the rare case of the sibyl she *has* access to the 'fecundation,' she is automatically deprived of the understanding necessary for the 'travail.' The Church's present resistance to women priests is no different, whatever the specious (canonic) arguments given, such as lack of

---

3 In *Mademoiselle de Maupin* (1835), by Theophile Gautier, the beauty-seeking d'Albert writes to his friend that women understand no more of poetry than do cabbages or roses, which is natural since they are themselves poetry: the flute cannot understand the tune played on it (1966, p. 206). And Mademoiselle de Maupin herself (disguised as a man) obligingly echoes these views. Women (she writes to *her* friend) are usually deprived of the feeling for beauty, because they possess beauty, and since self-knowledge is the most difficult knowledge they naturally understand nothing of it (pp. 301-2, my rendering). Pound to H.D.: 'You are a poem though your poem's naught' (H.D., *End to Torment* 1979, p. 12).

4 Hawthorne to his publisher, praising a contemporary woman 'domestic' writer, Fanny Fern, author of *Ruth Hall:* 'The woman writes as if the devil was in her; and that is the only condition under which a woman ever writes anything worth reading. Generally women write as emasculated men . . . ' (Ticknor 1913: pp. 141-2, quoted by Voloshin 1976).

biblical authority or inversely patristic authority against: *taceat mulier in ecclesia.* The true reason is the same time-honoured, self-assigned prerogative: the divine and metaphoric power of producing one thing out of another thing through the word is deeply felt as a male power. The priest, who with the Holy Spirit produces Christ the Body (the Logos), parallels the poet, who with his genius begets and labours to produce not only metaphors (Aristotle: a sign of genius) but motherless sons. Interestingly, the resistance to women priests corresponds exactly to the varying versions of transubstantiation from full metaphor (the bread *is* the Body) to a mere symbol: the Roman Catholic Church says no, never; the Anglican is in agonized compromise, the Lutheran and other Protestant Churches have mostly accepted.

It is thus almost normal, if such a contorted logic can be considered 'normal' that beneath an apparent general acceptance and praise of women in literature and the arts, there should still lie in men's unconscious, and therefore in that of society the deep phallocratic fear of women as memory, as birth, as death, of writing as the death of memory, and hence as birth and death, leading to the total occultation of women from the writing process and the resulting but equally deep conviction that women cannot be 'great' artists of 'genius' or even serious 'creators' with a possible posterity. As men can. As a few exceptional women have been, but they were influenced by men and they are dead, their posterity has been accommodated, it is not a new and threatening future posterity. Moreover, women writers can only write disguised autobiography, that is, 'life,' but consigned to death because (a) not male life and (b) not 'creative.'[5]

---

5   See Kolodny 1975, p. 77, even on a successful feminist author, about reviewers and TV hosts insisting that Erica Jong reveal the 'autobiographical underpinnings' of her novel *Fear of Flying,* so that, 'by attributing its narrative to autobiography, the inherently sexist view might be maintained that women's productions are attributable to something less than fully conscious artistic invention.' The observation is just, and men who use autobiography are seldom so plagued, or are tacitly assumed to have 'transmuted' it. A few pages later, however, Kolodny seems to contradict herself when she insists on feminine experience: 'To cavalierly label Kate Chopin's Edna as immoral, or Joan Didion's Maria as mad [...] is to ignore the possibility that the *worlds they inhabit may in fact be real, or true,* and for them the only worlds available' [italics mine]. Feminists cannot have it both ways, or at least Kolodny should define 'real' and 'true.'

And yet, in artistic creation, by anyone whatever and given the necessary initial conditions, life and death are shared by all, and the begetting is also the travail and vice versa.

To be an experimental writer

I am aware that in this return to my main topic, the sudden juxtaposition of 'experimental' writing with 'genius' may seem to be equating the two. In fact I don't even like the word 'genius' and have only been using it to point up a deep-lying contradiction. Clearly there can be trivial as well as truly innovative experiment, just as there can be trivial as well as important writing in wholly familiar forms. I shall not here define Greatness, or the Sublime, or Imagination, or Literature. But I should perhaps try to define 'experiment.'

I have so far put the word in quotes, because it seems to mean so many different things. What is 'experimental' art, or an 'experimental' novel? Is it *a genre?*

People often talk as if it were, although most experiment either widens the concept of a particular genre or explodes the notion of genre altogether. Yet a writer, or a group of writers, is put into that category, as if it were equivalent to Science Fiction, the Fantastic, Romance, Realism.

For Zola, the father of a certain kind of Realism, the 'experimental novel' meant a novel which had been carefully researched and backed by 'experiment' in the scientific sense of verification (of slaughterhouses, mines, peasant life), or what we now call documentary. The narrative voice had to be objective, impartial, 'scientific.' In other words, a new kind, or school, of Realism, called Naturalism, almost a new genre.

For Hardy it meant, as we saw (according to Boumelha's interesting readings), experiment away from Naturalism, the 'search for a form' revolving round the problem of female characters, provoking 'an uncertainty of genre and tone which unsettles the fictional modes in a disturbing and often provocative manner.' But the 'experiment' in question turns out to be (for me) chiefly Hardy's odd but by no means novel manipulation of viewpoint and a curious 'blend' of traditional forms for different purposes. If this is 'experimental,' then every writer who develops his art is experimental, and there is indeed a sense in which every writer is. But at least Boumelha is genuinely concerned with formal experiments as they are related to the themes of the 'New Woman' fiction of the nineties. Today, on the other hand, the word 'experimental' is often used by feminists to designate new feminist *themes,* that come out of feminine 'experience' (as opposed to 'experience' of mines and slaughterhouses), whether or not these create new modes or structures.

Conversely, in the Formalist and then the Structuralist periods, the underlying opposition was often felt to be Realism *versus* Experiment, that is, a complete reversal, with the privilege of seriousness on the 'experimental' side, since the presuppositions of Realism were being thoroughly requestioned. It is often forgotten that the *nouveau roman,* when it burst out in the fifties *against* the traditional realistic novel, first acquired the label *nouveau realisme,* and was linked to phenomenology, just as earlier literary 'revolutions' had been made in the name of a greater realism. Only later did it come to be seen as, and further developed into, a much more complex poetics, linked to 'postmodernism,' but this was because of its radical changes in the *form* of the novel.

So 'experiment,' although part of the tradition/innovation opposition, was caught up in that of realism/formalism—which itself had meant different things from Hegel on: for Hegel (and for the Marxists after him) 'formalist' meant superficial (Preface to *Phenomenology of Mind),* but for the Russian Formalists (much condemned by the Soviet regime at the time) it meant rigorous attention to literary structures and conventions, in other words, poetics. Thus 'experiment' is often regarded as 'merely' formal, tinkering with technique (conceived quite logically as something external in just the way Plato considered writing as external), tinkering with the signifier irrespective of the signified, the 'content,' the 'truth,' the 'real,' and other such idealist concepts; the implication being that the real exists independently of our systems of looking at it, and even that such tinkering is not accompanied by any valid 'content' at all, let alone 'value.' Baudelaire was complaining of this already in 1861 in his essay on Gautier.[6]

Years ago (1956) Nathalie Sarraute reversed the realist/formalist opposition and said that the true realists were those who look so hard at reality that they see it in a new way and so have to work equally hard to invent new forms to capture that new reality, whereas the formalists were the diluters, who come along afterwards and take these now more familiar forms, pouring into them the familiarized reality anyone can see. Sarraute's reversal in a way goes back to Hegel (formalism as superficial), for it calls the imitators formalists and the innovators realists. But such a reversal, although expressed in terms of an older dispensation (forms to capture a pre-existing reality), is basically sound, for it insists on the link between innovation and a completely different way of looking, which is after all another way of defining genius, for example in science. Today one would push it much further and say, not that new ways of looking necessitate new forms, but that experiment with new forms produces new ways of looking, produces, in fact, the very story (or 'reality' or 'truth') that it is supposed to reproduce, or, to put it in deconstructive terms, repeats an absent story (see Brooks 1977, Hillis Miller 1976, Chase 1979, Culler 1980).

Both aspects of the opposition, whichever way one takes it, are as necessary to the continuity of art as they are to that of life. Both occur in all art forms across the spectrum of genres and subgenres, both can be practised and achieved by men and women of all origins. And the prejudice against the unfamiliar affects all who experiment.

To be an experimental woman writer

Nevertheless women writers, not safely dead, who at any one living moment are trying to 'look in new ways' or 'reread' and therefore rewrite their world, are rarely treated on the same level of seriousness as their male counterparts. They can get published, they can even get good reviews. But they will be more easily forgotten between books and mys-

---

6 'Among the innumerable prejudices of which France is so proud is the common notion, naturally found heading the precepts of vulgar criticism, namely that a work which is *too well* written *must* be lacking in feeling' ([1868] 1921, p. 266, my translation and italics).

teriously absent from general situation surveys or critical books about contemporary literature, even about contemporary 'experimental' (or, for now, 'postmodern') novels. They will not ultimately be taken up by the more attentive critics. Even 'the great Virginia herself,' who had the best possible environment in the Bloomsbury Group to be so taken up, and her own publishing firm, who was called a 'genius' by her husband and friends, not only became ill with agony over the reception of every book by the then predominantly male literary scene, but was not fully and widely appreciated until well after her death. And she is the 'best' case, the token case. Similarly Nathalie Sarraute, another token case, was nearly sixty years old when she won recognition, at the time of the *nouveau roman* and thanks to the label, although her writing was and remains quite distinct from that of its male representatives.

It does seem, in other words, not only more difficult for a woman *experimental* writer to be accepted than for a woman writer (which corresponds to the male situation of experimental writer vs. writer), but also peculiarly more difficult for a *woman* experimental writer to be accepted than for a *male* experimental writer. She may, if young, get caught up in a 'movement,' like Djuna Barnes, like H. D., like Laura Riding, as someone's mistress, and then be forgotten, or if old, she may be 'admitted' into a group, under a label, but never be quite as seriously considered as the men in that group.

Perhaps one of the safest ways of dismissing a woman experimental writer is to stick a label on her, if possible that of a male group that is getting or (better still) used to get all the attention. Fluttering around a canon. The implication is clear: a woman writer must either use traditional forms or, if she dare experiment, she must be imitating an already old model. Indeed, the only two advantages of 'movements' are (1) for the writers, to promote themselves (hence they are usually men), and (2) for the critics, to serve as useful boxes to put authors into. But women are rarely considered seriously as part of a movement when it is 'in vogue,' and then they are damned with the label when it no longer is, when they can safely be considered as minor elements of it.

It may well be that women writers do not like new 'movements' and still shrink from declaring all over the place how revolutionary they are. Political women, and hence feminists, have had this courage. But, as well as 'muted' women (Ardener, see below), many artists, male or female (rightly or wrongly), evade the overtly political, and it seems to me that the combination of woman + artist + experimental means so much hard work and heartbreak and isolation that there must be little time or energy for crying out loud.

And here we come back to the canon, in the form of another ancient opposition within the idea of belonging: traditionally, men belong to groups, to society (the matrix, the canon). Women belong to men. And in so far as women, emancipating themselves, also behave in the same way, they are said to be imitating men (and so to belong to them again). All emancipation apparently has to pass that way, just as it has to pass through a 'separatist' stage to find its strength and identity. But every individual needs a mixture of withdrawal and belonging. And it seems to me that the woman artist needs more withdrawal and less belonging. She needs to withdraw, either from the man she is with who may be consciously or unconsciously punishing her for or otherwise stifling her creativity; or from society (ditto). She will try less hard to belong, because she needs it less deeply. Thus she will tend to belong neither to a man nor to society. At best she will belong to what Ardener calls the 'wild' zone, as described by Elaine Showalter (1981).

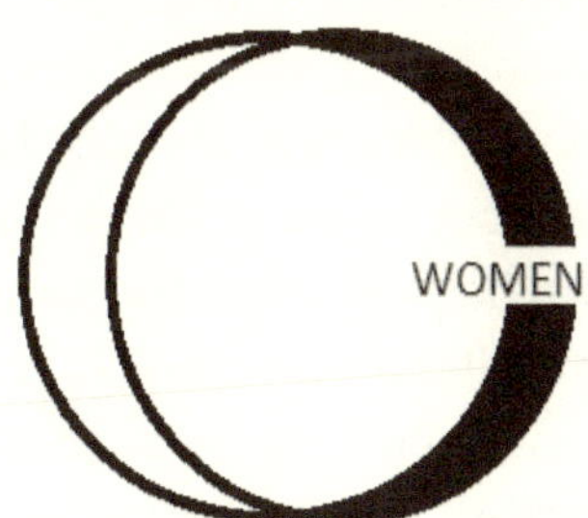

FIG. 10

Showalter gives Ardener's diagram of the 'muted' and the 'dominant' group as one circle over another, the 'muted' circle shifted slightly to the right (whereas in Victorian society the 'woman's sphere' was conceived as separate and smaller). (See Fig. 10).

Showalter points out that spatially and experientially each group has a crescent-shaped zone inaccessible to the other, but that 'metaphysically, or in terms of consciousness,' the wild zone

> has no corresponding male space since all male consciousness is within the circle of the dominant structure and thus accessible to or structured by language. In this sense, the 'wild' is always imaginary: from the male point of view, it may simply be the projection of the unconscious. In terms of cultural anthropology, women know what the male crescent is like, even if they have never seen it, because it becomes the subject of legend (like the wilderness). But men do not know what is in the wild. (p. 200)

If this is so, there are not only very few truly experimental writers of the 'wild' zone (to my knowledge only Angela Carter and Helene Cixous at her least self-indulgent succeed here, though my knowledge may be limited), but in theory they must also know, and accept, that they cannot enter the canon (unless of course men were to open their minds, and abolish the notion of canon). Except, perhaps, a female canon.

But then, the very notion of a female canon (the new geography) is a contradiction in terms. Feminists have not quite faced that problem, but I cannot deal further with this huge issue here, beyond noting the danger: not only can the new boldness of feminist themes seem in itself sufficient renewal (the wild zone perhaps turned into a new chunk of reality to be sold), it can also help to create the stamp, the label 'feminist writer' or even 'woman writer.' As I have suggested, one safe way not to recognize innovative women is to shove them under a label, and one such label is 'woman writer.' Women may feel that the dismissive aspect comes from men, but I am not so sure. Naturally it must be comforting to be backed and hailed by a sisterhood (a female canon) but that sisterhood is, with some few exceptions, generally so busy on feminist 'themes,' on defining a 'feminist aesthetic' and on discovering or reinterpreting women authors of the past (rather as the Deconstructionist School in America paid little attention to the deconstructing 'postmodern' literature all around them), that it has no time to notice or to make an effort to understand, let alone to back, an unfamiliar (experimental) woman writer who does not necessarily write on, or only on, such themes, but whose discourse is, in Elaine Showalter's phrase (1981), 'a double-voiced discourse, containing a "dominant" and a "muted" story, what Gilbert and Gubar in *The Madwoman in the Attic* call a palimpsest.' If the 'wild' zone writer is inaccessible to most male readers, she is at least appreciated by feminists. The 'double-voiced' writer (unless he is a man) antagonizes both, she is in the sea between two continents.

In his book *On Deconstruction* (1983), Jonathan Culler has a chapter called 'reading as a Woman,' where he quotes Shoshana Felman (1975): 'Is "speaking as a woman" determined by some biological condition or by a strategic, theoretical position, by anatomy or by culture?' And he applies this to the divided structure of woman's reading: women can read, and have read, as men, and have learnt to identify with a masculine experience presented as the human one. Today, women face this problem, and 'try to bring a new experience of reading for both men and women, a reading that questions the literary and political assumptions on which their reading has been based.'

It would seem, then, that the androgyny that some men have claimed for *all good* writers at the *creative* end has willy nilly been acquired by women at the *receiving* end, but not by men, who rarely identify with women characters as women do with male ones. Whatever the case, it would surely be a good thing if more men learnt to read as women (even the wild zone), so that the bisexual effort, which they have metaphorically appropriated at the creative end, should not remain so wholly on the women's side at the receiver's end. Both should read as both, just as both should write as both. And one of the ways in which this delightful bisexualism should occur is in a more open and intelligent attitude to experiment of all kinds by women.

Bibliography:

Ardener, Edwin, 1977. 'Belief and the Problem of Women' in *Perceiving Women*, ed. Shirley Ardener, London and New York, Malaby 1975, 1-27.

Boumelha, Penny, 1982. *Thomas Hardy and Women: Sexual Ideology and Form*, Totowa, N. J., Barnes & Noble / Sussex, Harvester.

Brooks, Peter, 1977. 'Freud's Master Plot: Questions of Narrative,' in *Yale French Studies* 55, 280-300.

Brown, Norman O., 1966. *Love's Body*, New York, Random House.

Burgess, Anthony, 1981. 'Grunts from a Sexist Pig,' *The Observer*, June 21, 37.

Chase, Cynthia, 1979. 'The Deconstruction of Elephants: Double Reading of Daniel Deronda,' *PMLA* 93, 215-27.

Culler, Jonathan, 1980. 'Fabula and Sjuzhet in the Analysis of Narrative: Some American Discussions,' *Poetics Today* 1/3, 27-37.

1983. *On Deconstruction—Theory and Criticism after Structuralism*, London, Routledge & Kegan Paul.

Derrida, Jacques, 1972a. 'La Pharmacie de Platon,' in 1972b, pp. 91-5.

Derrida, Jacques, 1972b. *La Dissemination*, Paris, Seuil; transl. *Dissemination*, Chicago University Press 1982.

Felman, Shoshana, 1975. 'Women and Madness: The Critical Phallacy,' *Diacritics* 5, 2-10.

Frye, Northrop, 1976. *The Secular Scripture*, Cambridge, Mass., Harvard University Press.

Gautier, Theophile, (1834). *Mademoiselle de Maupin*, ed. Genevieve van den Bogaert, Paris, Gamier 1966.

Gilbert, Sandra, and Gubar, Susan, 1979. *The Madwoman in the Attic: The Woman Writer in the Nineteenth-Century Literary Imagination*, New Haven. Yale University Press.

Hegel, G. W., (1807). *The Phenomenology of Mind*, transl. J. B. Baillie, New York, Harper 1867.

Kermode, Frank, 1979. *The Genesis of Secrecy*, Cambridge, Mass., Harvard University Press.

Kolodny, Annette, 1975, 'Some Notes on Denning: a Feminist Literary Criticism,' *Critical Inquiry* 2/1, 75-92.

Miller, J. Hillis, 1976. 'Ariadne's Thread: Repetition and the Narrative Line,' *Critical Inquiry* 3/1, 57-77.

Miller, Nancy K. 1981. 'Emphasis Added: Plots and Plausibility in Women's Fiction,' *PMLA* 96, 36-48.

Rabaté, Jean-Michel, 1986. *Language, Sexuality and Ideology in Ezra Pound's Cantos*, London. Macmillan.

Sarraute, Nathalie, 1956. *L'Ere du soupgon: essais sur le roman.* Paris, Gallimard; transl. Maria Jolas, *The Age of Suspicion*, London, Calder & Boyars 1963.

Showalter, Elaine, 1971. 'Women Writers and the Double Standard,' *Women in Sexist Society*, ed. V. Gornick & B. K. Moran, New York, Basic Books, pp. 323-43.

Showalter, Elaine, 1981. 'Feminist Criticism in the Wilderness,' *Critical Inquiry* 8/2, 179-205.

Voloshin, Beverly, 1976. 'A Historical Note on Women's Fiction: A Reply to Annette Kolodny,' *Critical Inquiry* 2/4, 817-20.

Woolf, Virginia, 1929. *A Room of One's Own*, London, Hogarth Press; New York. Harcourt Brace 1957, Panther Books, Granada 1977.

The Logaλφageis of kLeub^h: /la:ʃ/; /lʌv/

Chretine Broke-Prose

BUT don't you think Ms Grampion, professorial voice issuing from beyond the sarcomensa, that pal-latal diphthongisation in fourteenth century Kentish may have been optional? Polite tone smothered in gravel rising from the other side of the grave.

Candidate conscious only of opposing hirsute bulk—shaggy whitening blond hair clouding matching moon-face curdling down in side-whiskers to a startling handlebar moustache—Grendel's mother modernised bleached by myriad seas. Here the final battle in slow-motion, submerged.

Staring at the papered text on the table, well—I—er—yes, twisting forelock nervously round finger. How to avoid such a nonsensical question. A mediaeval bureaucrat briefly palimpsested: Chaucer's Sergeant of the Lawe who semed bisier than real proclaiming, from 23:59:59 on the 16th April 1340, palatal diphthongisation will be optional in the County of Kent.

Whimsy banished, surely sir, sirring habit relicked from service to menarch and country, surely the problem is really whether the diphthongs would have been rising or falling? I mean, that's what affects the metre and in this case, my interpretation. Leading with the chin lasering the monster's gaze, I'm only concerned with the poetry.

Dr Reeves glancing at the candidate from the other end of the interminable table, yes of course. A nouvelle approach. But you're dealing with a dinosaur language you know. Plump handsome face younger than the others equally Nordic. Philologists always seeming Nordic, seeking Old Norse souls in lost sounds syllababbles. Thesis supervisor sitting between the soles: fleshy bald taciturn. A toothless wyrm.

On and on. Grendel's mother nothing if not meretriculous holding a sheaf of notes perused point by point monopolising the interrogation;

grossly unfair. Would Dr Reeves have as many queries? If Dr Reeves would, Professor Grave Voice allowing no interjectory opportunity: quoting obscure insightations from other texts convincing Ms Grampion these texts remain unknown alas, but the candidate obstinately spruiking written Eve(r)dense in defence.

O-on page 327, flicking open to it wretchedly, gazing blank-brained at previously familiar typescript now a tenth century figment of a forgotten epic once copied by a neurotic scribe, your footnote refers to Dan Michel. What do you think o-of his preterite forms, in this particular instance?

Well these are irregular. I mean, from an Old Kentish point of view.

Ask an idiotic question receive an idiotic answer. Somewhere over the reignbough, Dr Reeves smiling at the wall. An Old Kentishman appearing peering out of the ninth century at the preterite forms used by Dan Michel in the fourteenth, head shaking muttering, most irregular. A tempting to adapt, Ms Grampion mimicrying the ludicrous jargling of the sexagrammarians.

Ordeal eventually ended. Presumably and by the skint of the teeth fledged as a Doctor of Philosophy fembodying a multiplicity of philistological sins.

Candidate emerging refreshed from the ladies room, Dr Reeves in a duffel-coat strolling the corridor stopping, come and have a drink. You must be feeling pretty dazed. Two full hours of it.

I knew they'd try and trip me up on philology, excluding the steward from the textaminers' triumpirate. It was very kind of you to adopt the defending role, smiling. My supervisor just seemed to disown me.

Perhaps Dr Reeves' doctorship recently acquired as painfully. But no; apparently sailed stormy weather with flying cullers, having inspected all the works of the rexaminers in order to know, even if too late, how many archademic noses the candidate would soil-rub.

You did very well. We're paid to grill you if we can't robber you. The nexaminer's identity briefly reasserted abruptly dropped, left like the hexaminer's gown at the hall-desk. Withershinning together through the rotating doors of the building. Walking to the cars parked in the drive, stopping in front of nothing so banal as the latest econo-import, instead a pale green restored Lambretta, affixing the briefcase to the curved front.

Do you mind riding my delightful decadence? I have to go to Piccadilly afterwards and don't want to return for it. Smiling side-saddling back-seat gingerly, thesis handbag hugged bodily. Better keep one hand free to hold on to me. Give me the great work and I'll put it in front.

Lambretta coughing heaving finally gliding forwards smoothly until snarled in Tottenham Court Road traffic. Leaning neatly down a small side-street stopping outside a wine bar.

What do you want with a PhD anyway? Handing back the thesis, you're not the academic type—just look at those corpses, smirking, you should be writing social commentary whodunnits.

Praised with faint damnation? Blushing, decoded as you seem much too attractive to shrivel up fade within academia. Not as your thesis just won't make the grade. Do I look like a female novelist? I thought they were all battle-axes, tone sharpened, since whatever career women do, they have it much tougher than men. Women are bound to look like battle-axes by the time they retire.

Oh come off it. Female novelists start in high school these days. Before they've matriculated they've attracted six-figure advances.

Dr Reeves skewing the conservative portrayal of the arcanademic; candidate scrupulously avoiding arrogant exclamations such as oh come off it what utter nonsense replacing these with might you be mistaken you may be right I would suggest, as scholarly opprobriate. Dr Reeves brash and blasé, likely to spout that sleeping around publishes a novel as soon as perishes it.

Deflating expectations, clasping an arm leading Ms Grampion inside the bar crammed with grey-suited grey-haired men: editors from the pubeshilling houses still clustered in the district, learned Arsinstant Keypurse from the British Mausoleum. Where oh where are the queans? Different worlds overlap in the Blooms of the Borough Bury; even after the years studying Ms Grampion bedevilled with unfamiliarity.

I think you need more than wine after that trial by fire. Two gee and tees, please. Quick, that table outside is free, grab it will you?

Sitting stunned mullet thankful at a practical stranger's assumption of the right to barbitrate even if only something alcoholic—perhaps an associate lectureship in the offing?

Bulky in duffle-coat managing two glasses a saucer in one hand briefcase—empty of the report on the great work?—in the other weaving round tangles of people towards the table.

So, pulling out the chair opposite sitting, that's better. Let's drink to Dr Grampion—no on second thoughts, you can't drink to yourself. Here's to Middle Kentish diphthongs, ^{rising} down the hatch _{falling}.

Generous helping of gin dipsonguising cramped empty stomach: three olives from the tabled saucer chomped. What'm I go'n' to 'o? Anguish muffled in the mouth stuffed with greens & blacks.

Glance embracing *carpe diem*, have a solid lunch I should think. Do you smoke? Displaying a blue leather cigarette case with a large gold frame. Another anachronism.

'o, swallowing, I mean yes thank you, head inclining towards the lifted cigarette lighter, I meant about my career. Mellowed with drink voice solemn draped in little-girl-lost air role-casting Dr Reeves *anders*. Not the pexaminer kinder handsomer than the others although still severe, not the jocular *uomo di mondo* motor-scooting to the bar, but a gentle pateritarian mentor meant friend guide offering to shelter the philledgling under the scholastic ala. Exhaling noticing slack flesh under chin creased brow eyes corner-crinkled white hair mingling thinly with fair. Miracutaneously sage safe suave.

I mean, I only just scraped through that. I'm not really good enough to be an academic . . . I'm too . . . erratic.

Tapping nose-tip eyes periwinkling, pretending incompetence to make yourself sound more intriguing? There's plenty of work in your field. Come and see me in my college, I can suggest several articles—

Paid?

Good god no. We're not trade hacks.

But I—er—have to look for work. It's April now and my grant stops soon.

Ignoring the lament rising walking to the bar counter with empty glasses, standing chatting with the barman, returning with refills.

Ours is an overcrowded profession, grinning, too many brilliant products of the Welfare State.

I'm a product of the Welfare State. Not brilliant though.

Really?

Assuming the ignorance of dangling modesty deliberate, I haven't worked my way up to brilliance from humble origins, even if it is the fashion these days.

What nonsense--we're not in the middle of the last century. Have another cigarette.

No thanks, hair twirled behind ear dizzyrentated by Dr Reeves. Too self-assured *au courant* for an arkendemhick, not a wit, fexaminer's manner saturating any shop-talk.

My education was a reward for services rendered, glass raised in salute, quite undeserved—just a few years military non-action. I've bluffed my way through all along.

Oh come off it you've a very fine brain and a lively critical approach—stated during the viva reminiscent of a refugee acquaintance writing popular books called *Brooke-Rose: A New Approach*, *Brooke-Rose and the New Critics: An Approach*—the trouble, Julia—I can call you Julia yes? Dr Grampion is a bit of a mouthful, and of course you must call me Bernard—is that you can't be a mediaevalist without being a philologist.

Oh.

Cigarette talking half-smoked in the mouth jogging up down with each word like a toggle very irritating. I sympathise, Julia. People like you and I don't really fit in, bracketing flattering tempting a grateful collegial smile, I'm tolerated but only as an eccentric. My interests are rather off-beat literary aspects.

Really? Your publications—thesis articles checked crammed with aphrodite discussion of dialect forms mannerscript problems—are all fairly orthodox.

Precisely. One has to be able to produce it.

Gentle Aplatodemic air-brushing from the superior.   Inhumed hungry filled with pick-me-up gin put-me-down pity crestfallen face inducing solicitous smile.

You're tired. Take a holiday.

Can't afford it.

Haven't you a home to go to? Somewhere outside London? What about your parents?

Glass half-full of excessive fascination, hating the query always resulting in apology, my father was killed in Africa. My mother in Afghanistan.

I'm very sorry.

Cheeks flushing smiling reverting to brusque fillerlogy, what on earth does it matter how *ea* was pronounced in fourteenth century Kentish anyway?

As an item, *nada.* But one can hardly discuss the literary merits of a poem without being able to place and date it and emend a doubtful manuscript.

Voice annoyed, of course. But I'm not interested in that; enough people are busy poking over the bare bones of language. I prefer to work from edited texts. Pure phonology is hopelessly old hat. The Department of Afro-Asian Philology uses very different methods. They don't apply the old-fashioned concepts of sound and grammar to those languages. It's a science using the latest technology, thinking of someone's acoustic tonometer borrowing cutting-edge cleverness.

Yes I know, quietly, and would be useless on the dead unless a spiritualist could recall the scribe of the Beowulf manuscript, thick lips curling, and even then a device wouldn't be much use. I'd be asking the reason for introducing all those Northern elements when the scribe so obviously hails from the South West.

Leaning forwards, demeanher conspiratorial, slightly euthanolised, you know I don't *believe* in pal-palat-tantalisation.

Snorting, the Professor o-o-only has a mild stutter Julia, go easy on the gin perhaps? Palatalisation isn't a matter for belief. It happened, at certain stages in the development of the English language, affecting how people pronounced things all over the place, the way poets rhymed words and balanced sounds. No basic difference exists between that and finding out how a live African speaks. The bare bones of language, *your* label, are our only means of communication, with each other and with the past. Aren't you interested in nuance?

Knowledge not flooring that argument: sponge-brain gin-soaked Phil has lost Log (hic!). Hmm . . . you rarely find anything as subtle as nonce from physterical heronetics. Of course, head briefly shaken infokussing on blue eyes, Chaucer is very witty sending up the Northern Daleks in one of his tales, but the difference is texterminated to us, hazarding gestures haply round the bar at grey suits. A snob joke is only funny if the norm is so natural you're unconscious of the norm. Like BBC World English and Yorkshire comedians. And those are just risible.

I wasn't talking about snob humour, friction sparking, I meant the glimpses of life seen via the very sound-changes.

Sound-changes! Almost drove me mad. I still dream them, gulping the last of the aphromnesiac, I wake up working out every stage by which *odium* becomes annoy, or how *cognitum* becomes quaint. But the change of meaning is much more interesting, setting the glass CLUNK on the table head tilting to one side, it has and has not mutated: hatred is after all most annoying and cognisance is a very quaint affair.

Studying the qualified Doctor delighted interest ignited. And yet, reproof wagging a mocking finger, if you didn't know from phonology the words were the same, you wouldn't know the semantic development, would you? Even a pure sound change can animate something of the past. Think of the Old French word *escarn*, bolting off to catch the Southern English change from *o* to *a*. It's the only Norman word to do so. *Scorn*, the voice me-me-king the νόημα, why should *scorn* be borrowed so much earlier than other Norman words with *a*? Casts a fascinating light on the psychology of occupation, don't you think?

Blinking at Bernard's Walter-Scott attitude to philology, *such* a drought-ridden subject! Having exhumologically gested: stupidity, thy name thine self Julia.

Oh why did I take all this up, grimacing, when all I can do now is to go back to my garret and starve while I write novels? The sort wrapped in garish jackets: breast-sellers.

Laughing, you don't really live in a garret? Where?

A top-floor bedsit in Gower Street.

What number?

Disclothed.

I'll pass by and see how the word-count is progressing. But now I'm afraid I must toodaloo. I'm rendaynouing my fumb for lunch and I'm tray tart already.

sExiting the bar thanking him Lystlessly.

Holding hands longer than neutrally adequate nodding, good luck. Don't worry. Take a holiday—you're bound to feel *kaputt* after all that effort. As the idle python says, look on the bright side—something will turn up, no doubt about it. Clambering astride the Lambretta scooter-ing towards Oxford Street no backward glance.

Walking a jay to spread the traffic jam of St Giles imagining the star-ring role as victual of a hit-and-run eating in the cafeteria noisily em-bowelled in sLyfones Körner wasHouse.

Le Diner

Nadine Mainard

Bernard's wife, ever fanatical about French standards in food and wine, deciding to serve a perfectly floating *soufflé au fromage de chèvre* accompanied by a lightly chilled *Vouvray*. Despite Nicolette's excellent cuisine, no-one would laud the dinner for publisher, academic, his wife, and his lover an overwhelming success.

Justin, intent on discussing the recent shortcomings of Bernard's manuscript, *Courtly Love*, and having cast Bernard as the architect of the latter's own downfall, will proceed to assist in laying the foundations for it.

—You know, old chap, Justin placing his napkin neatly across his lap, your original text was rather remarkable. *As it was.*

—Yes well, Bernard forking a mouthful of *soufflé* and swallowing quickly, it was a little light on. Needed a bit of backbone. Rather gappy in places.

—Fiddlesticks. All those footnotes, endnotes, asymptotes and anecdotes are a Gorgon's glare. Tortured tangles of serpent.

—Oh come on. I've a standard to uphold here.

—What? In pedantry? You'll have the readers either falling asleep or reaching for a Harlequin.

Bernard, enjoying a mood of elated irrepressibility and equally intent on warding off Justin's slings and arrows of outrageous exaggeration, having Julia to impress and his wife to possess.

—Utter nonsense. The topic would be considered a frivolous one otherwise. Readers appreciate these minor digressions.

—No, Justin waving a dissenting fork, they prefer reading about the major indiscretions. Courtly Love has gone from being a light romp to an armoured joust.

—Precisely, Nicolette gesturing expansively with the wine bottle before pouring, why armour was invented. To ensure the survival of the knights. The riff-raff belt each other up with wooden staffs. If you adopt such a slap-happy approach to scholarship, you may as well throw intellectual integrity out the window.

—Weeding out these off-shoots of obfuscation, Justin raising his glass, hardly constitutes slap-happy. Merely prudent gardening. Sante! Sipping his wine and smiling thinly.

—How do you suppose the public, let alone the University, Nicolette smoothing her sleek brown hair behind her ears, would react if I started popularising my work on early Latin graffiti by including the latest rap homeoptotes?

—You could, Nicolette darling, but don't expect a slew of offers for the film rights.

—If you want to build a prestige list, Justin, and that was rather your point in commissioning Bernard, you'll just have to accept that there's a limited audience for such works.

—Bernard does not for one minute fall within our prestige list, Justin's finger tapping lightly on the cloth-covered table, and if he had wanted to write Courtly Love as an endeavour in true scholarship, he should have sent the manuscript to Cambridge or Oxford or Edinburgh, since they have the funds to support such a cause. But that wasn't the kind of book Bernard chose to write, placing his cutlery together on his plate and leaning back in his chair.

Julia, previously silent, delighted at the excuse to meet Bernard's wife and inspect the apparently fading allure of her charms, oscillating between agreement with Justin and attraction to Bernard and annoyance with Nicolette. Consequently supporting the wife and simpering at the husband and sallying forth against the publisher.

—Nicolette has a point, though, Julia twirling her hair around her fingers and eyeing Bernard. Courtly Love is a scholarly work and readers will expect a certain amount of learned asides. You can't really be thinking of stripping out its rigour, Justin. Why, Tweedie and Tweedie would look as though it were only interested in publishing sub-par theses.

—Footnotes are essential, Bernard reaching across the table to pat Julia's arm, to a text of this depth.

—Footnotes will just nose-dive this text, Justin dabbing his mouth with his napkin. Excellent nosh, Nicolette. Your soufflés must have been the inspiration for Bernard's original treatment of mediaeval matchmaking. 'Fraid it has rather sunk now.

—It's terribly erudite! Julia shaking her head, the wine colouring her cheeks rose.

—Justin, you have no idea, Nicolette collecting the four empty plates deftly and rising from the table, as to the precision and attention to detail the baking of a perfect soufflé requires. Shall we drink our coffee in the salon? Just give me a few moments, won't you?

—Terribly being the operative word, Justin offering his arm to Julia pushing back her chair, her acceptance awkward, Bernard frowning and following. Nicolette reappearing, holding a tray bearing pewter-framed glass demitasses filled with espresso, and setting it on the low table between the two lounges. Justin sitting beside Julia, manoeuvring Bernard opposite to share a couch with his wife.

—Darling, you know gays make the best chefs, Justin sprinkling brown sugar crystals over his coffee. There's a reason we're also the most successful in publishing.

—You flatter yourself, Justin, Nicolette laughing and watching her husband watching Julia still twirling her hair round her fingers.

—Oh come off it, Bernard relaxing back against the couch, you don't seriously expect me to believe you're better qualified to judge Courtly Love than someone in an academic position, do you, Justin?

—Someone in a missionary position, perhaps? Julia picking up her coffee quickly, the glow in her cheeks deepening. On the coffee table, Bernard arranging his spoon with two sugar cubes lying on each side of its flank and pointing towards Julia.

—Kitten, the *Kama Sutra* makes better reading than Kinsey, whichever position you're in.

—*Bah oui*, it's that Oriental streak in you, Nicolette stirring her coffee, you're just being perverse, Justin.

—Look, it's Bernard's book, of course, Justin flicking his black hair back from his almond-shaped eyes and steepling his fingers. But since you want to insist it's an academic work, I'll have to check the contract, swallowing the last of his coffee, because we charge for excess alternations in the proofs. The printer's bill will be astronomical, popping a *petit four* in his mouth and pursing his lips. Anyway, I'll talk to Tweedie —umm, delicious chocs, Nicky darling—tomorrow and let you know.

—I'm sure we can—er—arrange something, Bernard offering the plate of *petits four* to Julia, taking one himself and passing the plate to Nicolette. You know, I've been thinking about London University. Such a top institution. It's not just about the learning, being at the pinnacle of the profession. It's about London. So cosmopolitan, the centre of the arts world, really.

—So true, Julia curling her hair around her fingers, the provinces are just completely—

—Provincial, Justin winking at a frowning Nicolette, her mouth pinching at the corners.

—So much more going on. People to meet, places to see, not just colleagues—

—Far too many distractions, Nicolette clattering her cup down on its saucer. A really English university, Bernard, with a proper scholarship like the one I wanted to take up, now that—

—That, Nicolette, is called a backwater.

—It's all very well if you have friends outside, of course, but the social life at the post-grad level is, well, pretty uneventful. Julia looking at Bernard; Justin smirking.

—Having an English education hardly confers any particular advantage.

—Justin, you're just being contrary again.

—Right, well, contrary or not, Justin standing and shaking out his legs, it's been a—er—delightful evening. Nicolette, you could do just as well with Michelin stars as with Latin lexicons—it was a lovely meal. Julia, can I drop you anywhere?

—Oh! That's very kind of you. I—er—rather thought I'd—er—well if you don't mind, Nicolette, nodding and smiling at Nicolette nodding and smiling at her in return, I thought I'd discuss the other book with Bernard. Since we didn't quite manage that.

—No, darling, we didn't. Somehow Bernard's book commandeered the conversation, Justin smiling at her knowingly. Pity—you could have persuaded me about the worth of yours. Some other time, perhaps?

—Oh yes please. That would be—that is—well, when you've had time to read the sample chapter.

—I've read it, sweets, Justin shrugging and broken-wristing an indifferent flutter, Julia leaning forwards, hesitating, sinking on the cushions. But no, you stay and talk shop with Bernard. Hopefully you don't succumb to annotationary temptations.

Nicolette walking him to the door, both lip-puckering the air around each other's cheeks.

—Bye, Justin. Thanks for coming.

—Of course. It's always a pleasure, Nicolette. Now go and keep an eye on those two before they lose themselves in that new tome.

Nicolette closing the front door behind him as the lift chimes its arrival. Later, Bernard will drive Julia home to a protracted farewell at a different front door.

Everything You Always Wanted to Know About Christine Brooke-Rose's Distant Relatives (But Were Too Poststructuralist To Ask)

Joseph Andrew Darlington

On September 11th 2013 my plane touched down in Austin, Texas. I'd been travelling for twenty-five hours and had lost count of the number of times I'd been taken aside while submachine gun-swinging guards rifled through my visa papers.

"And what is your purpose of travel today, sir?"

"Research."

"And what kind of research is that, sir?"

"Studying a writer. I'm going to the Harry Ransom Centre in Austin. They've awarded me a fellowsh—"

"Very good, sir. And who is this writer, sir?"

"Christine Brooke-Rose."

"And who is that, sir?"

<u>Exam Question</u>: Five-Minute Oral Presentation:— Explain the works of Christine Brooke-Rose to a border official operating at high alert, following a sleepless transatlantic flight after having passed through enough anti-terror scanning systems to give you the radiation signature of a dirty bomb.

I couldn't help being reminded of *Between*, Brooke-Rose's 1968 novel of transnational transit and cultural confusion. What if the novel were written today? Surely the lack of military-grade high-tech checkpoints would be notable by their absence, like servants in a Jane Austen novel. Rather than adrift in an ocean of foreign signification I was excruciatingly aware of being broken down into my component parts: face, fingerprints, citizenship documents, proof of employment—the nails by which we're hammered into official history. Popping a couple of melatonin tablets, I dozed my way out of September 11th.

The Harry Ransom Centre itself is tremendous. The tiresome process of visas and travel are immediately made worthwhile as you realise just how much historical material they hold there. I was being funded to produce research on the relationship between Brooke-Rose and Paris after May '68, but to stay on-message is near impossible. Letters between Anthony Burgess and William Burroughs, Zulfikar Ghose and B.S. Johnson, the Graham Greene archive, the Doris Lessing archive and not forgetting the rest of the Brooke-Rose papers—all were there for the viewing. It was with a real sense of urgency that I opened up the box containing Brooke-Rose's notes for *The Dear Deceit*—a novel I had not at that point read—and immediately encountered a note in Brooke-Rose's handwriting: "the man who does not respect his ancestors is unlikely to do deeds for which posterity will respect him".

Now I have never been too interested in ancestry. At the first flowerings of the internet my granddad signed up to *ancestry.com*, or some such, only to find that a distant Mormon relative had mapped our entire family history in the interest of posthumously dragging the entire Gospel clan off to Mormon heaven. Considering this included some Jewish ancestors I felt the practice somehow distasteful. Nevertheless, amongst the notebooks and manuscripts Brooke-Rose had compiled here enough materials not only for a family tree but for a working history of the Brookes, Roses and Poulin families. At the centre of this came a sheet marked "The Dear Deceit: Notes on Fiction Vs. Fact". For those interested, some sample contents:

—Philip vaguely based on my first husband, Rodney Bax, and Weirwood Abbey on Bletchley Park

—Cordelia: my father's sister, letters read. Her name is Dorothy Gordon Forbes . . . no stranger would recognize her

—Muriel: real, legacy story true, real name Muriel Rose. Now dead."

—the mother: everything real throughout novel, ditto the Bertrand family is the Brooke family

—Vernon Manning = Rev. George Chambers, rector in Ventnor . . . Wld recognize himself, but wouldn't mind

—Lambertines = Benedictines

—Alfred Hayley is of course Alfred [Northcliffe] Rose

It was this last that the novel is all about. Alfred Northcliffe Rose was Christine Brooke-Rose's father who left her mother at an early age and went on to live a life marked by what acquaintance Henry Watts describes as a "general attitude . . . of brazen indifference".

The novel is structured as a kind of backwards-facing bildungsroman. Bookended by a fictionalised version of Brooke-Rose's ex-husband doing the research work of Brooke-Rose herself, it takes the reader backwards from the reading of the will through to the mischievous youth of Alfred Hayley. By reversing the traditional form, Brooke-Rose encourages us to think like biographers rather than readers of biography. We are presented with an eccentric, pompous middle-aged publisher who, in a fit of drunken mischief, replaces the doctor's names in a medical directory with obscenities and is charged with libel. We know from his funeral of his profligacy and womanising. Now, as we move backwards through the brief snippets of information presented to us, are we supposed to explain the present by the patterns of the past? The cause-and-effect implications of the bildungsroman form appear more starkly when the process is shown in reverse. We look backwards over a lifetime and choose which parts we want to see. As historians we're standing beside Heraclitus' river of existence, scooping cups of only the clearest water into our buckets.

As an academic, it is tempting to highlight which parts of *The Dear Deceit* match up with which documents in Brooke-Rose's research: perhaps in the interests of sifting fact from fiction. A moment near the end of the novel when young Northbrooke lifts his nightshirt "like a living statue in the window-frame" (p. 300) and shows his "considerable" (p. 301) genitals to the crowd below, for example, is quoted almost directly from Francis G. Walton's letter of 28th August, 1957, right down to the "living statue" image. Walton was a childhood friend of Brooke-Rose's father with whom she corresponded and visited during the process of research. Other details, such as the mother "volunteering for the Censorship" (p. 16) department are confirmed by official Ministry of Information documents (Eastburn), while the claim to be descended from

Charlemagne (p. 148) is justified by the twenty-five generations outlined in *Chronique de la Famille Brooke*. I found nine direct parallels between research and final novel; a record I lay down for future researchers to break.

What is perhaps of more interest are the untold stories. Chief among these is the figure of Northcliffe's mother, Mary Rose. Along with her husband, the Roses were appointed joint custodians of Shakespeare's birthplace on 29th June 1900, according to Liam Fox, director of the "Trustees and Guardians of the Birthplace". A prominent member of the local Shakespeare Club, Mary Rose presented a lecture on "Shakespeare in Fact and Fiction" to an audience of over 100 people defending Shakespeare against the growing accusations that Francis Bacon was the true author of his works, stating:

> Remembering that biography, as they understand it now, was unknown in Shakespeare's day, that the modern memoir writer then has no existence, the right attitude to the subject was never to wonder there was so little, but constantly to marvel there was so much.

The speech was quoted in the local paper, *Stratford-upon-Avon*, on September 11th 1908. Afraid that the then current custodian could have taken exception and sued for libel, Northcliffe's mother Rose does not appear in *The Dear Deceit*, although two of her published papers—"Women in Shakespeare" and "Baconian Myths: Notes on Two Great Englishmen and their Defamers"—appear in the Shakespearean bookshop of semi-fictional Northcliffe's fictional mother (p. 170).

See how quickly we have returned to the text.

But the case is to be made for doing so. We find in the fan-mail folder a number of readers all wishing to remark how successful Brooke-Rose was in capturing their real life friends and acquaintances and often suggesting corrections to the story where they feel she had got some event wrong. One letter from an Ivan F. B. Parker opens with a paragraph condemning the book's unusual choice of structure before explaining that he bought Mr Rose's lease from him in 1930 and that Northcliffe had had with him a "charming young lady" at the time—"I am wondering which character she was in the book". One could be forgiven for suspecting that, having met Alfred Northcliffe Rose once, Parker felt he might even have had a chance of appearing in the book himself.

The question arises: for how many readers was *The Dear Deceit* a cleverly concealed biography? It's a question we can't answer, and I forgot to count the number of letters which might suggest that type of response. It was certainly more than one. Is that a useful amount? For the benefit of future academics, all e-books could conclude with surveys in which readers are invited to Respond To the Text. Biometric scanners could chart brain activity, pulse, pupil dilation and map results against text present on the screen—the resulting metadata could be fed inside literature producing machines capable of creating greater and greater thrills, shocks, suspense, romance; erotic impacts exponentially generating in feedback loops to the point where W. H. Smith would be stocked with novels too potent for human consumption. Having become a matter of national security the government would be obliged to fund libraries again—the shelves stocked with intercontinental belletristic missiles . . . missives? Brooke-Rose makes this look easier than it is.

But what does merit record if not the material most capable of producing response? Recent linguistic studies have shown that non-specific signifiers produce sensations of profundity when the reader considers them to emanate from a position of authority. Is this a scientific explanation of literary theory? Does this explanation only work because it satisfies the prejudices of those who were against literary theory in the first place? Does the answer change when I reveal that the studies were a fictional construct inspired by a tweet, or a blog, or some other piece of ephemera such that I am being neither informative nor particularly creative by bringing it in at this point? Have critics finally gotten over metafiction yet?

A "what if?" scenario: three possible novels about the family history which Brooke-Rose never considered:—

The Looting of Maryland: Richard Brooke, a Catholic Englishman living in the time of King James 1 flees for America after a resident of his town, Guy Fawkes, is caught attempting regicide. What follows is a family saga following the rise and fall of the Maryland Brookes; a family whose name is still held by the three towns of Brookeville, Brookefield and Brooke Manor. The title refers to a joke made by the unnamed author of *Chronique de la Famille Brooke* in referring to another book, *The Pillars of Maryland*: "Pillars signifie piliers, non pillards!" (p. 2).

The Butterfly Cage: The American Frances Livingstone Butler-Brooke was fluent in French, German and Dutch. Her love of music brought her to Europe where she married a Baron. Finding herself lost among European aristocracy she retreats to her music, committing a number of indiscretions and faux pas before the Baron ultimately divorces her. The title comes from Roland P. Falkner's wonderfully mixed metaphor in which he describes his aunt as "something of a butterfly that bruised itself against the walls of a cage" (p. 15).

A Catholic Yankee in Pius IX's Court: Dismayed by the Pope's support for the Confederacy, President Abraham Lincoln turns to the chaplain of the United States Senate, Clement Butler (father of Frances Livingstone Butler-Brooke), to correct this "misunderstanding of facts". Although able to read French and Italian the American cannot speak them and so finds himself wandering the Vatican with only Church Latin as a means of communication. Hilarity ensues. This novel is also inspired by the work of Roland P. Falkner.

These stories, appearing as they do in slim volumes of family history, would have perhaps been destined for obscurity were it not for their minor role as inspiration for Christine Brooke-Rose. As it is, they are stored safely and securely in the Ransom Centre vaults in Austin, Texas, with as much care taken over their maintenance as if they were original Shakespeare manuscripts. None shine enough intellectual light upon Brooke-Rose's works to be referenced in an academic paper; their read-ers will be limited to a handful of scholars who, although momentarily interested, will inevitably move on to more useful Brooke-Rose related materials. The manuscripts for *Thru* are fascinating, by the way.

I find it peculiar that I'm reading these histories. Even if I paid some credence to the visions of Joseph Smith, I have no business welcoming the Brooke-Roses to the Darlington family's heavenly estate. Is the interest "purely academic"? What do we learn from this exercise? The *Chronique de la Famille Brooke* lists the family traits of the Brookes as "intellectualité, ambition, humour, gout d'indépendance, autorité" (p. 2). The *Histoire de la Famille Poulin de Geneve*, written in 1942 by Francis Brooke-Poulin (sitting out the second world war in Switzerland) describes the character of the Poulins in terms of "le gout de la simplicité et de la vie de famille; et le respect des traditions". These authors, currently done the disservice of being quoted by a non-French speaker to make some abstract point about identity and history . . . who knows, maybe they're right? Surely it makes as much sense to attach traits to a family as it does to that disparate, momentary, thing-of-context we call a personality?

I wonder about the NSA, GCHQ, Prism and Tempora. I wonder about what data is stored in those hangars in the desert and by what metadata they determine the traits of terrorists and foreign diplomats. I realise that everything we write can and will be used against us in a court of history. Maybe this is the message of *The Dear Deceit* when read in the twenty-first century. All the while we go on living forwards through time unaware that, as creatures of information, we come into being only by looking backwards. Maybe "national security" is existential. A programme of total surveillance is a blueprint for immortality. The four eyes in the retrovisor reflect nothing but TEXT.

Then I'm stepping off the plane in Manchester and I haven't slept and I have undergrad seminars to teach in two hours. The customs officer scans the barcode on my passport and scratches his beard:

"This you in this photo?"

"Yeah."

"It an old picture?"

"Yeah."

"Don't look n'thin' like you."

And I walk out of the door and towards the exit through a corridor NOTHING TO DECLARE.

Bibliography

Brooke-Poulin, Francis. *Histoire de la Famille Poulin de Geneve*. Undated [post-1942].

Brooke-Rose, Christine. "Note". Undated. Enclosed in Falkner (see below).

——*The Dear Deceit*. London: Secker and Warburg, 1960.

——"The Dear Deceit: Notes on Fiction vs. Fact". Undated.

Chronique de la Famille Brooke. Undated.

Eastburn, G.J. (Major). Official testimonial for Evelyn Brooke-Rose, dated 9th June 1942.

Falkner, Roland P. *Descendants of Rev. Clement Moore Butler, D. D.* 1933.

Fox, Liam. Letter to Christine Brooke-Rose, 14th November, 1957.

Parker, Ivan F.B. Letter to Christine Brooke-Rose, 5th February, 1961.

Stratford-upon-Avon, 11th September, 1908.

Walton, Francis G. Letter to Christine Brooke-Rose, 28th August, 1957.

Watts, Henry. Letter to Christine Brooke-Rose, 8th September, 1957

Aubade

Christine Brooke-Rose

Morning numb aches
through the innumerable swerves of night,
stretches a bruised angular light
on the thrumming of young hours,
bares a golden shoulder
to the calyxed hand
that darkly unseen wakes
from the steep fashioning of farewell vows
only lovers understand.

Reading the Horoscope After Christine

Scott Beauchamp

Of course, as you drop the paper to the floor, it falls open to the most titillating parts: $5 million homes being considered by charmed yuppies (perhaps . . . perhaps . . .), a roadside vigil for a dead kid (is that a *Family Guy* balloon?), adverts showing juices pooled in the contours of feminine lips, the paused implication of motion almost agonizing (but not to you, to an implied you, a dumber and more generalized you). And you wonder who reads the paper any more anyway. You do, of course. But not the implied you. Not the generalized you. Your generalized and implied (i.e. market) self is watching youtube videos, eating junk food, laughing at a flatscreen television.

You've wondered if throwing the paper down and letting the pages fall open on their own might be a wonderful technique to read the news, a sort of I-Ching of modern media. Imagine the variables that would combine into the outcome: subconscious control of tiny wrist muscles in the toss, the heft of certain pages weighted with more ink than others, the microscopic flaws in the fabric of the paper, the airflow across the Mid-Atlantic, the dirty architecture of the city, and finally through the geometry of your lonely apartment. Scattershot randomness to illustrate how arbitrary the idea of random actually is. Using randomness to transcend randomness. Patterns inside patterns (perhaps THE pattern of all patterns: universal significance). After a gentle and relieving self-admonishment for thinking a thought so paranoid and colorful (a healthy dose of self-loathing to keep you stable), you notice the Horoscope.

Chaldean wisdom not nearly as old in the Occident as we pretend. Rubbish. Trash. If the lottery is the poor man's Stock Market, the Horoscope is surely his Analyst. Not really good for anything besides a smirk (admittedly, it does feel good to be so superior). But no, this is a complicated and troubled world in which we live—revolutions, disease, starvation—and we don't have time for self-delusion. Stock footage of calamity rolls through your mind—so real that you're almost swatting flies: lines of orphaned children march across a dusty landscape, a man in a white protective suit slowly waves a Geiger counter across a city of rubble, landfills on fire, corpses lining streets. Of course it's not just stupid to read occult stuff in times like these but immoral, worse than a waste, distracting us from our most pressing calamities.

You sip your coffee. You run your large toe across the the unfolded newspaper on the floor. You read your horoscope anyway:

Taurus (April 20—May 20)

> *However deep you go down the rabbit hole, Taurus, remember that understanding is better coming from your heart rather than your brain. Instead of trying to decipher surface clues, feel the answer from within using intuitive logic. Your environment is too complicated to analyze its component parts— instead of categorizing, try reaching equilibrium with your environment. Never forget that you are one of those pieces within the larger environment—and the universe is incomplete without you.*

Rabbit hole—unfortunate that it's smudged with overuse from lazy 60's counterculture baby boomers—can't say the words without conjuring faded polaroids of your parents' friends' RV trip to Lake Placid ("We called it Lake Acid" "Very clever, dad") to listen to the Dead and chill out. Down the rabbit hole. A wonderful phrase, what a waste that its accounts were depleted by suburban teens fifty years ago. And what wonderful advice for Alice, this particular horoscope. Alice who was born on May 4, was a Taurus of course, could have used some of that wasteful advice herself. She could have used someone telling her that she wasn't outside of the story—dropped into it, sure, but into it she was, and once there just as enigmatic as any Cheshire Cat (I've seen a story without an Alice, but I've never seen an Alice without a story)—

her universe incomplete without her Taurusly plodding along the pages.

Being ruled by Venus, Don Quixote must also be a Taurus. A translation of a story of a translation of Alonso Quijote the hidalgo also caught up in, not necessarily horoscopes, but dangerously frivolous literature of his time—the heroically misinformed hidalgo, the gentleman of the sad face who surely surely surely would have played the Lotto were he here and were he now, and maybe would have even occasionally pretended that he had won (cheering himself through his losses, buying used cars on credit and lavishing gaudy gifts on friends because BIG THINGS ARE COMING MY WAY)—didn't tradition have him born on April 23? The day before the death of his one-armed sailor Creator—the same day as the death of the Other Creator—Shakespeare—and so without textual evidence it seems proper to have the The Man of Woeful Countenance loping across the Spanish plain like a Taurus. He thinks he's the matador but he's the bull. I'm American. I understand that.

You press down hard on the corner of the paper with your big toe and, carefully lifting your leg diagonally, turn the page.

Either in jest or confirmation of something that you had already suspected, on the very next page is an Astronomy article illustrated with a large photo of a blue/purple explosion, a bubble with folds set into a dark matrix. The explosion occurred some time before the earth was created and wasn't an explosion at all (math being the more accurate language in which to translate the event) but some sort of "traumatic cosmic event" that you wouldn't even be able to visualize were it not for computer graphics programs able to assign colors to levels of radiation not originally on the visible spectrum. Impossible to imagine having witnessed the event from space itself—no sound or light, just waves of energy moving over distances equally impossible to imagine. Impossible to imagine yourself being able to physically interact with a phenomenon so simultaneously fundamental and esoteric. But the article ends with a cryptic promise of The Event somehow bringing us closer to " . . . understanding the laws of physical existence." Half hinting that there might be another type of existence.

The Event had occurred in the Taurus-Auriga Complex, the "closest cluster of star creation to Earth" according to the caption. And the large orange dot in the background is Aldebaran—"the follower" in Arabic—often considered the jewel set in the center of the Tauran bull's head. Of what use is any of this? You pinch half of the paper between your toes and gently close its pages without leaving your chair.

In the Labyrinth, translated by Christine Brooke-Rose: A Review

G. N. Forester

One rests here, for the moment well-saved. Upside it shines. Upside, fingers walking head lowered hands shading eyes staring ahead at a few squares, a few squares of glazed surface; it is cold, the pointer flows through black glyphs twisted and straight, the pointer flows through the dotted and crossed, selecting whole groups in a high-light, in a highlight, highlight, blinking as shadow against the white background. Nearside it is yellowed, there is no glow from behind, no light to shine a path, fingers walking head lowered hands shading eyes staring ahead at an oblong, a few oblongs of matted surface where the focus flutters forwards and backwards, sideways, circles around and

<pre>
    d

      o

        w

          n

            to a f
                   f
                   f
                   f

            o   r   k

      o   r   k

      o   r   k

      o   r   k

      o   r   k

      o   r   k

      o   r   keep to the right and mind the gap
</pre>

                    o   r

                    o

                         n

                    e   could turn to the

                                        l

                              e

                         f

                    t

              fingers

         walking
    head
lowered
hands
shading
eyes
staring at the next level shadows, shapes blurred with a brush; the
artist arranging glyphs of movement and objects: the bird standing, the
spear throwing, the mammoth falling, the person bending, on the surface not shining not matt the surface crumbling with age, dust settles in
parallels in circles in furrows everywhere on the skull lying on the
floor.

The string has no message, the string has no theory, the string has no
music, the string has no series.

Downside it is **black**ening, it has ████ened, it will **blacken**, it is **black-**
ening. The masses s____l____i____d____i____n____ga   p   a   r   t
         themassesbunchingtogetheroneononetopupsidedownrightsideupinsideout
mind   the   gap
please remember to take all belongings off the car
                                        ou
                                        sel
                                   before interring watch the

       ssss tttteeep
     ssssssstttttteeeppp
       ssss tttteeepp

     ssss tttteeepp
   ssssssstttteeeppp
    ssss tttteeep

      ssss tttteeep
    ssssssstttttteeeppp
     ssss tttteeepp

  ssss tttteeepp   id
ssssssstttttteeeppp   br   ge
   ssss tttteeep crossing the   and ferry-boating to the other side.

Out side, it sunshines. Outside, tripping head lowered hands shading eyes staring ahead at a few stones, a few stones of old golden sand; it is warm, the breeze blows through the vines of the climbing rose, the breeze blows through the blooms, swaying the long limbs in a swing, in a swing, swing. Outside, the statues bend and straighten and wave hello, pointing the path to the patio, to the person smiling ahead at the roses.

—I wasn't sure you'd make it.

—Well, GPS. Otherwise these lanes are a maze. Thank you for letting me visit.

—It seemed to take a while to organise. But I'm glad you're here. You must be tired and thirsty. Would you like something to drink?

—Oh no. I'm fine, I don't want you to go to any trouble.

—It's no trouble for me, I just have to ask you to fetch the drinks tray.

—Of course. Inside?

—Yes, just through to the wheeled table. Valérie left everything organised for us when she was here this morning.

The patio door creaks open, head lowered eyes staring ahead a few metres to the trolley, a few metres to the trolley laden with a large glass pot filled with a red liquid, two glass cups, scones, jam, cream, plates and cutlery, two white cloth napkins.

—This is marvellous! She looks after you well.

—Usually, yes. Today in particular.

—What sort of tea is it? Very nice.

—*Rosa canina,* mostly. Help yourself to the scones.

—Delicious.

—*Alors . . .*

—I wanted to ask you about the first translation, first. The Robbe-Grillet. Why did you use present tense in English and not the continuous, since he used the participle? And you changed the metaphor?

—Which one? There were quite a few, even though he supposedly preached rejection.

—The swing, for example. And you used present-perfect where he hadn't. Why? Since you were both pretty fixed on the implications of Narrative Sentence and past tense and . . .

—All a very long time ago. Let me explain . . .

Brief notes:

Required reading to understand how working with Robbe-Grillet deeply influenced Christine Brooke-Rose's thought and development, more so than the narratives of Nathalie Sarraute, despite the daughter of the latter claiming Robbe-Grillet had stolen all her mother's ideas[1] (true, according to Jonathan Meades, suggesting Robbe-Grillet was better at marketing than Sarraute, hence becoming the more successful of the two[2]). Although Brooke-Rose performs due diligence on a number of authors, including Sarraute, to whose critical ideas and theory she gives credit for seeding some of her own (specifically Sarraute's *Age of Suspicion*), and indicates the strands of writing style and concerns which at-

---

1 "Robbe-Grillet a tout piqué à maman", *BibliObs avec Le Nouvel Observateur*, 02 February, 2008

2 "How to Misread Robbe-Grillet", *New Statesman*, 06 March, 2008.

tracted her attention and dominated her interest, such as the humour of Maurice Roche and Beckett[3], it is to Robbe-Grillet she frequently refers as the impetus for taking a new path.[4]

Robbe-Grillet's camera intrigues her most (she will later admit the tedium of recording each detail was not the path she wished to follow[5]), because Robbe-Grillet avoids indicating who holds the camera—no narrative presence indicates a revelation, pronouns are eschewed, and it is these facets she will develop in her fiction, in conjunction with the use of "scientific" (objective, what "hits" the consciousness and is reported) present tense, repeated passages of text subtly altered (most often with witty and multilingual neologues) to continually reflect the themes which occupied her (attributed to her readings of Pound[6]), although she will tread different paths when she introduces new constraints, such as excising all conjugative instances of verbs denoting existence[7] and possession[8], or writing wholly in the future tense while simultaneously avoiding an oracular tone and constative sentences.[9]

Reading *In the Labyrinth* creates the feeling of being inside such an object (as if the title alone were not enough to suggest it), but overlaid with the eerie camera perspective of dark, surreal landscape still-shots, where scenes blur and confuse the watcher, never sure where in time or space the camera is located, or what exactly the watcher watches. Dismissing the novel for lacking the elements of "story" is questionable- the plot is that of winding through a labyrinth, trying to find the way to the centre or the exit, trying to make sense, trying to locate—commensurate with if not greater than the tension of an A to B narrative—and the narration reflects this in the character observed, the character ob-

3   Interview with David Hayman, *Contemporary Literature*, Vol 17, No 1, Winter, 1976, pp. 14-5.

4   "The Author is Dead, Long Live the Author" first given as a lecture at the University of Helsinki, September 1999, and published as "Narrating Without A Narrator" in *The Times Literary Supplement*, 31 December 1999, pp. 12-3; *Invisible Author: Last Essays*, Columbus, The Ohio State University Press, March 2002, pp. 130-55.

5   Justin Jacob, editor at Tweedie & Tweedie, refused the inclusion of yet another footnote (see *The Languages of Love*, forthcoming edition Verbivoracious Press, 2014).

6   Interview with David Hayman, *Contemporary Literature*, Vol 17, No 1, Winter, 1976, p. 10.

7   *Between*, London, M. Joseph 1968.

8   *Next*, Manchester, Carcanet 1998.

9   *Amalgamemnon*, Manchester, Carcanet 1984 and Illinois, Dalkey Archive Press, 1994.

serving (the labyrinth between writer and reader: who sees? Who speaks? Who reads?), and the lack of commenting author guiding and interpreting and providing the reader with a sense of (false, because how should a book be a moral compass or substitute for responsibility of decision and consequence) security, precisely reflecting Robbe-Grillet's concern with eradicating omniscient past tense narrative sentence, the anthropomorphism of objects and perspectives (a camera sees and creates no metaphor, but equally any way of observing an object or situation on different levels is metaphoric), and the author as omnipotent deity.[10] Setting could not be more richly described!

The caveat being that the style may become wearing: the constant specificity of description, minute details necessarily creating the atmosphere as well as the distanced camera, equally requiring a sustained concentration perhaps difficult to achieve given the superimposition of similar yet different images—similar to wandering routeless through a gallery filled with surreal images displaying a few variant scenes depicted in tones confined to white, sepia, and black, apart from the rare splash of colour serving as counterpoint. Passages of text are repeated, slightly altered, to generate the dream sense of déjà vu, as would be experienced in a labyrinth; both setting, action, perspective alternately disorientate and yet are oddly familiar. Perhaps one of the finest examples of form generating content to have been written in the twentieth century, even to the motif of a labyrinth, under the scrutiny of the camera, patterned in the twists and turns of naturally occurring phenomena. All accolades, well-deserved, and *The Observer* applauded Christine Brooke-Rose's 1968 translation for its flawlessness, the British Arts Council awarding her its Translation Prize in 1969.

---

10 Robbe-Grillet, Alain, *Snapshots* and *Towards a New Novel*, translated by Barbara Wright, London, Calder and Boyars 1965.

Troglodyte

Christine Brooke-Rose

My friends were a little dubious when I announced my decision to become a troglodyte. But after all, I had made the decision partly in order to get away from the dubiousness of my friends. I should have spared them their dubiousness, I suppose, by not telling them. On the other hand, it is the telling that strengthens a decision from a vague idea to an obligation and from an obligation to an accomplished fact.

So here I am in my cave, which is, as Cortado said, cool in summer, warm in winter. Cortado was not dubious at all, and from the first, aimed to raise the eventual rent of his cave by pretending hard to sell me something I didn't want. Wouldn't I prefer to rent a *casa* on the hills behind the city, viewing the island's central mountains on one side, and on the other the distant sea? His pricing eye cash-registered my shapeless dress of glazed cotton, then my shabby suitcase. Something *más económico* perhaps, a very small *casa*? But he knew quite well that I was serious in my foreign eccentricity, and I knew quite well that he couldn't really put me in the way of renting a villa, any more than I rent one. All the same, he behaved like an estate agent to the end.

'Cool in summer, warm in winter,' Cortado said. 'And this cave is among the best in the village, as you can see, it's not every cave that has its own private staircase.'

This is true, in a way. The steps, gleaming white-washed in the sun, climb over the roof of the cave below, which juts out like a porch, a squashed sort of porch on account of the steps climbing up one side. But the steps are only there because Cortado's cave happens to be the first of a row to which some access had to be made from the lower row. Cortado's cave, like the others in the row, is set back a little, so that a ridge of flat rock winds along in front of the caves and above the porches underneath. This ridge is bordered with a parapet full of geraniums, forming a kind of long balcony for all his neighbours to the left and of course for his own front door. My front door, now.

I haven't yet found out whether Cortado pays rent for his cave. The other troglodytes are very reticent on the subject, unwilling to help me work out just what Cortado's profit might be. Presumably anyone originally able to build a front wall and door to any one of these caves thereby established a right to it, but the village as it has now stood for generations may well have evolved a system of sales and transferences and nominal rents to someone or other. I only know that Cortado was fairly zealous to let me have it, and found somewhere else to sleep with remarkable ease.

'The Guanches made the caves,' he said to me on his first courtesy call after I had moved in. I nodded as I handed him a thimble cup of syrupy black coffee. I knew the history of the islands and had seen many of the caves, some as abandoned small black holes distantly high up a mountain face that looked from afar like a disease, some more accessible as developed villages, gay and painted and alive. This one was fairly high up, and the path below ours edged a mere three feet wide between the caves and a sheer drop. 'They made the caves to hide from us Spaniards.'

He caught my look of mock surprise, melting it into amusement. For despite the visibly more recent African blood in his veins, he had first proudly told me that he himself was a Guanche, embroidering a little too fast about his family owning the cave for generations and being descended from Princess Guayarmina herself. His black pupils glittered in the sun that flecked his face through the battered brim of an old straw hat as he sat on the penultimate step, sipping his coffee. He refused to come inside now that I was his tenant. The glitter in his eyes dismissed his earlier boast as salesmanship.

'*Café solo* is bitter,' he said, so simply and with such a distant look towards the mountains that it did not seem at all rude, or in any way connected with the coffee he was drinking. 'It tastes nicer with a little milk, but still strong. We call it *café cortado*.' Still watching the mountains, he grinned with pleasure at this elaborate joke, which he must have told many times, since it was the explanation of his nickname. But his eyeballs had moved imperceptibly in my direction at the climax, and his pleasure was partly derived from my appreciative smile.

He got up suddenly, placed the tiny cup on the parapet, bowed and said with careful politeness: '*Señorita* should not be *sola* either. *Adios, Señorita*, and thank you.' He went slowly down the steps, turned back at the bottom and raised his hand in farewell, almost but not quite to the brim of his old straw hat. Then he walked on along the narrow path below without looking back and vanished round the corner of the mountain.

Some of the other caves, I have discovered, go deeper, with a second and sometimes a third room at the back. But Cortado's is a bachelor flat. It is sumptuously furnished, for a cave, I mean. There is a wooden table that wobbles on the uneven floor, a stool and a huge old bergère with its insides strewing a bit. A shelf with hooks for coat-hangers has been nailed or screwed into the rock and a cretonne curtain hangs over it. There is a brazier for cooking and a marble-topped washstand with china jug, basin and soap-dish in matching roses and lilies, and a china slop-pail from another set with cherubs and ribbons. The chamberpot has marguerites. There is also a grandfather clock that chimes, and finally a brass double bed with a mattress of stuffing, not straw, some blankets for the chilly nights and a pair of sheets. I do my own laundry, that is, I manage my personal things in the stream further down the mountain on the communal wash-day, but Maria Nieves, who lives below me, does the sheets for me. She spreads them on the rocks with a stone at each corner and they dry on the same day, bleaching in the sun.

Like my neighbours, I am living almost entirely on *gofio*, the toasted maize flour which is mostly eaten as a kind of porridge, but can also be mixed in soup or spread on bread or used as flour for frying, when there is anything to fry—pimentoes, chiefly. So I am getting fat. The sea is too far to go swimming, and although I do my small shopping and other chores, I can only walk for exercise in the cool of the evening.

And then I prefer to sit, for that is when everyone else sits, just outside their front door, in twos and threes, gossiping, and one doesn't want to singularise oneself. So I sit outside my door, receiving, or I sit outside someone else's door, visiting. During the day I sit inside my cave, in the broken bergère, gazing at the hole of bright light and meditate. The troglodytes are not in the least dubious about this.

'The *señorita* is meditating,' they shout down the path if children are making a lot of noise or anyone officious-looking is on the way to disturb me. I meditate to the noise of Maria's radio from below. Maria's radio is permanently on, and Maria would, I feel sure, feel naked in her waking hours without its enveloping noise. And soon I too learn to dress into it and to undress out of it, and to sit in my clothing of noise, staring at the hole of bright light outside my cave.

Through the hole of bright light I can see, beyond the geraniums on my parapet, another wall of caves, sideways, to the right, and to the left a more distant ridge over other caves, topped by a cluster of young palm trees, blowing sometimes in the breeze like shingled heads; and beyond all that the sky and the slope of an orange mountain. It is astonishing how hypnotic a hole of bright light and colour can be when stared at from a darkness, for of course, although the walls of my cave are whitewashed in pale pink, they seem quite dark compared to the hole of bright light. Sometimes I have visions. I only mention them in passing since I am not sure which kind they are.

'The *señorita* should not be *sola*,' Cortado said for the sixteenth time when he came to collect the rent for the sixteenth time, today.

'But I like being alone, Cortada.'

'You spend much time with Maria Nieves, don't you?'

'She is a kind person.'

'You like her cave better, perhaps?'

'No, no. Of course not.'

'It is bigger. But then she has a large family.'

'Naturally.'

'She has, too, a radio.'

'Indeed she has.'

'But Cortado,' I added after a pause, 'I don't want a radio here. I assure you, I am quite, quite satisfied with looking at the sky. I have visions sometimes,' I said shyly.

That was two days ago. This afternoon two men struggled up the narrow paths with a large cardboard box on a porter's push-trolley. All the troglodytes came out to watch and cheer their efforts, and I went out too, cheering with them. But when I saw that everyone was giving excited directions, pointing at me, my heart sank. Cortado was nowhere to be seen.

The push-trolley reached my steps at last. The two men lifted the big box off the trolley and carried it up. Carefully they deposited the box on the floor of my little forecourt and started to cut the string.

'What is it? If it's a radio, I don't want it.'

They shook their heads and said together, shouting above the nasal sobs from Maria's radio: '*Momento señora, momentito.*'

I waited.

I nearly screamed when I saw the two antennae of the portable aerial. The two men grinned at my childish excitement. It was not until the familiar dead window peered out of the packing straw that my voice found the right frequency again.

'Take it away,' I said calmly but loudly above the lament of Maria's radio. 'I don't want a television set. No television.'

'Where is the electric plug?' one man asked above the strumming from Maria's radio.

There was a long silence, that is to say, there was only the strumming from Maria's radio. The strumming broke into a wail. The troglodytes were crowded on the row up the steps, and behind me on the parapet.

'Cortado said there was electricity.'

'Not in this cave,' I said, triumphantly, above the lament from Maria's radio. 'Oil lamp. See?'

'But the radio?'

'Cortado said it could run from the same plug.' They were shouting both together, above the twanging from Maria's radio, and pointing down at the sound as if it proved something. 'We brought a two-way adapter and a very long flex. Here, you see. Over the parapet.'

'Maria's radio,' I said as the song whirled to a stop, 'is a battery radio.'

Everyone started talking at once, drowning the announcer on Maria's radio.

'Some of the caves have electricity.'

'Yes, but only down below.'

'It's not far.'

'A hundred metres.'

'Fifty.'

'You could have it down there and visit it.'

'Maria nearly had the electricity brought up.'

'That was last year.'

'I always said—'

'Then we could all see it.'

Cortado came this morning to stare morosely at the unborn television set which is standing on the marble washstand. The jug and basin had been removed to a dark corner of the cave floor, and when I need them I place them on the wooden table.

'I thought, I rent, you enjoy the pictures, you pay me higher rent. The *señorita* should not be *sola*.'

I was touched, but firm. 'I am not alone, Cortado. My cave has been crowded with visitors all day. Even without pictures, the set fascinates them.' I added gently: 'You will have to take it away, Cortado.' He looked pained. 'You see, I prefer to look at your beautiful sky. It makes much prettier pictures.'

'Yes, the sky is fine. But you should not be alone.'

It was then that he gave me his dark look. Until that moment I had not at all understood what he was getting at. 'Cortado, you are not a marriage agent.' I put it nicely to save his sensibility. 'I enjoy being alone. And besides, I know what I look like.'

That was my first mistake. I will not pretend that I do not feel sensitive about being so patently an English old maid. It was precisely to avoid those hunters for free sex among frustrated female tourists that I came here, away from even the cheapest of hotels. But one should never draw attention to one's own defects.

A string of compliments followed.

I was disappointed with Cortado. I had not expected that of him.

'Who, in any case,' I asked, as ever clumsy with compliments, on account of trying so hard to remember that they are false, 'who would want to keep me company?' That was my second mistake.

'There are *señores*,' he said with a flourish of his brown hand.

The jug and basin are back on the marble washstand. The unborn television set now sits on the floor near the table, like a stool, although nobody would dare to use it as such. For it is much revered by most of my visiting neighbours, who have all heard of television and are convinced that it works for me alone. They tend to sit hypnotised in front of it, hoping that they too will be vouchsafed a vision, and perhaps believing that they have been. Little Dolores, Maria's second eldest aged eleven, seems to think it is a new kind of magic mirror in which I can see her future when she sits before it. Old Paquita Jimenez, who tells fortunes, is quite annoyed.

Maria had advised me to keep all this popularity of mine from Cortado, who prefers me to be *sola*, so that he can go on trying to persuade me not to be. On the whole, however, they come in the evenings, when their work is done, and leave me to myself by day. They respect my solitude as a visionary. Cortado does not respect my solitude, at least, not as a visionary. I shouldn't, perhaps, have told him about my visions, for he has become more and more dubious. This morning he came like a destructive angel.

'I have a friend.'

'I am glad.'

'My friend is an electrician. In the capital.'

'Cortado, please don't insist.'

'He can bring the electricity up from the lower caves. For me he will charge nothing. The cable he will steal from his shop.'

'I cannot receive pictures through a stolen cable.'

'Well the *señorita* may pay for the cable if she wishes.'

Winter has come, and the hole of bright light is less bright. I have had to borrow extra blankets.

'It *could* be warm in winter!' Cortado darkly altered the tense when I queried his original promise.

The pressure of these hints continues. Either Or, Cortado seems to be saying.

So here I am in my cave, or rather, in Cortado's cave, he has moved back in. Spring has come and it is so hot that Cortado just sits in the broken bergère with his feet on the cardboard box full of straw that once packed the unborn television set. As he sits, he draws a small income from the television set, which has now been born at last, down in one of the bottom caves, the big one which is the troglodyte village Shop, and the Shop makes small profit from allowing people in to watch at ten centimos an evening. Even Cortado goes down, and I feel a little lonely, deserted by all my friends. But by day he just sits, with his feet on a cushion on the cardboard box full of straw, and from the cool depth of rock he gazes at the hole of bright light and the orange mountain, to the noise of Maria's radio. He says he is meditating. He hardly moves except to remove the cushion and use the cardboard box as a private table when I serve his meals.

I eat at the wobbly table. I cook the *gofio* and do the small shopping and mend his socks and wash our clothes in the stream further down the mountain on the communal wash-day. I have learnt how to beat the sheets clean because I can't afford to pay Maria Nieves any more. They dry on the same day, bleaching in the sun, now that the winter drizzles are over. I also pay Cortado his rent on which we live. I don't have visions any more, so it doesn't matter where they came from.

It was lovely being a troglodyte, but I am beginning to feel a little dubious about it. Perhaps I shall go back to London soon. Before the winter sets in, anyway. Or after the winter, before it gets too warm again.

Landscapes of My Childhood

Wee Teck Lim

Note to the Reader

This poem is inspired by the techniques used by Christine Brooke-Rose in *Between*, which uses extensive wordplay, as well as multiple European languages and European cultural references to meditate on the fluidity of identity and on what it means to be a multilingual dual-culture woman living in Europe in the 20th century. Growing up in Singapore, a former British colony which is multicultural and multilingual, those themes resonated deeply for me, and recalled my own struggles to reconcile my different cultural influences as a South-East Asian boy of Chinese ethnicity heavily steeped in British literature. The poem is annotated with an explanation included showing how those influences are interwoven and used in the poem.

That Sunday we were late getting away.(1)
The Causeway(2) jammed with holiday seekers,
horns blaring, each car a moving furnace
we swam through waves of heat.

The passports stamped—thank you nadri(3) xie xie(4)
and terimah kasih(5)—then to KL(6)
we drove with barely a glance backwards at
the uncles and aunties(7)

Entigerbalmed(8) in heat queuing cursing
kan ne na bei(9) why so long I kena(10)
mati(11) under the heat I surely die(12).
Kastam(13) fucking(14) officers.

(1) This is an allusion to Philip Larkin's poem, "The Whitsun Weddings", which starts "That Whitsun I was late getting away". See also note (42) below.

(2) The Causeway is a bridge linking the island city of Singapore with peninsula Malaysia.

(3) "Thank you" in Tamil, (4) in Mandarin Chinese, (5) in Malay. The main ethnic groups are Chinese, Malay, and Indian Tamil. The most common Chinese dialect spoken here was Hokkien, but official government policy in the 1970s has seen its erosion in favour of Mandarin. Government offices often have signs in all four official languages: English, Chinese, Malay, and Tamil.

(6) Acronym of Kuala Lumpur, the capital of Malaysia.

(7) An honorific in the local English dialect to refer to older men and women. It is an adaptation to English from the Asian practice of showing respect to such persons. Nowadays, the terms may also be used in a mildly pejorative way to refer to old fashioned, usually working class, older men and women.

(8) A play on embalmed and "Tiger Balm", a popular mentholated cream smelling strongly of eucalyptus oils used often to cure headaches and disguise bad smells. Particularly popular among "uncles and aunties".

(9) "Fuck your mother" in Chinese Hokkien. A popular swear term.

(10) "Struck" and (11) "Dead" in Malay.

(12) Repeats the idea of "kena mati"

(13) The spelling in Malay of "customs"

(14) Repeats the idea of "ka ne na bei"

The green road stretched the long road wound on
through rows of perfectly spaced trees of palm
rubber palm rubber(15). Then, speeding? Where got?(16)
Robber palm greased(17)—thank you

Nandri(18) xie xie(19) and terimah kasih(20)—
we drove again on the long road winding
through green wet heat, cooled air(21) blowing upon
my sunlit sunhit face.

Wau lau(22) jua(23)! Air panas(24) rè(25) hot hit then
when out we got at Air Hitam(26)
Black Water watering stop to Kay Ell(27)
for a spot of Green Spot(28).

How long more I whined as now refreshened
I lost myself on the road with Julian,
Dick, George, and Anne(29) back in the motor car
but I, Enid Blightened,

Cycle through green spots of butter cups and blue
bells tinkling on cows drinking at cooling
streams of sunlight through dappled leaves cooing
doves and cool air blowing.(30)

And so my head with stories filled(31), we reach
long day's journey's end(32) at the Klang cornered(33)
city water shed of its Britished(34) past.
The day's heat breaks at last.

(15) The highway to Kuala Lumpur was (and is) lined with rubber tree and oil palm plantations.

(16) In the local English dialect meaning something untrue and a literal translation of the Chinese Mandarin, na li you, expressing the same.

(17) A notorious practice among Malaysian traffic police was to stop vehicles with Singapore licence plates to accuse the driver of speeding. A small bribe was passed to the officer, tucked in the folds of the demanded passport, as a common way of making the accusation vanish.

(18) "Thank you" in Tamil, (19) in Mandarin Chinese, (20) in Malay.

(21) Cooled by the car's overworked air conditioning unit.

(22) An exclamation akin to "wow" or "OMG".

(23) "Hot" in Chinese Hokkien, (24) in Malay, (25) n Chinese Mandarin.

(26) Air Hitam is a tiny town in Malaysia, a popular stop for drivers travelling from Singapore to KL. "Air" is pronounced I-yer in Malay, meaning "water", "Hitam" is "black" in Malay: Black Water town.

(27) KL rendered in syllables.

(28) A popular brand of orange soda in South-East Asia.

(29) To pass the time on the long drive, I would read. Enid Blyton was a favourite of mine and many other English educated children in Singapore. The four persons refer to the four of her popular children's series *Famous Five*. The fifth member was a dog, Timmy.

(30) This landscape was a frequent feature of Blyton's books. Growing up in the tropics much of it was enticing but also puzzling.

(31) An allusion to the last line of William Wordsworth's famous poem: *And then my heart with pleasure fills / And dances with the daffodils.*

(32) An allusion to the title of Eugene O'Neill's play, "Long Day's Journey into Night".

(33) KL is located at the confluence of the Klang and Gombak rivers.

(34) KL was part of the former British colony, British Malaya.

Monsoon's water dropped on kopi(35) cups blue—
nga telang(36) changing green spots blaring horns
on the bullock-blocking streams of teksis(37)
che(38) trishaws. Cayell filing

past, all in a rush. It's KL see see(39).
But in my head I only saw landscapes
alien to me. Black zi che noodles(40)
can't compete with blancmange(41)

stories told to a child. Frustration fillled
that little heart sharpened to an arrow
and loosed out into the darkling future
somewhere becoming pain.(42)

(35) "Coffee" in Chinese Hokkien.

(36) The local Malay name for the butterfly pea flower, correctly "bunga telang". The flower is blue; "blue-nga telang" is a pun.

(37) "Taxi" in Malay; (38) "cars" in Chinese Mandarin.

(39) A reference to the KLCC (Kuala Lumpur City Centre), a large mall in KL's centre, part of the Petronas Twin Towers. I couldn't resist the pun.

(40) Noodles fried in dark soya sauce (hence black). A popular street food in Malaysia, the stall in KL was famous for cooking it particularly well. "Zi che" is a pun; the correct term, "zi cha" is a Chinese Hokkien term meaning "cook fry referring to a style and variety of street cooking of Southern Chinese dishes popular in Singapore and Malaysia. "che" is Chinese Mandarin for "eat alluding to the reference to eat ("manger" in French) in "blancmange".

(41) A common food reference in Enid Blyton's books, utterly mystifying to me as a child.

(42) Philip Larkin, "The Whitsun Weddings": *We slowed again,/And as the tightened brakes took hold, there swelled/A sense of falling, like an arrow-shower/Sent out of sight, somewhere becoming rain.*

THRU my WORDS

Silvia Barlaam

"whoever you invented invented you too"
Thru, Christine Brooke-Rose, p. 54

THRU

in the circularity of things, we all die. Our life is narrated thus, en plein air, open spaces of remembrance where our names and dates (portrait us)—this is me, and ME was made of these numbers and these letters, and if you combine them differently, other characters appear in my story, no longer my own. Christine Brooke-Rose's story started in 1923 and ended in 2012. But there are other dates too: she was first published in 1954 and her last work released in 2006. Between these, poems, criticism, and novels were produced: each with a date of beginning and of ending, when she first had the idea until that well transformed to something else, when the first word was typed until the last word was written. Yet, many more dates exist: the first reader, the first editor, the first critic, each single article and commentary, interviews, sales, each starting and finished at a set point in time—a convention, as we know, computed in abstract ways making it average, available, world-spread, so I can say I first sat to write this at 12.35, 6th September 2012, but really the idea was there before that, only there was no computer date stamp in my brain to assess it and certify it.

Where does one end (and) start?
(Who says that's not the correct sequence of events)
(causality of one and the other being like Schrödinger's cat)

existing / at / the / very / same / time / **thru** / time / same / very / the / at / existing / **not**

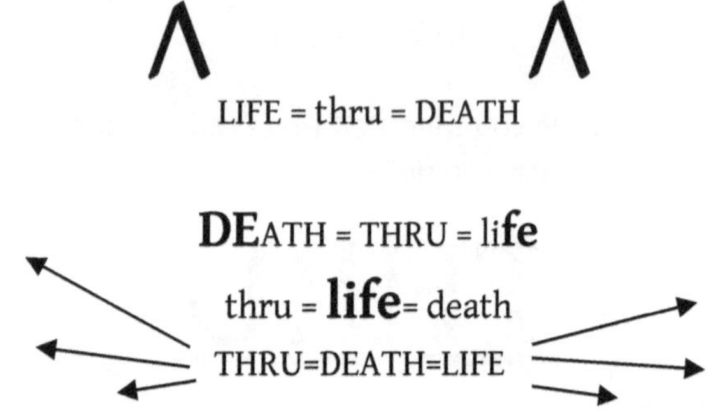

Equations are statements, complex mathematical imaginings for long and twisted conversations among numbers, values that are equal to each other, but THRU always meant more than just an equal sign, a passing through of meaning from one state to another, from person to person, from thought to sound, from life to death.

MY WORDS

deconstruction of narrativity
the signage of language is giving meaning to sounds like droppings of birds falling from
the
sky

who's listening?

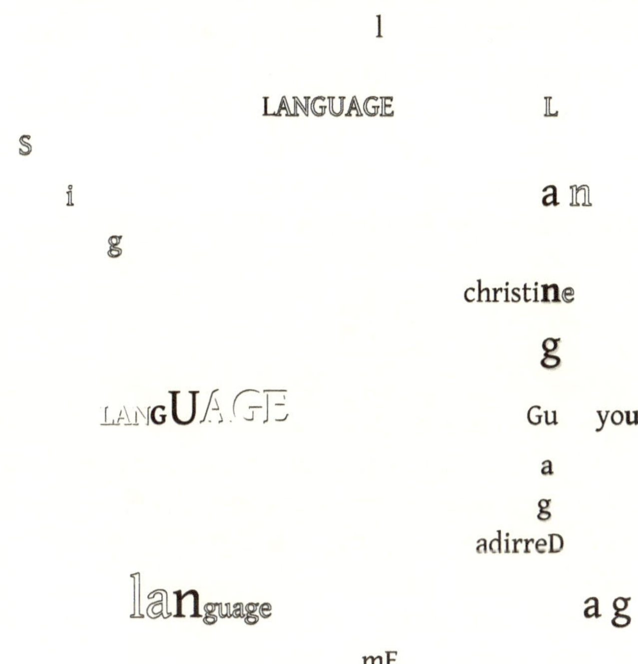

My mother dies on October 15th, 2009. It's a Thursday. The following year, the 15th of October falls on a Wednesday. In the year 2011, Friday is the 15th of October. This October, the 15th was a Tuesday. My mother dies / has died / is dying / will be dying / has been dead on all of these days, and in time, she will have been dead each single day of the week, one week after the other. Where does my mother's life start and where does it end? I'm alive bearing witness to her existence, through my memories and recollections of words and gestures and photos—some already greying under the patina of time—some aching as a bruised soul —all vibrant with the essence of being / having been. At some point in this projection my mother and Christine Brooke-Rose will be dead at the same time, and alive at the same time, narrated by their words left behind, and the words grown upon those and those birthed from those in never-ending proliferation propagation production and ululations of sounds and meanings THRU all of this and more and all of us and more and that little seed hiding in the box is growing and not growing, and all these numbers of death and birth still don't begin or end one's narration of one's life, because experiment connects to discovery and discovery connects to games and games become explorations of possibility, the joy of the multilayer and multistrata and intersections interactions interconnections and the possibilities, OH THE POSSIBILITES!

<u>AN</u>

we are inventions constructions conversations, of body and soul and brains, cogs in a wheel forever spinning hurling burning at apocalyptic speed THRU ⟵ the neurons and ⟶ electrons and ⟵⟶ ions and participles ⟵⟶ and particles ⟵⟶ of our essence

but not **Nouveau Roman,** not that, not for Christine Brooke-Rose:

I was very much thinking of death as the meaning of life,

she says in 'A Conversation with Christine Brooke-Rose', Ellen G. Friedman & Miriam Fuchs, *Review of Contemporary Fiction*, Fall 1989, Vol. 9.3

and THRU is ***an intertextuality about intertextuality, a fictionality about fictionality*** she adds later
and then goes   on saying

there's always a representative function simply

because language is representative

<u>HOMAGE</u>

Ambiguity plurisignificance intelligibility communication destination sender receiver emitter transmitter irony sign signification and all those other sweetmeats of the brain for the tongue, the poetry of jargon, the metaphor of space/stage, of language for the ears, of ink on the page, names and dates jumbling in space and time to connect with each other

(shaken by theoretical borders walls assumptions predispositions limits contextualized within/out with fictions)

and become

a story
a narrative
a linguistic game
a puzzle
an interplay of meanings
Derridean allusions
acrostics on the stage
a **writer**
Christine Brooke-Rose

Christine Brooke-Rose and the Liberty of Literature

David Auerbach

*I shall not be 'nihilistic' or 'deconstructive', but neither
shall I impose a system, or use one theory.*
Christine Brooke-Rose, A *Rhetoric of the Unreal*

Christine Brooke-Rose, a preternaturally mature writer, wrote in an immature time of theoretical upheaval. Her first fictions in the late 1950s and 1960s exist both stylistically and chronologically between the French nouveau roman and deconstructionist texts. Yet unlike her continental peers, Brooke-Rose maintained a far wider range of reference that integrated continental influences (not only deconstructionist and structuralist ones, but also sources from Dilthey to Roman Ingarden to Stanislaw Lem) with many diverse strains of Anglo criticism: she was able to situate the mythopoetic analysis of Northrop Frye and F. O. Matthiessen alongside I. A. Richards' and William Empson's rhetorical studies, Eric Havelock's theories of oral culture, and J. L. Austin's ideas of linguistic performance. Her claim as one of the most important critics of the latter half of the 20th century resides in her wide-ranging cosmopolitanism[1] in a time of increasingly cloistered specialization. Poised roughly between Frank Kermode and Roman Jakobson, she was able to borrow aspects of each without being beholden to either.

A central and representative insight of Brooke-Rose's was that the exhaustion of conventional narrative required a reinvigorated polyvocalic approach (cf. Bakhtin) rather than a solipsistic one. She was unstinting in her criticism of the direction that the experimental novel was taking in first-world countries, and while many were rushing to praise the expansive fictions of Latin American writers from Cortázar to

---

1 By "cosmopolitanism" I mean an ability to travel between artistic, theoretical, and societal parishes without claiming an exclusive membership in one or two alone, nor rejecting a foreign parish for methodological disagreements or misalignments with a more familiar parish.

Fuentes to Donoso, Brooke-Rose saw why it appeared to hold such fertile promise, particularly to the Anglo critical establishment. In an essay on such "palimpsest histories," as she termed those superior works, she called out the domestic problem as a simultaneous lack of knowledge ("Knowledge has long been unfashionable in fiction") and a lack of interest in gaining it:

> The English novel has been dying for a long time, enclosed in its parochial and personal little narrated lives, and if American postmodernism has seemed at times to bring new vigour and a breath of fresh air, it is often still too concerned with the narcissistic relation of the author to his writing, which interests no one but himself. The reader, although frequently addressed, is only taken into account with reference to this narcissistic concern in a 'look-what-I'm-doing' relationship. Here I'm thinking particularly of John Barth, who also writes big novels, or of Gilbert Sorrentino's Mulligan Stew. But these have little to do with history, and more to do with either the form of the novel or the modern American Way of Life, or both.[2]

Brooke-Rose identified a common thread between both the "realistic" work of Cheever and Updike and the "experimental" work of John Barth and Robert Coover: a retreat from any curiosity toward foreign experience and into the reflective mirrors (be they flat or curved) of the mind, an area which Beckett had already mined brilliantly, but to exhaustion.

> The writer cannot do without imagination. Dostoevsky understood this. And mere homework is not enough either. But a great deal of this homework done by the classical realist was sociological, and eventually led, in the modern neorealist novel we are all familiar with, to

---

2   Brooke-Rose, Christine. "Palimpsest History", *Stories, theories, and things* (Cambridge: Cambridge University Press, 1991), p. 183.

> slice-of-life novels about miners, doctors, football-play-
> ers, admen and all the rest. Back to the personal experi-
> ence of the writer in fact. Now personal experience is
> sadly limited. And the American postmodern attempt to
> break out of it rarely succeeds beyond fun-games with
> narrative conventions—a very restricted type of know-
> ledge .[3]

In a brilliant passage, she pinned the unified cause of this avoidance of knowledge to a rhetorical shift that strove to minimize the author as those ashamed of the subjective voice, attempting to disavow narrative authority by claiming it at a higher level:

> Formally, as we have seen, the sentence of Represented
> Speech and Thought can be similar to the Narrative
> Sentence, indeed identical with it when deictics and
> other signs of E[xpression] are not linguistically
> present, but only the perceiving character. This formal
> similarity led, inevitably, to these two distinct poles be-
> ing fused, and the sentence of Represented Speech and
> Thought being used as narration, to tell, to give narrat-
> ive information—whole summaries of a situation, for in-
> stance, or analepses (flashbacks) of a whole past, which
> are clearly there to inform the reader and not to repres-
> ent a character's perceptions, save at the cost of making
> them rather gross, or at best wholly artificial. This can
> go on for pages. Such misuse is extremely frequent in
> the average modern neo-realist novel, including most
> classical Science Fiction that imitated the worn-out
> techniques of the realist novel in an attempt to be re-
> spectable. This misuse is a direct result, not only of the
> post-Jamesian (and Aristotelian) condemnation of
> 'telling' in favour of 'showing', but also of the concomit-
> ant attempt to eliminate the author: and since narrative

---

3   *ibid.*

information must be given, the easy solution was to 'filter' it all through a character's mind, however implausibly, thus thoroughly weakening the device into its opposite.[4]

Yet as comparisons with the rich "palimpsest histories" show, these tendencies only exacerbated the problems they were meant to correct: represented speech and thought, rather than supplanting narrative, became only a more greatly inflected and limited form of the selfsame narrative. By exposing "Show, don't tell" to mean "Tell this way, don't tell that way," where "this way" is merely the approved style of the predominant literary idiom (be it "realistic" or "experimental"), Brooke-Rose exposed the common root of the problem not as "showing" or "telling," but in the ever-encroaching negation that quashes imagination and curiosity: "Don't."

Brooke-Rose diagnosed both the promises and limitations of the nouveau roman, dissecting Robbe-Grillet and Sarraute sympathetically but also opening up the temporal and spatial mechanisms of their work as few could, bringing utter precision to the interaction of language and idea. There is little slipperiness in Brooke-Rose's criticism, and always the sense that any position presented, no matter how provisional, has been worked out to the nth degree. (One might ask: is there any other way in which a position should be presented?) Only such rigor could allow for her later analysis of Joseph McElroy's science-fiction novel *Plus* ("The New Science Fiction in *A Rhetoric of the Unreal*), which fills in the critical story she began in her criticism of the nouveau roman over a decade previous. Her taxonomy of the novel's terminology reveals that Robbe-Grillet and Sarraute neither invented nor perfected their chosen forms, but brought new variations to a continuum of literature that were then drawn upon decades later by the mercurial American McElroy, a novelist as widely-read as Brooke-Rose. Aside from illuminating McElroy's tricky work, this essay in particular provides much insight toward inferring the underlying processes of Brooke-Rose's own mid-

---

4 Brooke-Rose, "Ill Locutions", *op. cit.*

period novels like *Such* and *Between*, which, like McElroy's work, extend the pointillistic impressionism of the *nouveau roman* in more semantically and narratively rich dimensions. In her fiction, Brooke-Rose's particularly intricate combination of surface word-play and submerged idea-play requires much decoding, and her criticism is a crucial tool toward that end.

Her ambitious critical work *A Rhetoric of the Unreal* draws together these threads by demonstrating, among other parallels, an isomorphism of the French new novel and less formalist postwar Anglo fiction. Examining the "defocalisation" (in her apt term) used by Thomas Pynchon, Robert Sukenick, and other writers, she argues, in a lucid structuralist analysis influenced by Jakobson and Barthes, that the manipulations of content in the Anglo novels are the result of processual variations analogous to the technical and syntactic manipulations of Robbe-Grillet and Sarraute. Both are responses to a more universal aesthetic "mimetic crisis." To that end, the Anglo experiments with content retained the same "defocalising" traits of the more blatant *nouveau roman* experiments with

> a return to distance by rejecting narrative of speech (wholly in Nombres) for narrative of events (diegesis, maximum of narrator), combined with slowed-down scenes (mimesis, maximum of information).[5]

(She did, however, note one key difference: "One quality is scarce in the French experiments, that of humor.")[6] Arguing vertically, across micro- and macro-levels of fictive content, the coup of the book's argument lies in a long analysis of James' *The Turn of the Screw*. Her micro-readings of the syntax build to an architectonic analysis of "masculine" and "feminine" events of the story that show the injection of the "unreal" into James' work to prefigure the very same "defocalisations" of the 20th century: the human desires an elaboratory framework for "intensification" and "coherence," which the narrative and the super-

---

5   Brooke-Rose, Christine, *A Rhetoric of the Unreal* (Cambridge: Cambridge University Press, 1981), p. 327.
6   *ibid.*, p. 338.

natural elements alternately provide and undermine:

> the frame is constantly being expanded and shrunk, like the narrator's consciousness at the beginning, and it positively bursts, expanded to metaphysical heights and shrunk to sordid suppositions and trivial though passionate questioning as the figure of Quint, in the last chapter, appears and disappears at the window . . . [7]

Hence the germination of the ensuing mimetic crisis.

Brooke-Rose's achievement in creating this majestic synthesis was rooted in her view of literature as a self-contradictory delta of theoretical streams intermingling with one another. That sense of provisionality was key to her ability to move between different systems of thought without being beholden to any. Without the sort of catchy slogans of a Stanley Fish, Brooke-Rose's work went less noticed, possibly because to listen to Brooke-Rose is to undermine Fish's easy promises of certainty. She identified the collapse of structuralism in its enslavement to a painfully reductive system, a fault which also quickly overtook deconstructionism, as the trace and the deferral became indisputable terms of art, never to be questioned:

> Narratology was thus immensely useful. But in the end, it couldn't cope with narrative and its complexities, except at the price of either trivialization or of becoming a separate theoretical discourse, rarely relevant to the narrative discussed, when discussed. In other words, it became itself a story, or set of stories, of narratives not only extradiegetic, metalinguistic, transtextual, paratextual, hypotextual, extratextual, intertextual, but also, yes, sometimes, textual, all at the same time. And so, yes, a 'good' story. Nevertheless, the study of narratological phenomena, as happens so often, turned into an endless discussion about how to speak of them. The story of narratology became as self-reflexive as a 'post-

---

7   *ibid.*, p. 187

> modern' novel. But after all, every age has the rhetoric
> it deserves.[8]

Nowhere was her criticism more pointed than of the most dogmatic strains of feminist theory of the time. For her, the denotation and ostracism of extant structural and rhetorical forms as "masculine" posed a great danger of restricting women's artistic expression, arresting its growing autonomy.

> The twentieth century in general, from the Surrealists
> and much misunderstanding of Freud onwards, has ten-
> ded to enthrone the Unconscious as the latest substitute
> for dogmatic truth, rather than as a language to under-
> stand, a language to come to terms with and to explore,
> exploit, imaginatively. The Unconscious (or the pre-
> Symbolic) by definition is inaccessible, like the ontic,
> except through conscious effort and analysis, which
> automatically means structuring and schematizing and
> rehandling, to which all perception is subservient: we
> already rehandle a dream the moment we try to capture
> it and write it down. The Unconscious as Truth, the
> 'music of the womb' as 'more real'. Feminism is be-
> latedly repeating the same gesture, and I am not at all
> sure how 'subversive' it really is, on its wombish own.
>
> Flux and chaos and primitive perceptions, for all their
> undoubted vitality and necessity as a means of achiev-
> ing tolerance, integration, wholeness, are nevertheless
> at the moment more in danger of threatening all that
> we hold dear in civilization today. Moreover, control
> and logic (etc.), as well as 'symbolic' rather than purely
> 'semiotic' expression can hardly be said to be absent
> from the best and most incisive feminist criticism—it
> couldn't make its points without them. Cixous and

---

8 Brooke-Rose, Christine, "Whatever Happened to Narratology?" in *Stories, theories, and things* (Cambridge: Cambridge University Press, 1991), p. 27.

Kristeva, who seem to be the highest feminist reference, are the two most highly qualified, intellectual, and intelligent literary women in France. Feminist critics usually hold jobs in academia, with all its internecine power-struggles, and presumably they partake in those, using 'male' structures. Naturally there is still unfairness and difficulty, but to compete they presumably do not turn to the music of the womb, but to tough preparation for tough examinations, dissertations, conference papers, publications. It seems to me unacceptable to live in these relative sinecures and continue to talk about the desirability of flux, chaos and pre-Oedipal sensibility.[9]

In contrast to the exclusionary narrowing of one's voice in search of a non-existent authentic moral perfection, Brooke-Rose's counterproposal, as one would expect, was polyvocal. Beginning with Diotima's contribution to the polyvocal Symposium, she brings us to the present:

> It would seem, then, that the androgyny that some men have claimed for all good writers at the creative end has willy nilly been acquired by women at the receiving end, but not by men, who rarely identify with women characters as women do with male ones. Whatever the case, it would surely be a good thing if more men learnt to read as women (even the wild zone [cf. Elaine Showalter]), so that the bisexual effort, which they have metaphorically appropriated at the creative end, should not remain so wholly on the women's side at the receiver's end. Both should read as both, just as both should write as both. And one of the ways in which this delightful bisexualism should occur is in a more open and intelligent attitude to experiment of all kinds by women.[10]

---

9 Brooke-Rose, "A Womb of One's Own?" *op. cit*, p. 233.
10 Brooke-Rose, Christine. "Illiterations", *op. cit.*, p. 264.

For Brooke-Rose, women did not need to cast a miasma of suspicion on the forms of expression themselves (logic, rhetoric, rationality), but needed to redeem such forms through a process of supplementation and revivification, in much the same way that her "palimpsest histories" enrich the novel through their greater scope of knowledge and perspective. She makes the critical point that women writers such as Eliot and Woolf have already been doing so all along. Rather than being creatively oppressed, what we take to be indications of oppression and limitation in their works are often indications of our own limitations as readers, especially male readers. Yet Brooke-Rose would not excuse anti-rationalists of either gender from the charge of discounting the contributions of women writers of earlier ages, reducing their achievements to futile gestures against a supposedly all-powerful rationalist patriarchy, rather than illuminating their too-rarely sounded notes to whose resonances we should all be listening.

Brooke-Rose's account of the possibilities of literature is far more fecund than the arid, imploding ouroboros offered by Blanchot, Fish, and Derrida. In comparison, Brooke-Rose's bravery, curiosity, and sheer energy refresh, while the works of Derrida and Ronell leave one deflated, with little left to turn to but the new historicism which has supplanted them, in which literature's potential is subjugated to a "realistic" (though in fact fabricated and tendentious) historical model. Like the erudite philological works of Erich Auerbach, Karl Vossler, and R. B. Onians, Brooke-Rose's criticism presents the idea of literature as such an immense mass of potential knowledge and experience that it makes one ashamed of settling for anything less.

Ill Wit and Good Humour

Christine Brooke-Rose

This essay is more a light-hearted meditation on women and comic writing than a scholarly analysis, more the pursuit of an intuition, which may be wrong, than an exhaustive investigation. This is because, although I do not think the intuition is wrong, I do think that comedy tends to be killed by exhaustive analysis.

Soap-bubble or 'text-object'

In Umberto Eco's best-selling novel *The Name of the Rose* (1980), the solution to all those monkish murders lies in the library's secret possession of Aristotle's lost work on comedy—which is of course fictionally lost again as the monastery burns. This is superbly self-referential comedy, based on both knowledge of rhetoric in general and on the absence of a specific rhetoric of comedy. But I have often wondered whether that supposed loss of Aristotle's supposed work on comedy does not in fact represent the undesirability of theorizing about comedy or analysing it. I don't mean that theorizing about comedy is impossible, merely that it seems more murderous of it. Of course, there are rules, but rules have to do with craftsmanship and production. It seems, however, a peculiar contradiction in terms to analyse what makes us laugh. From Schopenhauer to Freud and beyond, laughter, or the joke, or whatever we call it, seems more like a soap-bubble than an analysable 'text-object.' Whereas human passions treated on a grand scale or the sadness of the human condition, from classical tragedy through domestic tragedy to the modern weepy, seem somehow more conducive to analysis. But of course, to say that something is unanalysable smacks of old-fashioned idealism, or even, as I. A. Richards put it over sixty years ago, of mystery mongering.

The difficulty of theorizing about laughter, as in Schopenhauer or Kierkegaard or Bergson (to the latter two of whom I shall turn below), is the very generality of theory, despite examples, compared to the apparently unique specificity of comic situations—an illusion of course. For this is partly due to the very social nature of laughter, compared to the essential solitariness of suffering, even when witnessed or shared—unless of course suffering is presented as comic. We have all experienced trying to retell a funny situation to someone who wasn't there. It only works as part of a new social situation, a re-enacting in fact, a re-creation. And naturally this aspect, so clear in the theatre, even varying from one performance to another, poses particular problems in the novel, the reading of which is normally a solitary activity.

The theatre obviously disposes of many comic elements not available to the novelist—gestures, facial expressions, timing, costume, props—in other words the combined talents of actor and producer. The novelist has *only* language. And although he shares its natural riches with the dramatist, his equivalent for the different reception (re-creation) according to different audiences can only be the different readings, which he can only experience from brief and scattered individual reactions if at all. Such individual reaction can happen in the theatre too, but it is submerged by the social situation—as for example the splendid scene in the Greek film *Never on Sunday*, when the call girl, played by Melina Mercouri, finds herself in an ancient amphitheatre where classical tragedy is being played, which she finds irresistibly funny. On a simpler level, every music hall audience knows that parodies (in Genette's sense) of famous extracts from tragedies can be a source of comedy. In this sense, comedy is perhaps simply a displacement of things taken seriously in one social context, to another social context. But this seems insufficient, and particularly so in relation to another problem.

Why no women?

To these two generalities—the difficulty of theorizing about what is funny and the essentially social dimension of laughter, I would like to suggest a third, which is the apparent—and if true, extremely strange—exclusion of women from the comic canon.
By this I do not mean that there have been no comic women writers or

that women writers are never funny—how could anyone say that within an English tradition that starts with Jane Austen? Nor am I presupposing an authoritarian exclusion of comic women writers, as opposed to others, by men.

No. I mean that, relative to men, women comic writers seem rare. I would look at it this way: women are now officially accepted as equal in every ex-male domain, from the arts to politics, from newscaster to sports commentator to city expert. But this has not happened at the same speed. Doctors came long before sports commentators for instance, and even now there are still pockets of resistance where a fifty-year-old discourse is still heard—the domain of engineers for example. I would like to suggest that, within the art of writing, where women (with varying difficulties) were accepted much earlier than in the other arts, there are still pockets of unconscious non-acceptance. Experiment is one, which I discussed in the last chapter. Comic writing may be another, but here the non-acceptance is complex enough to have created, in fact, a curious kind of *self*-exclusion by women.

For the general picture is of a tradition of women's writing which first flourishes in the aristocratic imitations of courtly literature from the twelfth to the sixteenth centuries in France, continues more 'seriously' with *La Princesse de Cleves*, but also with a crop of seventeenth and eighteenth-century ladies more or less regarded as blue-stockings or *femmes savantes*, if not *précieuses ridicules*, then blossoms to an unexpectedly balanced serio-comic perfection in Jane Austen, to be followed, grandly enough, by passionate romance (Mme de Stael) or passionate Gothic, domestic tragedy and portraits of society in the work of the Brontës, George Sand, George Eliot or Mrs Gaskell. All excellent writers, full of irony, but hardly comic writers.

Why, in other words, was women's writing, when allowed to flourish at all, so serious? The New Women protest novels of the eighties and nineties, which partly influenced Hardy, the stories of great romance or the streams of personal consciousness, all these poured out in profusion. And it is chiefly a certain kind of irony—acutely observed social nuances noted with wit and malice and gentle mockery—in other words what is already highly developed in Jane Austen—that flourishes in the twentieth century, from the popular detective story of an Agatha Christie to the passionate thresholds of consciousness of a Virginia Woolf. In the modern domestic novel there is much pleasure of recognition but little outright laughter. Such comic writers as did emerge seemed to develop as brilliant journalists rather than as novelists: Dorothy Parker is the archetype (and she died forgotten and wretched). Even today a great deal of specifically feminist writing of the type that refuses to 'conquer' or 'imitate' any male domain tends to manifest itself as free but deadly earnest descriptions of sex and expressions of flowing feelings (so in fact imitating earlier male freedoms)—free, sometimes highly experimental and poetic, opening up new horizons, but rarely funny, except perhaps unconsciously. There must be exceptions, and I am perhaps deliberately exaggerating to stress the impression I have—but I do have it—that between Jane Austen and Muriel Spark or, in different veins, Angela Carter and Kathy Acker, there is very little that would stand up to, say, the comedy of Dickens or Jerome K. Jerome or P. G. Wodehouse or even Edgar Anstey (to cite as many different registers as possible). Or, in modern times, to anyone from Evelyn Waugh to Kingsley Amis, from Joyce to Barth or Ishmael Reed.

This is extremely peculiar and surprising, since the comic spirit is perhaps the only successful weapon in any struggle for equality, far more efficient than complaint, aggression or segregation, and one, moreover, that men are far more afraid of. Why did women not turn to it in larger numbers and develop it more sharply? Other oppressed groups did and do still—Jewish humour and the humour of Black writing for instance—and both are sophisticated enough to include self-mockery, which feminist writing rarely does.

If this self-exclusion from the comic canon is true, it would, I think, be linked very directly to the social nature of the comic and, less obviously, to the difficulty of theorizing about the comic, in the sense that theorizing about women's writing has proved far more difficult and quicksandy than most Feminist critics would probably admit.

What makes women laugh—or not laugh?

The social aspect, like all social things including communication, has two facets, that of inception, and that of reception, and the latter (what makes people laugh) thoroughly conditions the former (comic creation), which is why I shall look mostly at what makes people laugh, for, as we shall see, it almost explains the strange situation. Here is a personal anecdote.

At a 1986 Conference, during an excursion, the bus had to brake violently for a car, which happened to have a woman driver. My companion, who admittedly was Germanic but belonged to my generation (and sometimes I wonder whether men move less quickly with the times than women do) immediately launched into the story of the statue of Boadicea on Westminster Bridge who, with the reins in her right hand, is driving her chariot in that direction but with her other arm outstretched to the left. The predictable punch-line was 'how like a woman, to signal one way and go off the other way.' I smiled politely, for I had first heard this joke some forty years earlier, and teased his trivial (and inaccurate) sexism. His reaction was interesting: Okay you're right, it's a very old joke. But it belongs to an old tradition, in which a bad woman driver is funny, a bad man driver is not.

Conversely that same month, there was an article in *The Women's Review* about slapstick, which observed that a man falling over is funny, a woman falling over is not. In other words, in audience reception, comic situations are sexually determined: women do not spontaneously laugh at jokes about women drivers or at sex-jokes except when trying to imitate and join males.

Historically, women have never been expected or allowed to be more than, at very best, witty in a society salon, that is, to add charm and general agreeability to an occasion, the icing on the cake, the spice to the dish—and it is interesting that I can only think of cooking metaphors. And even pepperpot charm would be restricted to a high-society milieu at certain relatively libertine periods—the Renaissance, the English Restoration, the eighteenth century, the English Regency or the nineteenth-century *fin de siècle*. It is difficult to imagine either a Puritan or a Victorian wife or daughter being allowed to make jokes at the husband's or the father's, or indeed anyone's, expense. For good humour is nearly always ill wit, at someone's expense even if it is one's own (the safest). Being funny, like talking too much or appearing intelligent, wasn't done, except perhaps by a mistress or a scarlet whore. And this was precisely during the period that women novelists at last emerged as other than aristocratic or blue-stocking exceptions.

This excluding attitude was partly due to the social protectiveness of men, in other words, to decorum. Women should not make themselves ridiculous, or vulgar, just as women should not fall over. But behind the decorum lies something deeper. It seems to me precisely because humour is such an efficient weapon, and feared by men, that it had to be either evaded by women or used very covertly. Even today, when in a quarrel a man laughs at something said by his companion, she tends to be disoriented or cowed, whereas when the woman laughs, the man's reaction tends to be fury or silent exit. For I believe that the situation of women in history is more complexly determined than that of classes or races, because although that of classes or races can be complicated by sex, it is not itself sexual but political and social, whereas that of women is itself sexual and can be complicated by power urges and social conditions. The slave or the oppressed worker does not love his oppressor in the same way as the woman may love her man, and be afraid to lose him. The slave fears his master and longs for freedom, whereas women's attitude to 'freedom' was for a long time, and often still is, much more ambiguous, with many even against it, and historically many conservative backlashes (like today's 'post'-feminism) may mean that every new start has to go back a bit.

'Feminists have no sense of humour, as Wayne Booth has shown.' This sentence is from an essay by Nancy K. Miller (1986) on 'Rereading as a Woman,' where she retells 'a celebrated moment at a symposium organized by *Critical Inquiry* in 1981 on "The Politics of Interpretation"' when Wayne Booth, 'then President of the MLA, came out as a male feminist.' I quote the relevant bit she gives from Booth with the Rabelais recall:

> When I read, as a young man, the account of how Panurge got his revenge on the Lady of Paris (as you recall, he punishes her for turning him down by sprinkling her gown with the pulverized genitals of a bitch in heat, then withdraws to watch gleefully the spectacle of the assembled male dogs of Paris pissing on her from head to toe), I was transported with delighted laughter; and when I later read Rabelais aloud to my young wife, as she did the ironing(!), she could easily tell that I expected her to be as fully transported as I was. Of course she did find a lot of it funny, a great deal of it is very funny. But now, reading passages like that, when everything I know about the work as a whole suggests that my earlier response was closer to the spirit of the work itself, I draw back and start thinking rather than laughing, taking a different kind of pleasure with a *somewhat* diminished text.
>
> (1986, p. 292; Booth, *Critical Inquiry* 9/1, 1982, p. 68)

The tone of regret, at having something taken away from him by a more feminist-sensitive reading, is a revelation in itself. Could feminism be an *impoverishment*? But sex-jokes, of which the above is an extreme example, are not the only comic situations which are sexually determined. This has not been greatly written about, but if we go back, first, to Bergson on laughter (*Le Rire*, 1900; 1984. Translated, 1911), we find that his analysis unwittingly explains this sexual determination.

Things

Bergson does not define the comic. His theory is that there is a vitality in the human organism, which is highly flexible, creative, alive, but that humans constantly fall back into lifeless matter, which behaves mechanically, inflexibly, killing the creativity of the 'lifeforce.' Laughter is the safeguard that wakes us up when we drop into the merely mechanical, behave mechanically, inflexibly. It has to be *people*: an object as such, or a landscape, isn't funny, unless connected to a human being or a human reaction. But humans behaving like things are the basic source of laughter. And inversely so are mechanical objects animated like humans (the jack-in-the-box, the marionette) sources of laughter (1984, p. 53).

Later Bergson further elaborates this opposition of life versus lifeless mechanism: life changes, the mechanical repeats itself; life is irreversible (or has irreversible series), the mechanical is reversible: life needs a minimum of individuality and self-containment, mechanical series are liable to reciprocal interference. These three elements, repetition, inversion and reciprocal interference of series (say plot and subplot) are the mainstay of comedy in Bergson's mechanical theory of laughter (p. 67-8). He further applies all this to language, for instance when language clogs thought or when cliches or dead metaphors are brought to life and so on (p. 99ff.). However, there is an interesting constraint: laughter is a corrective to all behaviour due to inflexibility, but as corrective it always contains 'an unavowed intention to humiliate' and requires a degree of cruelty: rather than sympathy.

Naturally I am not suggesting that women could have been aware of all these elements, but the elements do explain, in negative counterfoil, why women did not willingly go in for rousting comedy, but rather more for the wry smile or irony. Why should women, so long considered as things, and trained to react in a dutifully mechanical way, laugh at the thingness of people and the thingness of language they were themselves so inextricably a part of? Why should they, caught up in the irreversibility of life, amuse themselves with mechanically reversible situations and reciprocally interacting sequences? Why should they throw themselves into a genre which makes laughter incompatible with sympathetic understanding?

And yet, the inflexibility and rigidity of much masculine behaviour towards them and towards the politics of life, family and power could have given them splendid material. It did so, but more comfortably through gentle irony and emotional sympathy than through rumbustious or even sophisticated comedy.

Irony, humour, comedy

If what makes people laugh (reception) has an almost direct bearing on inception, so do generally received ideas of comedy as a genre, of humour as a faculty.

The traditional ideas about comedy were that it is 'low,' whereas tragedy is 'high'; that it is clever and cold and suggests superiority whereas tragedy is emotional and profoundly understanding; and that it has a happy ending. Clearly women were not expected to be 'low,' or 'clever,' and as to 'happy endings,' women certainly used them, but they are not specific to comedy. In the novel (where men used them too) they can be either sentimental, that is, not warranted by the elements of the story (for example, the ending of *Middlemarch*), but they can also be wryly happy endings, such as Jane Eyre finally marrying Rochester but blind and maimed, in other words castrated (for if some might argue that this savage irony is unconscious for the author, it certainly cannot be for us).

For Kierkegaard (1846), there were three spheres of existence, the aesthetic, the ethical and the religious. Between them are two buffer zones, irony and humour. This scheme could be represented as follows:

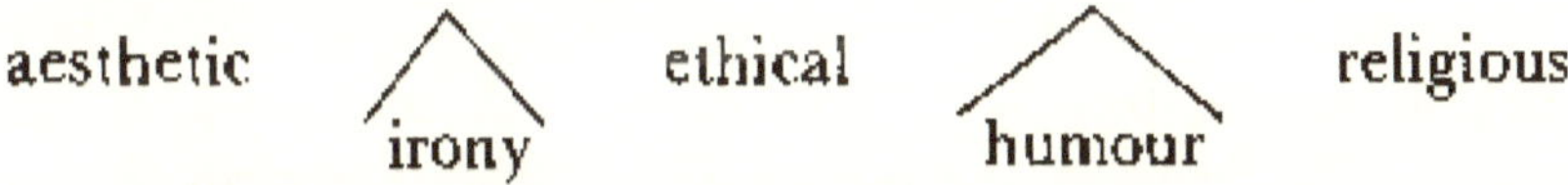

Although the religious is inaccessible to comic apprehension, humour seems to be closer to the religious because Kierkegaard thought that prayer, though expressing the highest pathos, is ultimately comical. And one could hardly expect nineteenth-century women to go along with that. He also thought it was a regression to childhood, though earlier he had said that the comical is a mark of maturity.

Michael Silk (1988) who discusses Kierkegaard's ideas but with a different purpose from mine (to show that comedy is autonomous and not a proper opposition to tragedy), tries to reconcile the various contradictions and unclarities, but these do not concern me here. I simply want to take the negative calque of these ideas, as with Bergson, and show how they could explain women's self-exclusion from 'humour' (comedy) as opposed to 'irony': women have always felt at home between the aesthetic and the ethical, but less so between the ethical and the religious. Their religion (in the eighteenth and nineteenth centuries) does not seem to have been a very profound affair, but more of a social *bienséance* (between the aesthetic and the ethical), and even an atheist like George Eliot was still 'concerned' with religion, but in a serious, philosophical and ethical way. Women's upbringing would quite prevent them from jesting with the Almighty. As to 'maturity' and 'regression to childhood' ('a startling anticipation of Freud's infantilism' as Silk says, p. 22), both are present in humour, but the infantilism seems more prevalent in the general idea people have of humour (men's jokes, the frivolous, the trivial), and since women seem to have been considered either as more mature (the mother-figure) or as child-wives, it is easy to imagine a double standard situation in which men's jokes, however regressive, were regarded as mature, and women's jokes, when made at all, as infantile.

There are also a few other persistent notions about humour and comedy and laughter which would exclude women: that comic laughter comes from ridicule and implies superiority (already in Hobbes, quoted by Silk who links this with Freud's aggressive element 'which turns pathos to bathos, tragedy to comedy'—p. 13); laughter is Satanic (Baudelaire); it degrades and materializes (Bakhtin); comedy is more materialistic than tragedy (Brecht, all these cited for other purposes by Silk). And the comic is of course intimately linked with performance, from which women were in fact excluded. All these images of the comic, which must have floated around as *idées reçues* long before they were expressed, go a long way to explain the strong preference women writers have shown for, on the one hand, serious topics, and on the other, for irony.

This 'negative' reading of what has been said on laughter and comedy may have suggested a false picture of women as utterly cowed, angelic, non-aggressive, withdrawn, profoundly understanding and so on. I hope it is not necessary to insist that I am talking about images of comedy, and ideal images that women must have had of themselves, as reflected by the expectations of society, and not of individual women with their angers and private cruelties. Much of what I describe has long disappeared, and I am talking of ancient structures, which, like all ancient structures, have left an inheritance, not only in the reception of women writers who are in fact funny, but also, perhaps, in women writers themselves. For just as a young girl could exhibit her skills at the spinet or pretty watercolours as extra accomplishments on the marriage market, but was never, never expected to compose or paint a fresco, similarly, when a woman did become a writer, she was benignly expected not only to imitate the male canon but within that to confine herself to familiar forms and to the domestic scenes she knew best. I would add, similarly again, that she was not expected to risk her precious person and become any kind of clown, certainly not on stage, but not even when safely hidden from view in the pages of a book. High comedy seems in a way the last bastion for women writers truly to conquer, not as exceptions but as the norm, like doctors, financial experts, and, why not, engineers. But:

Perhaps not?

Some critics have suggested (Jean Paul for instance) that the comic writer does not in any way distort the real but sees it that way (as mad). If this is true, then women were hardly trained to do this, but to accept the world as not only masculine but as sane and normal because masculine. Even if it is not true (and it belongs to the notion that the world is pre-existent and merely 'seen' by the writer, rather than created by him), comedy still requires not only a certain hardness of heart but an ability to 'see' at least aspects of the world as abnormal. It requires a degree of independent judgement that women took decades to develop.

Indeed, it may well be that women writers should *not* merely try to 'catch up' and develop the comic spirit as evolved by men over centuries: since the whole world is now 'seen' by all to be ab-'normal,' it may well be classical comedy that has died, and not, as everyone thought, tragedy, or even the novel: for it is true that comedy as commonly understood in the theatre-world is chiefly limited to boulevard, that is, to outrageous caricatures of the middle class in its most fixed image of inflexibility (which, because it is mechanical, women can write today as well as men). And those fixed images of the middle class are dead and gone—which is why they are popular.

But that's another story. The different 'view' of the world needed for high comedy, and apparently not acquired by women, might, however, also explain the lack of success (broadly speaking) of women in 'postmodern' experiment, where outrageous humour is one of the chief ingredients on the male side.

Bibliography:

Bergson, Henri, (1900). *Le Rire, essai sur la signification du comique, Oeuvres*, 4th ed. 1984, p. 381-485, Paris, Presses Universitaires de France; transl. C. Brereton and F. Rothwell, *Laughter, an Essay in the Meaning of the Comic*, London, Macmillan 1911.

Booth, Wayne C., 1982. 'Freedom of Interpretation: Bakhtin and the Challenge of Feminist Criticism,' in *Critical Inquiry 9-1*, p. 45-76.

Eco, Umberto, 1980. *Il nome della Rosa*, Milano, Fabbri-Bompiani; translated William Weaver, *The Name of the Rose*, London, Seeker & Warburg, New York, Harcourt Brace Jovanovich 1983.

Kierkegaard, Soren, (1846). *Concluding Unscientific Postscript*, transl. D. F. Swanson and W. Lowrie, Princeton, N. J., Princeton University Press 1941.

Miller, Nancy K., 1986. 'Rereading as a Woman: The Body in Practice,' in Suleiman 1986, republ. as book from Special Number of *Poetics Today 6*, 1985, p. 254-62.

Richards, I. A., 1929. *Practical Criticism—A Study of Literary Judgment*, London, Routledge & Kegan Paul.

Silk, Michael, 1988. 'The Anatomy of Comedy,' *Comparative Criticism 10*, Cambridge, Cambridge University Press, p. 3-37.

Walking a Disappearing Line: Christine Brooke-Rose's Treatment of Language Ambiguity in Xorandor

S. D. Stewart

In Christine Brooke-Rose's novel *Xorandor*, two precocious twins, Jip (short for John Ivor Paul) and Zab (short for Isabel), narrate their discovery of and subsequent interactions with a rock-like being that is feeding on the nuclear waste stored at a facility managed by their father. When this news breaks to a wider audience, the twins are drawn into the center of a global political drama, out of which arises the threat of nuclear catastrophe. While Brooke-Rose displays keen insight in her treatment of the global issue of nuclear waste and its politicization by world leaders, the linchpin of this novel derives from the questions it raises about the effectiveness of human language as a means of communication.

Xorandor was published in 1986, a moment in time when personal computers were still slow and expensive (Apple's flagship model, the Mac Plus, came out that year with a list price of $2600 and containing a mere 1 MB of RAM).[1] By using a hybrid computer programming language based partly on BASIC, forward-thinking Brooke-Rose, in her unique way, examines communication at a fundamental level, specifically considering the strengths and failings of human language in parallel with the logic and direct interface capabilities of computer code.

As the twins Jip and Zab attempt to provide an accurate and fact-based account of how they came to meet the being they eventually name Xorandor, and all of what happened as a result of that meeting, they struggle to prevent their emotions from distorting facts. Through their ongoing arguments about how to do this, the twins begin to deconstruct the act of storytelling, a topic that Brooke-Rose later explores at length in her collection of essays *Stories, theories, and things*. It is a

1 PC World, eds., 'The 25 greatest PCs of all time', http://www.techhive.com/article/126692/-greatest_pcs_of_all_time.html

testament to her own storytelling skill that she is able to approach the grave issue of a global nuclear threat through the words of two children smitten with the 'truth' of computer code, yet at the same time unable to resist the allure of telling an engaging tale.

Over time, Jip and Zab come to recognize the near-hopeless failure of communication between themselves and Xorandor when only using spoken human language. This is not a natural mode for Xorandor, who is used to communicating at an elemental level through programming language. The twins' solution is to use their hand-held computer Poc-com 3 to translate their human speech into machine-readable code and vice versa. While still imperfect, this method, dubbed 'softalking' by the twins, enables a more rapid form of communication allowing for accuracy and precision.

Brooke-Rose herself was bilingual, speaking French and English, having grown up in a trilingual household where French, English, and German were spoken,[2] giving her insight into the nuanced difficulties of cross-communication between languages and the feeling of 'loss of identity'[3] that can sometimes arise when moving between them. Yet by showing how the twins adapt through development of the 'softalking' technique, which they use to avert a severe communication crisis, Brooke-Rose explicates how this transition between languages can comprise a shift from a temporary feeling of loss to a sense of enrichment.

David Auerbach (2011) critiqued *Xorandor* and concluded that Brooke-Rose appropriated computer programming language to stand in for human language, ignoring the conceptual basis of the computer code and treating it strictly on a lexical level.[4] Auerbach is a software engineer with a passion for literature, giving him a unique perspective on this novel. He maintains that most of the code Brooke-Rose uses serves only to structure a narrative that could just as easily be told us-

---

2   Christine Brooke-Rose interviewed by David Seed, *Textual Practice*. 7.2 (1993): pp. 247-57.

3   'A conversation with Christine Brooke-Rose', *The Review of Contemporary Fiction*, Fall 1989, Vol. 9.3;   http://www.dalkeyarchive.com/a-conversation-with-christine-brooke-rose-by-ellen-g-fried-man- and-miriam-fuchs/

4   Auerbach, David, *Xorandor* by Christine Brooke-Rose, http://www.waggish.org/2011/xorandor-by-christine-brooke-rose/

ing natural language, and by disregarding the concepts underlying the code, Brooke-Rose roots herself in the post-structuralist time period in which she was writing, where so many writers suffered from the prevalent, in Auerbach's words, 'anti-conceptualist dogma of deconstruction,' a belief that it is not possible to discern the meaning underlying a text because of the uncertain and shifting nature of language.[5]

Auerbach bypasses some of the fictional premises of the novel to posit Brooke-Rose's disregard of the nature of computer code. Xorandor is not a computer, but a sentient being that utilizes computer logic in its communication. Thus Xorandor is an anomaly, without a real world precedent for how it should use that logic. Brooke-Rose treats the symbolic language that Jip and Zab use to communicate with Xorandor via Poccom 3 (the 'softalking') as an imperfect solution to bridging a gap between two languages: English and Xorandor's 'language', which should not be regarded as traditional computer code. Since this 'language' has been artificially constructed for the purpose of the novel, it cannot be effectively criticized as inaccurate or lacking a conceptual basis. Neither can Jip and Zab be faulted for a lack of programming knowledge. They are teenagers with enough code know-how and quick wit to manage a number of unusual situations, yet Auerbach states that one of their jokes is not true-to-real-programming life. Arising from two characters with a proclivity for wordplay, such jokes are unsurprising and completely fitting in context.

By focusing on what is termed the frivolity of Brooke-Rose's wordplay and her exploitation of computer code to accomplish the book's structural novelty, Auerbach appears to dismiss several of Brooke-Rose's linguistic insights. Through her portrayal of Jip and Zab's difficulty in communicating with Xorandor, she demonstrates how the ambiguity of human language with its unpredictable shifts in meaning distinguishes humans from machines (and machine-like beings). It is, after all, the flexibility of meaning inherent in many human languages that makes them so fascinating, and yet also maddening, particularly

---

5 Delahoyde, Michael, 'Structuralism, post-structuralism, deconstruction' http://public.wsu.edu/~delahoyd/decon.html

for non-native speakers and translators. In addition, Jip and Zab's persistent bickering over how to keep their own story real and true, while also interesting to readers, zeroes in on the human tendency to embellish a narrative of events during its telling, raising the question of whether it is indeed possible to elaborate on a narrative, and fashion it as a captivating story, without distorting its central meaning or purpose. Jip and Zab have opinions and perceptions outside the factual framework of the narrative they are presenting, and yet the continual question bandied between them is whether those opinions and perceptions add value to the narrative.

In order to probe both of these points, Brooke-Rose positions the humans with their natural language alongside machine-like beings with their programming language. This deep contrast allows the reader to see both the failings and the wonders of natural language. It is unnecessary for a reader to understand how computer code works in order to grasp the points. As such, Brooke-Rose's use of coding at a strictly lexical level seems entirely appropriate, suggesting the focus of Auerbach's critique is tangential to the central theme of the book.

By contrasting natural and programming language on a lexical level, not only does Brooke-Rose illustrate the pros and cons of natural language, she also hints at struggles inherent in computer-aided communication. For example, a human attempting to navigate a computer-guided help system over the telephone often experiences exasperation at the computer's rigid response expectations, a result of the system's lack of appropriate use-case scenarios necessary to account for the range of syntax, inflection, and word choice inherent in human language. This exasperation is reflected in Jip and Zab's attempt to communicate with Xorandor via voice alone. A gap exists that is difficult to bridge. Further evidence of this gap presents itself when Xorandor's 'child' perceives a human promise as a program, inferring that it should always lead to the same precise outcome. Unfortunately, this is a flawed analogy, as humans routinely break promises, thus rendering them 'corrupt programs' lacking in reliability. The foundation of a human promise is faith, which is outside the realm of machine logic. In this case, Jip and Zab are able to correct the misunderstanding through further 'softalking', though perhaps only because they are conversing with a sentient being, and not a true computer.

As Jip and Zab tell their grand story, they eventually come to see the value in supplementing the logic and directness of computer code with the embellishment that natural language affords them. They are aware of how their emotions affect the integrity of the narrative, seeing the potential to distort facts, yet they also know it is *their* story to tell, and for them to remove themselves from it completely would cause the story to deflate. It is this holistic awareness, the storyteller's consciousness, that Brooke-Rose seems to hold in high regard.

Christine Brooke-Rose presents a mindset akin to walking along the top of a fence, thus enabling a view of the entire field. She forever walks this line with eyes on both sides, keeping all possibilities alive, even as the line disappears into the brambles. Her texts reflect an interest in exploring, in prodding at linguistic boundaries within the lines of her stories, and the technical constraints she employed led her into new territories of thought. As she describes in *Stories, theories, and things*, 'the idea is formed out of the writing, the text *is* (generates) the idea, perfect or imperfect.'[6] For example, in *Amalgamemnon* (1984), she uses only future tense, which expanded thematically as she moved forward in the writing process.

> We're always living in this kind of future so that when a
> thing happens, it's always a big letdown, not to mention
> THE future of the death of the planet, which is hovering
> over all of us. This is something new that I wanted to
> explore, the sort of predictability of discourse in private
> situations. Even more so since sociologists and psycho-
> logist [sic] have analyzed it, and we all understand each
> other's hidden motives. This is something which has
> taken surprise and wonder out of living. So, the original
> technical motive acquires a thematic "motivation" (in

6 Brooke-Rose, Christine, *Stories, theories, and things*, Cambridge: Cambridge University Press, 1991.

the Genette sense).[7] Not the other way around.[8]

Ultimately, the kinds of questions Brooke-Rose poses in *Xorandor* don't appear to have ready-made answers, as is the case with most of life's interesting questions. On a basic level, *Xorandor* demonstrates that the ambiguity of natural language prevents these questions from being answered. There are too many ways of asking and the existence of any one answer seems improbable. Nevertheless, continuing to ask these questions in as many new and different ways as possible is important if answers are ever to be considered.

More generally, Brooke-Rose insisted on stretching the boundaries of language and of writing, and showed that when a misunderstanding presents itself, it is also the ambiguous nature of language that can act as a strength, for it is this ambiguity that also facilitates near-infinite possibilities in communication. Languages are capable of adapting to the changing needs of storytelling in all its forms. In order to put into words what so often feels inexpressible, it is the language users who must strive to shape these adaptations, even ripping words out at their roots and planting new seeds, if that is what is required to keep telling new stories.

---

7 Gérard Genette, French literary theorist associated with structuralism and narratological criticism. See his essay "Vraisemblance et *motivation*" ("Verisimilitude and motivation") for additional reading. The French version is collected in Genette's book *Figures II* (1969); an English translation by David Gorman appears in *Narrative* Vol. 9, No. 3 (Oct., 2001).

8 'A conversation with Christine Brooke-Rose', *Review of Contemporary Fiction*, Fall 1989, Vol. 9.3; http://www.dalkeyarchive.com/a-conversation-with-christine-brooke-rose-by-ellen-g-friedman-and-miriam-fuchs/

Reset

M. J. Nicholls

Imp: This here what follows is the sad and improbable tale of The Player.

Bat: Imp, you are not the Crafty Old Wordsmith (COW).

Imp: Our tale begins—

Bat: Our tale begins when I begin to tell the tale.

Imp: You are so comBATive!

Bat: And you are IMPossible!

Imp: Har-har.

Bat: This is the story of The Player, who led us through the perilous lava caverns, the perilous salty waterfalls, and the perilous spiky mountains—

Imp: Peril*ouch*!

Bat: —to rescue the Wise Old Woman (WOW) and defeat the Sick Old Wizard (SOW). All stories start at the start, don't they?

Imp: Good place to start.

Bat: IMPudence!

Imp: BATtitude!

Bat: At the start, our village had been reduced from the usual 4,000,000 pixel-optic shuttermap compression blips to under 2,000 gigaslams of sight—

Imp: Less technigargled!

Bat: Sorry! They burnt down our village. The SOW had sent a batch of flutterbytes to eat up our homes and bytenap the WOW, who held the secret code to rule the skies and move the bodies in our solar system. I was the only one—

Imp: Except me!

Bat: —including Imp, who could stop the SOW and save the planet from destruction like flooding or melting or freezing. The Player could speak to us through his keyboard and told us his name: *Hey dudes, my name's Mark-J-Kool!*

Imp: And off we went!

Bat: The Player took us over the valley. Across the dirty lake, where sneaky terrapins—

Imp: *Terrorpins!*

Bat: —poked their heads out to spit slime at us, and baby pterodactyls dropped eggs that cracked on the land to release anklebiters which clung to our legs and sucked our health until we drowned them in puddles.

Imp: One sucked me 'til I croaked!

Bat: But Imp, unlike me, was merely programmed to repeat my movements as made by The Player, and had infinite lives.

Imp: IMPortal!

Bat: That doesn't work, Imp.

Imp: Pooh-pooh.

Bat: The Player led us to the cave, up and over the bloody spikes, using my triple-wallop punchslapkick manoeuvre to fend off the baddies. I died for the first time when The Player tried to leap on a floating platform too soon and I tumbled in the bog and sank under! Back to the beginning for us!

Imp: IMPrudent!

Bat: On the way, we picked up the energy noodles and charged my health bar. The Player found a power brownie in a scrub, which doubled the size of my energy for one life. We picked up coins and ladybugs to barter. At the end of the first level, The Player typed a message to us: *Hooray, guys! We did it! On to the next!*

Imp: He was kool.

Bat: Yeah!

From the depths of childhood memory, he tried to re-imagine his grandmother's last few living months: a peaceful time spent

The Lonely Old Woman (LOW) sits watching daytime television on the sofa. Robert Kilroy-Silk is interviewing a victim of sexual abuse, pseudo-

alone in her upstairs council flat, *moralising about the very bad bad-* with occasional visits from her *ness of crime. She watches for two* close family. He hoped to author a *hours before returning to the kitchen* more tangible version of his past, *to check on her bread. She is making* to decode a childhood lost to long *her own gluten-free loaf in her bread-* years of solipsistic indulgence, idle *maker, to be eaten later with a packet* fantasising, and self-refusal. He *of McCoy's ready salted crisps and a* tried to imagine her life three *banana cut into slices. She returns to* weeks before her death, in the *the sofa to watch more daytime tele-* hope doing so would bring him *vision. Her daughter is coming* closer to an understanding of his *around to visit later. It will be the* grandmother, and make him seem *highlight of her day.* less disinterested in his childhood.

Bat: The Player took us into the Temporal City. This is where the Mad Old Watchmaker (MOW) lived, inside the huge clock tower. We crossed the perilous landscape, dodging baddies like the timewraps and thyme-wasps, pelting us with slowballs and speedoos until we were so dizzy we were bitten by a German resetter, and sent back to the beginning. This level really upset The Player, who struggled to reach the end.

Imp: Drove him BATty! You lost twenty-two lives!

Bat: He told us at the end: *That was a tricky level, guys! I need to concentrate a bit harder. Got stuff on my mind.* We were programmed with a number of responses to his responses—

Imp: Not like now, we've been new and IMProved!

Bat: —so I asked him how he was feeling about finding the MOW and begging him to warp us to the next level. He typed: *Feeling fine. Only I've been thinking about my gran. She's been unwell lately and I haven't been to see her in two years. She only lives across the street.*

Imp: Heavy!

Bat: Due to the limited program, I could only reply that we press on and meet the MOW to help us rescue the WOW. He typed: *All right!* On we went to the next level, the Aqua Opal. We had to restrict our breathing underwater, and swam past the chub-nosed Uzis, spanktons, stungeons, and swordfish.

Imp: Don't forget the maddocks, *malmons*, hellings, spikes, smacker-els, sorefish, pokerels, killbacks, and dead snappers!

Bat: We drowned forty-three times, missing our oxygen bubbles at the last minute, and The Player struggled in a duel with a bifferfish who kept inflating and deflating moments after he'd sent me to strike-dash.

Imp: You BATtered him!

Bat: Eventually. Soon it was time to speak to The Player again: *Awesome guys!* I asked how he was feeling. *I think I will visit my gran but only after we rescue the WOW. I think we can do it by the end of the week!*

Imp: IMPrudence!

Bat: We could only try.

Writing, he struggled to particularise his grandmother's experience from the generalities of an "old woman dying". He inserted scraps from his early childhood memory and assumptions not sustained by fact. He could have checked the particulars by asking his mother, but it would have tethered him to an official family version of events, when he wanted to author his own snapshot. A second-hand version would merely distance him from his own memory; re-imagining might take him closer to an understanding of the emotional inner life of his grandmother, which might atone for his blatant indifference to her.

The LOW is finding it harder to get up from the couch. She no longer leaves her flat to take the bus into town. She will never go outside again. She is able to make simple meals in the oven or microwave, from the food brought to her by her daughters. After long naps in the morning and afternoon, she listens to old records or watches television. Richard Whiteley is wearing a colourful tie and making weak puns about various words spelled by the contestants from scrambled anagrams. The records are by pretty-boy Catholic crooners like Daniel O'Donnell. She takes comfort in hearing them.

Bat: Remember the Arctic Labyrinth?

Imp: How could I forget?

Bat: We arrived at the igloo of the Frozen Old Wanderer (FOW), who told us the best way to cross the Death Forest to the SOW's castle was to melt part of the Arctic by tilting the Magnifying Eye in the watchtower at the snow. We paid him in energy snacks and went on our way. That's when we first met the Punguin.

Imp: The Painguin!

Bat: She followed us all the way to the Eye, making her puns!

Imp: Insults, mainly! She called us smellyphants, giriffraffs, rhinuisances, hywieners, hippopottymouths, crocodulls, bore-constructers, platywussies, Shetland phonies, punycorns, and dinosores!

Bat: Cheeky! We heave-hoed her and arrived at the Eye. The Player had to position me and Imp so we could push the Eye to make it point at at the snow, where the sun hit the glass and melted the landscape. Soon the Arctic was flooding and we used our sled as a surfboard and canoe to take us across the drowned forest.

Imp: Wheee!

Bat: On the way we had to paddle around pokey-out trees and rescue the drowning monkeys. We had to stack the monkeys on top of one other, so we had a pyramid of primates when we arrived at the SOW archipelago.

Imp: Arghipelago!

Bat: At the end of the level, I checked in with The Player again. Our program at the time only stored key words and formed questions around a bank of limited algorithms, so I asked him: How is grandmother? He typed: *Oh, thanks for asking. I haven't been over yet. Need to save the WOW first, right?*

Imp: And we could only repeat the last word of his text.

Bat: Right! He typed: *She's not going anywhere, is she?*

Imp: She!

Bat: *I mean, I can go over any time.*

Imp: Time!

Bat: *It's just I haven't gone over for two years.*

Imp: Years!

Bat: *So it's not very easy for me to see her since it's been ages.*

Imp: Ages!
Bat: *Oh well, let's keep going.*
Imp: Going!
Bat: Going, gone!

But writing, it became apparent that trying to re-imagine his grandmother's last days was merely a ham-fisted attempt to absolve his guilt, to apologise to the air for being a teenager too wrapped up in video games to visit her occasionally before she died. It became obvious that he never really knew and will never really know his grandmother, he can only recast the memories he has in different forms, and create variations on the same assumed events. His grandmother probably missed seeing him before she died, during the two years he never visited, but resigned herself to his absence, as she resigned herself to living alone in old age. She was loved. She was peaceful. End of.

The LOW struggles from her chair, shuffles over to turn off the television, and makes her way through to the bedroom. Checking the appliances and lights are all switched off, she goes to the bathroom for her final ablutions, then enters the bedroom. She switches on the main light, walks to the bed to turn on the table lamp, and undresses. She wears clothes that are easy to put on and remove. She switches off the main light and slides into bed. Getting in a freshly made bed after another long and tiring day is infinitely relaxing. She removes her false teeth and puts them on the bedside table, switching off the light. In a few minutes she is asleep, and in a few hours, her heart stops beating.

Bat: The SOW castle stood before us. A humungously scary red-bricked building with stone gargoyles shooting flame, bats dropping bile from above, and pitchforked sentinels patrolling the grounds. This was the tough stuff!
Imp: IMPortant!
Bat: We entered the Hellway, where we fought kickboxing butlers using the martial arts skills learned in Level Six. I ducked and weaved and bobbed and punched and sent those butlers flying back on their

butts!

Imp: *Buttlosers!*

Bat: The Player was concentrating really hard, because he kickassed his way through the labhorrortory with only nine deaths, fending off the nine-tailed radioactive porcupains, the mutant armouredillos, and the scary-looking circus cl*owwwns*, whose custard pie bombs killed on—

Imp: IMPact!

Bat: Before the final stage with the SOW, I spoke to The Player: *Guys, my gran died last night.* Ready to kickass? *I want to kill the boss first time. I can't believe she died so soon.*

Imp: Heavy!

Bat: What could I say, except let's save the WOW!? The SOW took forty goes for The Player to finally kill. He shot lasers from his eyes, nose, and ears, lasers that turned into maaarghots that latched on the skin and sucked energy. His eyeballs popped out of their sockets, his torso engulfed the screen, his legs turned fiery and icy and gluey and slimy. Only one vulnerable place could harm the SOW—

Imp: His bald spot!

Bat: Whenever he bent over, Imp or me would kickslap his pate, until finally his brain broke and he collapsed. At last, we could free the WOW! But the ending was not what we'd hoped for.

Imp: So sad!

Bat: When we got there, she'd already died from hunger and old age. But she'd left a note saying where her spell-book was hidden. We took the note and looked towards the sunset. The credits rolled.

Imp: All over!

Bat: One last message to The Player. He typed: *We were too late. We got there too late.* Thanks dude, you're awesome, I said. And we flew towards the end of the program.

Imp: Is our story done, Bat?

Bat: Seems so, Imp.

Imp: What now?

Bat: Now it's up to The Reader. Exit, replay, or reset?

A Conversation with Christine Brooke-Rose

Maria del Sapio Garbero

Les Maquignons (Provence, France)
21st August, 1991

Maria Del Sapio Garbero: You have been regarded as a "European intellectual," associated more with French and with American critical thought and writing than with English literary culture. Is that still the case? Or do you think that the context of the English novel is changing in a way that may make you feel more at home?

Christine Brooke-Rose: When I first starting experimenting with the novel I was very interested in everything that was happening in France, and later in America with postmodernism. But things have changed in England. I used to feel and be made to feel completely out, a mad Francophile, writing the *nouveau roman* in English and so forth. It wasn't true. I think the English have now absorbed what was going on in France, they've become less provincial. There are a lot of very interesting writers and critics in England. Also I've mellowed a bit myself, I'm less intransigent, so I feel more at home now in the English intellectual world.

MDSG: Certainly the English context is taking a more cosmopolitan and postmodern turn. And just as during the modernist period, outsiders again seem to be the leading figures on the British contemporary cultural scene. Do you think there is a relationship between being an outsider and transgressing the literary canon?

CB-R: Perhaps. It's interesting that more and more writers today come from elsewhere. That's not my case, I am English but I was born in Geneva and brought up in the Brussels. But there is this otherness and this awareness about other structures, not just literary structures but religious or cultural and so on. Some of the best modern writers in fact come from India or Japan or elsewhere. Many novels written in English have this other awareness, and I think that's a good sign. French culture absorbed foreigners earlier, Héredia, Supervielle, Ionesco and so on. I don't think a national literature should be entirely turned on itself.

MDSG: Your literary and critical concerns have always coexisted. How has this fact influenced your writing as a novelist?

CB-R: Very much so. From the start I was concerned with technical matters in literature. My first critical book was an analysis of metaphor and a technical metaphor in some form or another pervades my fiction. I've always had this rather technical attitude to what I am doing and I have often been blamed for this. English writers often seem to be against technique and against theory as if talent alone were all that mattered. It's a very strange notion, which no one would ever dream of upholding in music, or in painting. But with writing they seem to think that a thorough grasp of theory blocks creation. In my case on the contrary it absolutely inspired me. When I went to France and plunged into structuralism, and then poststructuralism, this awareness of how narrative was constructed and above all what it is, epistemologically, stimulated me. I am not ashamed of this. I've always pleaded for this technical knowledge which is not to be dismissed as "mere" technique. Of course technique isn't enough, you've got to have both. I hope I have both, but I've always found literary theory exciting, to understand how language functions, how narrative structures function and in my more recent work I have played with this.

MDSG: You make poetry out of this.

CB-R: I hope so. I make something else out of it.

MDSG: Perhaps what the critics dislike is the fact that this technique is foregrounded in your novels.

CB-R: Only in one novel. I've paid very heavily for *Thru*. I shall say a word on this later and try to put my work in context. But the technique is not foregrounded in other novels. There I played with it consciously.

MDSG: Following Barthes's definition, your novels can be classified as "writerly texts". You yourself say that you want to share the pleasure of your writing with your reader. But how can you accommodate pleasure to the fact that your reader has to be (to quote *Thru*) a "prepared consumer"? And how can you answer to the charge of being a difficult author?

CB-R: Yes, this perhaps would be the moment to try and put my work in context, because I am always surprised when I am called a difficult writer. My very early novels are not difficult at all, straightforward traditional novels. But I became very dissatisfied with this traditional way of writing, and I had been thinking a lot about narrative forms. The result was *Out*, my first, in quotes, experimental novel. Of course today it doesn't seem difficult compared to what came afterwards, but at the time few people in England understood it. First of all I imagined a reversal of the colour-bar in a future world unspecified, in the south somewhere. It all goes on through the mind of an old white man who cannot get a job because he is white. The technique seemed very unfamiliar, in fact this is the only novel where I was directly influenced by Robbe-Grillet who objectifies everything that goes on. You see, all the markings like "he thought," or "he said," or "she said" or pluperfects for flashbacks and so on, all that is taken out. And this was not at all familiar at the time.

Now everybody does it. In *Out* everything this old man sees and everything he thinks and everything that is said to him is, as it were, treated on the same level and in the present tense, not in a stream of consciousness where there is a lot of emotional gasping. Robbe-Grillet does this very well. It has been very badly imitated ever since though he would probably would not use it in this kind of "alternative world" fiction. I thought it was a very poetic way of doing things, and I use it on *Out* to express the confusion of this man. Everybody who is black or somehow yellow or brown or even pink has a better chance—you could be white but with a cardiac condition and you still had a better chance than the sickly unreliable feckless white people who are all suffering from some unspecified radiation disease from which the others have escaped. So there is a whole play of colours and chemistry. I can see that at the time it was very unfamiliar. Sarah Birch, who did an Oxford doctorate on me, brings out this aspect, that some of my early work now seems perfectly familiar. So it was the defamiliarization that the Russian formalists talked about which disoriented people.

And then came *Such* which was a sort of fantasy on the three minutes of someone being maybe dead, in fact who dies, and again I don't explain this, I don't go into whether he had three minutes of heart massage or is this a miracle like Lazarus. He is called Larry, but in fact the people in the psychic space I play with call him Lazarus. The realistic aspect is simply dropped out, there are never any explanations, so this have made is difficult, but in fact it's an extremely readable book. It's an adventure story, what happens to this person who meets this girl in outer space, and I use a lot of imagery from astrophysics as an ongoing metaphor for the distances between people. I think it's a very poetic novel, but again, there's this unfamiliarity, because what happens to him, I don't say who speaks, the voices just emerge and the characters emerge from that dialogue, there is no narrator-explanation. So these techniques interested me very much and I was called a difficult writer. But I think they have become much more familiar and these books would not be considered difficult now.

And then I wrote *Between*, where there are all these languages because the central character is a simultaneous interpreter in French and German, married to an Englishman, and constantly travelling, so the other languages act as a block, rather like the ideograms in pound. You know, you see "toilet" in Cyrillic script, etc. She may be trilingual, but she doesn't know everything, she has the same disorientation that every traveller has. Like the man in *Out* she has no name, she never says "I," except in dialogue, if there. There are all these sentences that she is translating simultaneously during conferences, juxtaposed with different discourses of her private life. So its quite difficult to read, but most people now don't find it difficult. I think there is a lot of unfamiliarity at first.

After that I wrote *Thru*, and here I admit that it's a very difficult novel. It has things printed downwards, in circles and so on. I was experimenting with typography. It is a novel about the theory of the novel, it is a text about textuality and intertextuality, it is a fiction about the fictionality of fiction. I am using structuralism and poststructuralism in a very, if you like, knowing way. A lot of people don't like me to be knowing, or to show knowledge. Nobody likes a woman to know. I am often accused of showing off my knowledge. I have never seen a man so accused; on the contrary, he is praised if he has a lot of knowledge. However, that was a parenthesis. I needed to write this book, because I had gone to France in 1968 and been plunged in all that very new theory and there I almost split apart, to go back to your earlier question. I needed to write this novel to bring the two "MEs" together again and I knew I was going to be rapped on the knuckles and I was. It was regarded as totally incomprehensible. I don't mind, I'm still glad I wrote this novel, and my real fans like that one best. You know, this is the book that is always quoted when people want to say I'm difficult. I absolutely admit *Thru* is difficult, very difficult. I accept that even quite serious critics can make misreadings. A lot of it is very ambiguous, it is undecidable who the narrator is, for instance, so critics who try and decide are obviously on the wrong track.

MDSG: And still it is often quote to illustrate what has been going on in contemporary literature and criticism.

CB-R: It is the most postmodern, when I got away from the *nouveau roman*. Well, I got away from it after *Out*. In *Thru* I really experiment. I've used that word, experiment, simply because it's always used with reference to me. But to experiment means that you never do the same thing twice. In each novel I do something different, which is probably one of the reasons that critics don't quite know where to place me. They are happy with a label like *nouveau roman*, or postmodern, or something. They have got used to this and that and so I mustn't do something different. But after *Thru*, you see, I changed again. I'd done that, I didn't want to do it again and *Amalgamemnon* is much more readable and easier. Since then I have tried to be less difficult. In fact, if you put it in the whole context, I think that it is largely unfamiliarity at the time which makes me seem difficult, and later in the context, with the exception of *Thru*, I don't think I am as difficult as all that. I do demand quite a lot from the reader, but I don't want to write a book where everything is given to the reader. That doesn't interest me.

MDSG: *Thru* is very much a novel about its own process of construction and destruction. Recently, however, you seem to have come to disapprove of an over-emphasised narcissistic preoccupation of the writer with his or her own writing. Can *Amalgamemnon* be considered a turning point?

CB-R: Well, yes and no. As I said *Thru* was exceptional and it is about the process of creation, but also about textuality and the fictionality of the fiction. The moment I create something I then decreate it. I break the fictional illusion. Other people have done that, it's not particularly original on that ground, but I think *Thru* goes further than they do and as far as that can be taken. But I also love to play with narrative structures and narrative conventions. I didn't stop doing that with *Amalgamemnon*. *Amalgamemnon* just tries to do something completely different, which is to use what I call non-realized tenses, mostly the future, but also the conditional, the subjunctive, the negative and so on, in linguistic terms, assertive non-modalised sentences, or, in philosophical terms, constative sentences, of which it can't be asked whether they be true or false.

As my best French interpreter Jean-Jacques Lecercle has shown, it's a "pragmatic lipogram." So that nothing is actually happening, nothing can be seen to be happening. But as to the future tense. Genette had said that the narrator need not position himself in space, but has to position himself in time, simply because he has to use tenses. He said narratives in the future are only possible in mini-narrative like a prophecy or an order. I was challenged by this and decided to do a whole novel. And that's what *Amalgamemnon* is about. It was originally called *Soon* but I decided to get away from my one-word titles. But there are also smaller and less visible tricks of narrative conventions, like the characters the author creates, for instance, out of constellations, who contact her as author and tell her she is doing wrong, which is what Genette calls metalepsis.

MDSG: The transgression of narrative levels?

CB-R: Yes. So I do play with that and I do so again, not in *Xorandor* but in *Verbivore*, and I do so in the next novel *Textermination*. So I haven't just dropped these things, I just don't do them with the intensity I use in *Thru*. It is true that *Amalgamemnon* is more readable than *Thru*, but there is a continuity with my earlier novels. It's not less or more readable than *Between* or *Such*.

MDSG: Of course you don't stop experimenting with narrative conventions and reflecting on those conventions and so on, but there is something else in *Amalgamemnon*: a wider concern with political issues and with what is happening in the world . . .

CB-R: Again I don't understand this stress on everything from *Thru* on. Perhaps because it is with *Thru* and *Amalgamemnon* that I got better known. But *Out* is extremely political and social. It's about the colour-bar. Can you have anything more social than that? And *Such* is about death and how this man who slowly comes back to life faces what's going on in his real life. That is much more social. *Between* is about identity but also about the futility of international conferences. People always think I've dropped plot and I am just experimenting with language. No, there is always a very strong idea. Whether it comes off or not this is another matter, it is not for me to say, but I certainly would not say that with *Amalgamemnon* I started being more political. Probably I was more competently political and that's a different thing. After living in France for a long time I did become more political than I was in England. But I would deny this idea that my earlier novels are just not concerned with the world; they are, but not overtly, they are not didactic, political novels.

MDSG: "Language is my material" you used to say. In your last novels, however, language itself is made into a political issue, related as it is to the problem of gender (*Amalgamemnon*) and to the problem of simulation versus reality (*Verbivore*). Is this an exact interpretation?

CB-R: Yes, I suppose so. I wouldn't say that *Amalgamemnon*'s chief idea is gender; it occurs, but it is not the main idea. The main idea is also the beginning of this simulation of reality that I try to do in *Verbivore*. In *Amalgamemnon* there is this professor of classics, of ancient Greek and Latin, who is made redundant, because nobody wants Greek and Latin now. And she is reading Herodotus and at the same time she is listening to the radio, and all these different discourses interfere. In that sense it's a very political novel: what happens to an intellectual who simply is thrown out of society because society changes. This is after all a very contemporary problem facing not just a professor but every worker, every manager even. The novel deals with what happens to her mind, which is extremely well equipped but can't quite cope with what is going on. Gender comes into it because she has these rather unsatis-factory lovers at the beginning and at the end. But the whole of *Amalgamemnon* is in fact concerned with her relationship to the characters she invents.

I don't think I've ever said this, maybe I have, but I did many versions of *Amalgamemnon* and it was only in the last version that I gave her more social substance, made her situation more explicit. Originally it started simply with what is going on in her mind and on the radio, and in Hero-dotus and so on, and this creation of characters. In a way it was a con-cession to the reader that I put it into a realistic context and I am very glad I did. The last version I think works very well. Naturally I had to rewrite the whole novels. I didn't just tack it on at the beginning, it goes all the way through and I had to work it out. I think it makes much better sense of the novel, but it was an afterthought. And I'm al-ways amused because that is what critics pounce on. They say it's a novel about a professor who loses her job. Well, in a way it is, but that wasn't my main concern. My concern was to explore this pseudo-future we all live in, through the media, all the speculation, you know, what's going to happen to Gorbachev or anybody else. And we are influenced by this. I then explored the media further in *Verbivore*, where it has become the main theme, but in *Amalgamemnon* it is interwoven with all these other things and this pseudo-future is reflected in the actual language. I think it is a social novel, but the gender thing is really almost incidental.

MDSG: But isn't simulation there also related to female language?

CB-R: Yes, of course.

MDSG: That's a question of gender.

CB-R: Absolutely, I'm not denying that there is gender, I am only protesting against you saying gender for *Amalgamemnon*, simulation for *Verbivore*. There is far more than gender in *Amalgamemnon*, but I agree it's there and certainly I use a lot of puns, one of which is "mimecstasy," "mimagree," and that of course connotes gender. But it's not simulation in the computer and media sense.

MDSG: Your bilingualism seems to be privileged biographical condition which allows you to contribute in very interesting ways to the deconstructive turn of contemporary culture. You actually work between culture, exploiting precisely the space of contiguity between the frontiers of discourses. Like Kristeva you seem to make your bilingualism the site from which the boundaries defining genres and cultural constructs of identity can be questioned. Would you agree with my view?

CB-R: Yes, certainly my bilingualism has always been very important in my writing, this awareness of other structures, this awareness of other structures. I think it influences the way I play with language. I think what was catastrophic in England after the war, was the way young writers dismissed what they called the "mandarins" who were, you know, Francophiles, Italophiles, Graecophiles. They said, English is enough and if you need a foreign literature, then read American literature, which of course does other things, but doesn't give you this contrastive sense of language, these contrastive structures in one's head which are there whenever one writes a sentence. However, I do think this has become a very common phenomenon. This is one of the things that Sarah Birch brings out in her thesis, in the bits of it that I've read, that a lot in my early work that seemed so unusual has now become not only more familiar but also more usual. A lot of people are living in a country which is not their own, partly because of the E.E.C.,[1] partly because of the refugees, the ex-British empire and so on. So I don't think that it's all that unusual now. But for me it's very important to have this distance to my language, both a deep understanding and a distance, that work together.

MDSG: In *Between* polyglottism seems to be associated with a constitutive female predicament. The space of contiguity between frontiers is exactly the space where a decentred female subjectivity posits herself. Here, as later in "Self-Confrontation and the Writer," the woeful personal problem of an elusive identity is interestingly recalled to be made into an issue concerning the writer's identity and the position of women within language. Nevertheless you say you were a bit anti-feminist in the early 1970s.

CB-R: I was and still am impatient with some types of feminism, but it's true that I have been very much concerned, especially in the eighties, with woman's place in language, and more especially the peculiar situation of the experimental woman writer, as opposed to the experimental male writer. I've written about this. But it is all part of my experimenting with different discourses, juxtaposing them and clashing them, rather than a specifically feminist concern.

MDSG: In *Amalgamemnon* you quote very effectively from Herodotus, about the Scythians being unable to learn the Amazonians' language, whereas the Amazonians learnt theirs, and therefore disappeared.

CB-R: Yes, I am glad you like that. Their disappearance is my addition. Certainly the bilingual predicament is probably stronger in women than in men, but I wouldn't say it is constitutive. It's difficult to say,

---

1 European Economic Community (renamed European Community in 1993).

there also many bilingual writers who are men, and in France particularly there is a long tradition . . .

MDSG: . . . Cassandra was bilingual!

CB-R: Yes, and it is interesting that you should ask that question because when I first started writing *Between* it didn't occur to me to make the central character a woman. Since the central character in the previous novel *Out* was a man I went on and I got completely blocked. Maybe I would have got blocked anyway, this happens often. So I put it away and wrote *Such* (also from a male viewpoint). I then took up *Between* again later. By then I had the travelling experience I needed. But I also decided to make her a woman, not so much because of bilingualism, but because of this idea that a translator merely transmits other people's ideas, and this is a sort of cliché about women, it's the view that a masculine world has and has had for many many centuries about women. And the moment I made her a woman it came out right, so there is something in what you say, but I wouldn't say it's because of her bilingualism. It is because of her status as middleman, passing on other people's ideas. And yet I had already explored the notion of the middleman in the last last of my earlier novels, a novel called *The Middlemen*, and most of these characters were men. So I don't think gender is specific either to bilingualism or to the intermediary status, but it did work better with a woman because of this—I think there is a sentence somewhere in *Between*, "existing as a woman but working as a man." And this was after all in the 1960s when it was slightly less accepted than it is today that a woman work as a man.

MDSG: Is it in the sense of a multi-layered subjectivity that the archaeological and mythological metaphor works in *Between* and *Amalgamemnon*?

CB-R: It certainly wasn't conscious. In *Between* it's simply part of the realistic background. Or at least the background motivates the metaphor. These interpreters go to conferences in many cities and go sightseeing, so the discourse of sightseeing is also one of the many discourses juxtaposed to one another. I wouldn't say it's a leading metaphor in *Between*. All the discourses are treated as equal and juxtaposed, and that is in fact the joke or the poetry, if you prefer, that comes out of it, the juxtaposing of these different discourses, and the vertical dimension is felt as an absence. There are these phrases about words going into the earphones in French and coming out in simultaneous German through the mouthpiece, which is a pun on moth and the actual mouthpiece of the interpreter's gadget. So in that sense, if you like the body is always there, as in fact you say in your book,[2] but it's all much more happening in the brain, "the distant brain way up." There are all these passengers in the plane, in the belly of the plane, and its brain is very distant. She lives in the world of discourses. And although discourse is in a way very physical, when you translate almost mechanically it's a much more, I wouldn't even say intellectual thing, but it is the brain at work whereas the body is practically at rest. And it is more in her private life, waking up in all these different hotels and not quite knowing what country she is in and so on, that these fusions between body and mind occur.

MDSG: Could the archaeological metaphor point more at a female multi-layered subjectivity?

CB-R: I would say so more in *Amalgamemnon*. I think that's very clear because she has all these layers, ancient Greek, and so on, and she calls herself Cassandra. That I think is very clear and it is tied up with herself as a woman in a feminist theme. And there are all these quotations from Herodotus at the beginning, of women being kidnapped and starting wars. I use the word "plagiarised" at one point which used to mean kidnapped, so there I think it's very clear. But in *Between* it certainly wasn't conscious. I think it's there, if you like, in an embryonic form.

MDSG: So there is something which looks forward to *Amalgamemnon*?

CB-R: Yes, I think every novel is already looking forward to another novel, not necessarily to the very next. There are these things you keep

---

2 M. Del Sapio Garbero, *L'assenza e la voce. Scena e intreccio della scrittura in Christina Rossetti, May Sinclair e Christine Brooke-Rose* (Napoli: Liguori 1991).

having in your mind and you use them differently in each novel. I simply wouldn't say that it is a guiding metaphor in *Between*. It is there but much more incidentally, as part of the sightseeing.

MDSG: In your recent book of criticism, *Stories, theories, and things* you maintain that the novel must again aspire (as in modernism) to the condition of poetry. And the impetus may come from the electronic revolution and the feminist revolution. Can you say something on this?

CB-R: This comes in a chapter which deals only with the so-called disappearing of the character in the modern novel. So it refers only to the character. And it is true that my characters aren't "well-rounded" characters in the traditional sense, but then, very often when I pick up a modern novel I do not actually believe in and identify with the characters as I used to and still do in great classical novels. When I say I am not a realistic writer I don't mean I don't admire the great realists or even the great realists today, but this process of identification has been very diluted, partly by the media. People identify with characters in soap and so on, so the process of identification still exists but on a much lower social level. So I tried to deal with all this in that particular chapter and I ended up on this notion that there might be a future, first of all in feminism which tries to understand the female psyche via Lacan *et al.*, and in the electronic revolution which is exactly the opposite, very masculine and binary and so on. And it was almost done tongue-in-cheek, I didn't work it out. It was thrown in at the end. But it does seem to me that just as the computer can introduce a simulation of a plan for an airplane or a very complex machinery, it is possible that one will be able to produce a character in a much more thorough way. I'm not for this, I'm just talking from a realistic point of view. But the computer revolution has and will change our mentalities, just as writing gave us complex characters not possible in oral literature. I don't think you should take it too seriously.

MDSG: But in your book you were not talking of the feminist revolution in general. You rather referred to those sectors of the feminist movement more interested in deconstructing binary oppositions, one of which is that between masculine and feminine.

CB-R: Yes, and I was quoting Lacan on the female pas-tout, not-all, whereas the masculine wants to be all, everything, the totalizing aspect.

MDSG: You seem to oppose the idea of women's writing. You seem to share Kristeva's and Cixous' idea that *écriture feminine* can exist in both masculine and feminine writing. What is specificity to you? Is there anything like this?

CB-R: Well, I have attacked the whole notion in my last book, at least as it is expressed. The radical feminists are very much against the androgynous-great-mind stance which was Virginia Woolf's. I am rather for it. Clearly any great mind or indeed any human being has a great deal of feminine and masculine in him, and all male writers have always had a lot of feminine in them. It's true they haven't always exploited it. Dickens's women, for instance, or even Hardy's, he tried, but it's always from the male point of view. And women have learned to go along with this, in fact for generations and centuries women have always read as men—Jonathan Culler has a very interesting essay on this—and it's time that men also learnt to read as women.

MDSG: You write about this in "Illiterations".

CB-R: Yes, I am absolutely against this notion of segregation. It's an interesting thing that all revolutions, including the black revolution, seem to have to go through this phase of "we're not going to have anything to do with the whites" (or with men and so on). I think this is a great mistake. Art can't just cut itself off from half its source. I mean there we are, men and women, and men have done the things that women claim are specifically feminine. I analyse this in an essay called "A Womb of One's Own?"—I rather like that title. And there I show that features feminists are claiming as specific are not only non-specific but not very much to their credit. They shouldn't actually want this, this going back to the primitive and flux and flowing and all that. They also talk about fragmentation—now fragmentation seems to me almost the opposite of flux. This has existed in modernist and postmodernist male writing and in much earlier poets . . .

MDSG: Which is why Kristeva herself has written mostly on male authors?

CB-R: Yes, but that's a different question. It's intriguing why the two top feminists in France, Cixous and Kristeva, find *écriture feminine* only in men, which seems to annoy the American feminists. But I think that's partly chance. As top women they are not all that interested in other women writers and so they find it in Genet and others. Similarly and it's quite interesting, the deconstructive movement in Yale, coming originally from France, was totally uninterested in the deconstructive novels of postmodernism that were being written all around them. They were deconstructing Shelley and Rousseau and Nietzsche and so on. I feel a little bit the same with the feminists. They plunge into theory and talk about all these things, the publishers are digging up—what I call scraping the barrel—forgotten women authors who sometimes had better remain forgotten, but they pay very little attention to the real interesting women writers around them.

But to get back to specificity, it's not tactically or even strategically a very good thing for women to back, because it is anti-artistic in its segregation. There is even someone, I mention her in my essay, I forget who it is, who wants all women experimental writers from Dorothy Richardson on to be treated as though there were no men before them. And you can't do that, it's just mutilating, and I don't understand, since they are so against men's psychic mutilation of women, why they are doing exactly what they accuse the men of doing. Now I don't mean to say that being a woman is not important, she will explore her experience just as a man explores his experience, she will imagine male characters just as men imagine female characters trying to get into them, some well, others less well, and so on. It is very difficult to imagine yourself as totally other, but if you can't do that you don't even begin to be a writer. And to write only about your troubles and your menstruations and your kitchen sink and your love affairs seems totally uninteresting now, a mere imitation of frank sex in the male novel earlier in the century. I suppose it can be well done, I am not just dismissing everybody, but I think it is a dangerous tack they're on. It's a little bit like what is happening with working class writers or black writers or any ethnic writer. I think it's an insult to treat them as a class. The working class writers are completely different from each other. D.H. Lawrence is not at all like Alan Sillitoe or any other. Similarly black writers are different. But to treat them simply with a label is as unfair as treating women as a "woman writer." These categories are not right. For the writer they are mutilating, they are debilitating. And the stress on specificity I think is just intellectually and I would say even morally wrong.

MDSG: Still, as you have already said, as an experimental woman writer you have had more problems than men.

CB-R: Yes, I have already touched on that and I did deal with it in my essay "Illiterations." I went all the way back to Plato and analysed how and why in a male society there is this deep conviction, that you still meet with today, quite unconscious, that women cannot create new forms, but can only imitate, either men, or their own lives (two different senses of the word imitate). To show how men appropriated as metaphors the whole creative process. There was the poet inspired (as penis) by God, impregnated but also gestating and giving birth (genius *and* labour). In Plato he may use a boy as a sort of titillating midwife, later it was women as muse or midwife: woman is beauty but she cannot create beauty. You get this still even in Pound, you get it in Gautier, this runs all the way through and I don't think it is conscious, but it does affect the experimental woman writer, who is, like men, trying to create new forms.

MDSG: Seriousness and humour. It is what you like in Pound and Beckett. How do you conciliate the two aspects in your novels?

CB-R: I don't have to conciliate them. They are just present all the time. I don't try to be funny and I don't try to be serious. It just happens. I think it's the result of my passion for language. Language is so funny. Discourse is so funny . . .

MDSG: Is language called to cover a certain amount of despair or anguish? I'm thinking of the frequent anagrammatic permutation of the title of your novel *Thru* in "hurt."

CB-R: Yes, I suppose so. But this is not a terribly interesting question to me. I don't know if you remember, but there is a scene in *Thru* where a Mali writer comes and interrupts Larissa, who is writing, and criticises her novels saying, "You are just escaping into language." In fact, much of that is personal. This episode did happen. And the moment I got rid of this man I just wrote the scene, absolutely verbatim. It's very rare in my novels, but I did. You know, he says something like . . . "this suffering and so on . . . and the moment you get to the real point . . . you escape into language . . . into a joke" and so on. And she answers (I can't remember the exact words): "Isn't the only thing to do with suffering to laugh at it!" So even if it's partly defence, it's not covering up because the suffering is there and the seriousness is there.

MDSG: You take up that point later on in *Thru* when you write that people are not interested in sharing suffering. "Only ebullience can be shared."

CB-R: I don't know. I don't remember that.

MDSG: So you work on suffering until it vanishes into language, something to play with . . .

CB-R: Well, I think this is the only way to cope with it. And also with seriousness, not necessarily suffering. But on suffering there are two completely opposite attitudes in society. One is that everyone regards suffering, or even bad characters, more complex characters, in novels as splendid. The happy people are rather dull! It's the old thing that God is so much less interesting in Milton than Satan and so on. But in real life everyone runs away from someone who is, say, in a crisis, or suffering, or an unhappy woman. Particularly women. People are rather sorry for an unhappy man but an unhappy woman, even if she is not talking about it, exudes unhappiness, and people avoid her. Nobody likes going to see people in hospital, you know, there is a fear of that, so their attitude to suffering in art is the opposite of their attitude to suffering in the world. But certainly I would say that I have nothing in particular to say on that question. It comes to me naturally. I don't strive for it and I've always coped with difficulties and suffering through humour. I love playing with forms, I love playing with language. It just comes to me so naturally and if anything I have to curb it.

MDSG: I was thinking of the Lacanian notion of lack and of language as a way of repairing this original lack. I rather see suffering in your novels as something which stems from a metaphysical preoccupation.

CB-R: Well, I suppose it's there, since I am deeply read in Lacan and Derrida, but, yes you can't do a lot with lack in language because language is present.

MDSG: It's both present and absent.

CB-R: Yes it's the subject of your book. And that is a very difficult topic which I try to handle in *Thru*, in fact I play with the notion of holding on to a structure until you fall through the empty space. The structure is like a diagram or a structuralist scheme. Life of course is much more complex than that. And Deleuze has gone right away from all these regular diagrams and talks about the rhizoma, he says you can't just deal in structures. But of course we are all the time having little structures in our life, every time we deal with a situation we are restructuring it already. We are structuring the chaos of the real and everything that happens, and we couldn't live if we didn't do this, and then the structure goes and it's like falling through the emptiness and you have to build a new one. So I do try to deal with this lack and this emptiness, but it's very difficult to write about, to write about nothing. Flaubert's great notion of writing *un livre sur rien*.

MDSG: Yes, yet lack is there in each novel you write. It is there in *Verbivore* where you suggestively quote Plato's *Phaedrus* (one of the dialogues) on the invention of writing—something, as he writes, which will deprive men of their memory and feelings,

CB-R: Yes, that's a very important dialogue which was taken up and analysed by Derrida. It's one of his earlier essays.

MDSG: *La pharmacie de Platon.*

CB-R: Yes, *La pharmacie de Platon.* It was my introduction to Derrida. It was the first thing I read by Derrida when it appeared in *Tel Quel* and then I read other things. I didn't know it came in *Verbivore.* It must be Zab who says it, because of the two twins of *Xorandor* who come back in *Verbivore,* she is the more philosophical one, so I expect she says it. No, I'm sure it's there, because lack is something we all have. There is always a lack, otherwise there would be no striving, that's a fundamental definition of mankind, I would say, this constant striving to fill up a lack.

MDSG: And also there is this sense of reality as constantly collapsing.

CB-R: Yes, I am fascinated by that. It's just very difficult to write about it. It's not a straight plot, you know, if everything is always collapsing . . .

MDSG: But that's the idea sustaining the narrative of *Verbivore,* the collapse of reality.

CB-R: Well, it's the collapse of the media, which are reality by then to everybody.

MDSG: Yes, it's a sort of second reality.

CB-R: I was trying to explore what would happen if we were suddenly deprived of the electronic media: would we go back to a pre-media stage. Well, we can't. Our entire attitudes, our mental structures have now been altered, and that's what I was exploring in *Verbivore,* the fact that this reality we are given every day is in fact highly organised. We noticed that yesterday when we watched news in Italian, and then the BBC, and I pointed out how differently structured it is. In fact people are just told what the *rédaction* want them to know. That's why I put this dish up on the roof because I am still very much interested in how we are being formed, not really brainwashed, it's too strong a term, but what we think is reality is an image we are given, which is presented to us that way. It was very clear during the Gulf War. So I am very interested in seeing German television, English, French, Italian and so on, to see these different realities and I wish in fact I had had my dish when I wrote *Verbivore*. I would have known much more about it.

MDSG: But again, I think there is a philosophical sense of absence in your novels, just because you are so interested in the simulation of reality.

CB-R: Yes, I go along with that.

MDSG: In "Self-Confrontation and the Writer," talking of yourself as a writer, you affirm the impossibility of coming to grips with one's "I" as a totality. Too many selves to confront (you say), too many of them asking for reunification. Do you feel that task of yours is accomplished by now? Or that your creativity thrives exactly on that impossibility? So that the effort towards reunification is part of the quest the reader (and critic) has to undertake?

CB-R: That essay was written very much tongue in cheek, and my only criticism of your book is that you start with that and take it all very seriously. I was asked, for a special number of *New Literary History*, to write on self-confrontation and the writer and I simply did it as a joke and it's really quite funny. In the end it turned out to be more personal but I don't think it should be a sort of basis. As you may have noticed I didn't reprint it in my *Stories, Theories and Things* and also it was written a long time ago. I'm not at all sure of all these identities. Now it's such an old-hat topic, this search for identity. It doesn't terribly interest me and of course I explore it mostly in *Between* where she is constantly split, with these different roles and different identities. This wasn't noticed at the time, but since I've said it somewhere everybody now picks on it, but I decided to write without the verb to be. Now there are two reasons for that. One is to get this constant sense of moving, she is all the time travelling, and it's a sort of constraint. I like working with a constraint. It forces me to find another verb which is usually a verb of movement, anyway more movement than just being. The other reason was this loss of identity through being an interpreter, interpreting what other people say and never saying her own things, and this constant travelling, and bilingualism, or trilingualism and so on. She never brings them together and I don't think she should, and I don't think a writer should, I don't think I should. We all accept that we are many different people and play roles even with our closest friends. In a way we are all playing roles, we are not exactly the same as when we are alone in the bathroom. There is a sense of continuity with the "I" I have always known and of course I've changed, but this is a perfectly common experience, we all have it. And I don't think that totalising is a good thing at all in the novel. I don't think a novel should go to "I" and "mine" and "who am I." No, that's not the point. In *Between* the customs office asks the usual question which comes all the way through the novel, "Have you anything to declare?" And she says, "No, just personal effects," and I think that's how the novel ends. One of these personal effects of course (in the context of customs) is just "what do you have in your suitcase?" but personal effects are also—

MDSG: Effects of reality?

CB-R: —yes effects of reality and what effect you have on people and people have on you. So, its quite a rich and ambiguous word. I think that's what literature is about. I don't think that one has to unify all these "Is". It's not a problem that actually worries me. Or perhaps it did when I wrote *Between*, I can't remember.

MDSG: Which is what is interesting in what you write. You affirm all the time that identity is a construct and no truth is possible even if one tells of one's I.

CB-R: Yes, I think that if one accepts that one is much happier as a person and more impersonal as a writer.

MDSG: The "I" is an illusion, as reality is an illusion?

CB-R: Well, I suppose there is a sort of fundamental I where you can think of your life, so "*that* was me," "*that* was me," and so on. You do have a consciousness that continues and most people would cling to that. That's why most people believe in afterlife, they can't believe that this fundamental I will just vanish. But I don't think that is a problem that has worried me very much. Perhaps as persons we all have to grow up and adapt and get on in the world and so on, and go through all our timidities and our fears and then our growing assurance and all that, but metaphysically it's not a problem that worries me very much. I played with it but I wouldn't think it's fundamental to my writing.

MDSG: There is a nice pun in "Self-confrontation and the Writer." You say biography is always bifography, as if to say that any attempt at truth always ends up in a fog, a false construction.

CB-R: Oh yes, I'd forgotten that. It's nice to have critics who come and remind one of the things one wrote many years ago.

Ganging Up

Christine Brooke-Rose

At a literary dinner in London last year, the conversation was wholly about who had reviewed what where. Unable to express an opinion when asked, I pleaded ignorance, explaining that in my job here it was difficult enough to keep up with all that has been happening since Structuralism. 'Oh,' said a woman novelist, 'is Structuralism over? Oh, *good!*' The notion that a type of investigation, having progressed, need no longer be bothered about, seems downright funny to me.

Structuralism, in linguistics, was 'over' with the advent of Chomsky, some twenty years ago, although it was taken up by Lévi-Strauss in anthropology, by Lacan in psychoanalysis, and by Barthes in literature, who caused a furore in academic circles at the time. In the early sixties, the review *Tel Quel* was founded by Philipe Sollers and Julia Kristeva, opening its pages to Barthes, Todorov, Genette, Derrida, Faye, and of course to many poets and novelists from the nouveau roman (the 'new novel') onwards (Barthes having rather oddly annexed the nouveau roman to Structuralism, with which it had nothing to do). All this, as always in France, was highly politicised, language being analysed in Marxist terms of exchange and subversion, so that Sollers could tell me recently, with absolute conviction, that '*nous avons fait la révolution.*'

Since then, much has happened, and *Tel Quel* has often given the impression, from the outside, of being indeed, as one English literary editor put it to me in 1971, 'a new theology' ('*C'est vrai,*' says Sollers, but proudly). Anyone who disagreed seems excommunicated or at least went off slamming the doors, often starting reviews of their own rather than discussing within the review: it would take 500 pages, says Sollers, the more 'imitations' there are, the more it serves us.

In fact the situation is more complex, reflecting genuine divergences. Todorov, Genette and Hélène Cixous founded *Poétique*, an international and chiefly university forum on literary theory, and Hélène Cixous has since started her own series of feminist publications. Jean-Pierre Faye, who had been chiefly responsible for the interest in the Russian Formalists (translated by Todorov), stated his own review *Change*, in 1968, one of its first numbers being devoted to the Prague Circle which, via Roman Jakobson, had led to Chomsky and the linguistic revolution of transformational grammar. All this may seem very strange to an English reader brought up on the New Criticism *et seq.*, all the more so since the same names (Mallarmé, Lautrémont, Breton and others) are taken up by the different groups, with different analyses.

A German called Sieburg once wrote a book, in the thirties, called *Dieu est-il français?*, imbued with admiration for France but also bringing out the curious capacity of the French for assuming, not only that all French good ideas are universal but that all other good ideas are French. During all the years of the New Criticism, for example, the French were still involved with the nineteenth-century criticism; they just didn't want to know. Then they had their revolution, through Structuralism—with curious side-effects, such as the discovery of 'polysémie,' in the sixties, as if Empson (1930, 1948) had never written. And now it's the English who don't want to know.

But Stucturalism is not French; it is Slav, then American. And one of the troubles with revolution, as opposed to evolution, is its tendency to become institutionalised. So the French Structuralists got stuck: a Structuralist grammar is ultimately a typology, semiology, incapable of 'generating' forms as a transformational grammar generates an infinite number of sentences and accounts for creativity in native speakers. Structuralist analysis, however useful in other ways not to be ignored, ceases to be a grammar—hence Barthes' later statement: 'there is no grammar of narrative.'

In the universities and in certain literary circles, many have remained within the bounds of traditional criticism, and even the work of Barthes is frowned on. Others have stayed with Structuralism (Greimas, Bremond, Todorov, for example), exploring texts as far as it will take them. Others still have adopted Derridean philosophy, or Lacanian analysis, or Klossovsky, Deleuze, Lyotard, and so on.

Barthes himself has withdrawn into a highly individualistic, but always elegant, position, exploring sociological, psychoanalytical and rhetorical encodings in text (in *S/Z*), and stressing the role of the reader, by discussing—as for instance in *La Plaisir du Texte—la jouissance*—which I gather has been translated as 'bliss,' thus suppressing the very specific sexual connotation and making him sound like Longinus on the Sublime. Julia Kristeva, plunged in an intricate semiotics of her own, has reversed many concepts, notably that of causality and that of *langue/parole*, language being no longer Saussure's 'treasury' from which one fetches up words, like currency, but a continually expanding treasure, produced by the practice of writing. Her husband Sollers, editor of *Tel Quel*, himself an interesting practitioner and polemicist on literature, has taken up Joyce, Burroughs and other writers who subvert language, subversion being of course a revolutionary activity.

Yet ultimately the position of *Tel Quel* is an individualistic one, literature being now in perpetual crisis: the 'literary series' is autonomous with regard to the 'political series,' two parallel lines which touch only in infinity (Kristeva admitted to me that this also produces 'un moment de tristesse'). To join them leads to totalitarianism, and the real cultural revolution is to 'creuser le singulier.' *Change*, in particular, wages an incessant war against these 'misconceptions.' For Jean-Pierre Faye, whose monumental work on totalitarian discourse reveals, precisely, the deep structures underlying many of Hitler's or Goebbels' or Himmler's statements, *Tel Quel* is merely trendy: first Communism, then Maoism, now 'neo-Surrealism,' psychoanalysis, drugs, mysticism (Julia Kristeva is called Mme Blavatsky in the latest number).

Leaving aside the lapses of tone, regally ignored by *Tel Quel*, I find *Change* extremely exciting, despite its occasionally extravagant claims for itself (from which no one is exempt in Paris). It has left Structuralism and Semiology far behind, and is now exploring transformationalism and its highly experimental (and difficult) application to literary forms. It has published the work of, and interviews with, Morris Halle and Sam J. Kayser on deep structures in poetry and especially metre, as well as that of Jacques Roubaud (poet and mathematician), Jean Paris, Sam Levin, Ann Banfield and the extraordinarily bright Mitsou Ronat who is waging her own war on the 'regressive' (Structuralistic) mess of generative semantics (as opposed to generative grammar or syntax). *Change* sets these investigations in an international context, where they belong, and it is in touch with people all over the world: except, of course, England where, Faye tells me, there are 'no echoes,' though he was there recently—invited by a Czech. He has also published Chomsky's *Blood Baths*, and the whole account of its suppression in the U.S.

I have concentrated on these two reviews (or 'gangs') because they are the ones, with *Poétique*, that interest me the most, but there are many others, representing every tendency: the old *NRF*, *L'Homme*, *Esprit*, *Minuit*, *Diagraphe*, *Dialectiques*, *Communications*, and so on. One of the most lively aspects of France is, precisely, this vast forum for discussion. It is the publishing houses which usually finance the reviews, even, like Seuil, rival ones (a good capitalist principle which Sollers is proud to exploit). And the reviews sell, except, in this time of crisis, the very traditional ones; if not outright, always eventually (between 4000 and 8000 per number), both in France and abroad. Some years ago I asked an English publisher to back such a review, which I hoped to edit with Frank Kermode, to be called, at the time, *Paradigm* (or, privately, in a skittish mood *The Franker Mode*), but after some initial interest the publisher got cold feet. Hence there is no forum in England, and hence the parochialism of English literary life: Is Structuralism over? Oh *good.*

'Letter From Paris', The Spectator, 27 March, 1976.

(W)rite of Passage

Nicolas Tredell

I lost my virginity as an interviewer with Christine Brooke-Rose. It was not an initiation I would have chosen.

At that time, I was closely associated with the magazine *PN Review*, and its editor, Michael Schmidt, the director of Carcanet Press, had suggested I might do some interviews for it. Christine's name was not mentioned at first; the two initial targets, as I recall, were Christopher MacLehose and Frank Kermode, and Michael wrote to them asking if they would be interviewed by me. But before any response came, Michael rang to say that Christine was coming over from Paris to launch her book *Verbivore*, published by Carcanet, and asked if I could interview her—he knew I had an interest in experimental fiction and I had written quite a lot about modern literary theory in *PN Review*.

I agreed, but contemplated the event with some trepidation; I had never done a serious literary interview before and had only met Christine briefly once, at a launch lunch at Bertorelli's. While I much admired her fiction and criticism, I was alarmed by the formidable persona her texts, particularly her critical ones, projected. But I set to, re-reading her work and finding myself constantly astonished by the way her novels from *Out* onwards differed from run-of-the-mill fiction; among her earlier books, I was especially impressed with *Such*, which seemed, and still does, enormously original. I prepared myself as fully as possible, unaware that I was laying down a pattern of thorough preparation that would stand me in good stead in subsequent interviews.

I rang Christine to confirm our appointment and joked: "I'll wear a bowler hat and a dandelion so you'll recognize me". I was glad that she laughed (on a later occasion, I made the same quip to someone I hadn't met before and it took us some time to rendezvous at Oxford station because they were looking for a man who really was wearing a bowler hat and dandelion). Christine's laughter, I felt, showed she had a sense of humour and made me feel slightly more relaxed about the forthcoming encounter.

I arranged to meet her in the lobby of the Park Court Hotel in Bayswater. This hotel had sub-literary associations for me which it is not perhaps quite irrelevant to mention here. My father used to stay there on business trips from Leicester and at a certain point I discovered that this was where he had indulged a secret vice: writing. It was here, at the end of the business day, that he would sit down at his portable Imperial typewriter (a notable Leicester product at that time) and work on his solidly realistic novels. These never were published and perhaps this contributed to my later sense that realistic fiction, whatever its merits, was not quite what writers should be doing in the post-1945 era. Christine herself had of course started as a realistic novelist of a sort and had made the break into a very different kind of fiction.

I wasn't wearing a bowler hat and dandelion but I did display my copy of *Verbivore* prominently as I sat in the hotel foyer, near the main entrance, and anxiously watched the ladies who entered. One problem was that I didn't know what Christine now looked like; this was 1990, long before the present-day proliferation of images on the internet, and the idea I had of her was that of the elegant young woman in an Yves Saint Laurent scarf on the cover of the copy of *Thru* that I had brought for 50p as a remainder copy in a Brighton bookshop years ago. But *Thru* had been published in 1975; even Catherine Deneuve could hardly look like that now. The woman who turned out to be Christine looked more like a public school Senior Mistress, furtively smoking off duty (this was a time when it was still permissible to smoke in English hotels).

I took her up to the room I had booked and the interview began. She had just come from another interview, I think with a *Time Out* journalist, and she started speaking quite quickly about *Verbivore*, pitching it on what struck me as a simplified level; for the first time it occurred to me that she might be nervous too. But as the conversation went on and

I tried to show that I had read her work carefully, we both relaxed and our discourse moved to a more sophisticated plane. When she laughed when I used the word "mimesis", pronouncing it with a long "e", I thought I might have blundered, but she observed that my pronunciation was the American one (I hadn't realised this) and that in the English pronunciation, with a short "e", she always heard the phrase "my missus". It was this pun that had amused her, and that struck me as a piece of pure Brooke-Roseana. Apart from my relief that I had not made a pronunciatory *faux pas*, I felt delighted to have provoked it.

I was also struck by her irreverent attitude to one of the key post-structuralist tenets of the time—that mimesis was a bad thing, a mode of mystification that concealed the fictionality of fiction and the free play of language. As I began to broach this point, she said, with amusement, "That was just a phase" and that everybody knew now that fiction was made of words. This was a revelation; I had previously assumed that Christine would firmly deprecate mimesis and that this attitude still reigned in Paris; but here, from a person who had been at the very heart of the *grande révolution* of deconstruction and post-structuralism, was a clear indication that times had moved on, that the anti-mimetic thrust that was still preoccupying supposedly leading-edge English critics, had run its course in its place of origin.

I had a further surprise when I spoke about Joyce. Liking James Joyce seemed to be another essential feature of an avant-garde late-twentieth-century writer; and when Christine casually, but with evident sincerity, remarked "I don't really like Joyce" I had to recalibrate my expectations again. I had the sense—and I think it comes through in her criticism too—that her attitude to Joyce was not far from Virginia Woolf's: "a queasy undergraduate scratching his pimples."

If Christine was not anti-mimetic, she was, at the time I interviewed her, anti-autobiographical, averse to the idea of using her own experience in her fiction. She said that "just to reproduce my own little life, that doesn't interest me at all." Even at that time, I thought her belittling of her own life questionable—it seemed pretty interesting to me —but it is only in retrospect that I fully realize how remarkable and unusual her life was, with its cosmopolitanism, its multilingualism, her early work at Bletchley Park ("my first university"), her Oxford studies, her life in literary London in the 1950s, her move to Vincennes at the height of the post-1968 tumults, her marriages, and, above all, her writing. Later, when she felt she would not write another novel, Michael Schmidt suggested she try an autobiography and she did so—though of course, with Christine, it was not be a conventional autobiography but one full of distancing devices and signs of textuality that heightened the awareness of life as a construction, made of words—but no less a life for that, indeed more of one, a full and moving set of remade experiences. Both *Remake* and *Life, End of* are classics of autobiography and add to Christine's achievement as a fiction writer and critic.

After the interview, I kept in touch with Christine and corresponded with her, and her communications always put me in a state of high alertness, as our first sustained encounter had done. As time went on, I came to feel, as one sometimes does with very old people, that, despite her increasing physical frailty, she would never die, that she would always be there. It was a shock to learn of her death from a request in my junk mail, from the *Independent* newspaper, to write her obituary, a task to which I instantly gave my full attention—even posthumously she had the power to raise my game.

Her books are an immense gift to all who read them but, on that March day in 1990 at the Park Court Hotel in London, she gave me another gift: confidence in myself as an interviewer. After the interview was over, I asked her to sign a couple of her books, *Thru* and *Verbivore*. It was clear that she took the act of inscription seriously, feeling impelled to choose the right words: in my copy of *Thru*, she wrote "a faithful remainder" and in my copy of *Verbivore* "intelligent interviewer —rare bird". This last phrase was like a benediction, a sign that I had successfully completed my (w)rite of passage; and, thus emboldened, I would go on to do interviews with nineteen more people, which were published in *PN Review* and eventually as a book, *Conversations with Critics*—with Christine, fittingly, as the first subject.

29 November 2013

A Long Way to San Francisco

Emily Rhodes

The rising tide lifted the crazy old boats of Battersea Reach in the water. As they lurched afloat, a collective shudder passed through their owners, as each fretted about their craft's particular holes, patches and other weaknesses.

The barge-owners were gathered for their Sunday meeting on Lord Jim, a flawless converted minesweeper. Little had been decided: the easy-flowing current had eddied against a rock of disapproval when Willis, owner of Dreadnought, had asked the others not to mention its various leaks to potential buyers.

Now, as the boats slipped on their amphibious form, it was silently acknowledged that the meeting was over. The owners were impatient to return to their boats, certain that only their presence would protect the flimsy wooden vessels against the fierce flow of the Thames. Richard, the owner of Lord Jim, wished them goodnight and watched them scramble off the deck. They slunk away in the gloaming, making their way back to their boats along precarious gangplanks, picking a path between the litter of ropes, buckets and oilskins.

'I wish you'd stay and have a drink with us,' Richard said to Nenna, owner of Grace, as the others dispersed.

Nenna sensed Richard's dissatisfaction with the unresolved meeting. Waves of anxiety rippled away from him like those from a pebble flung into the river. 'I wish I knew the exact time,' she said, hoping that he might feel better if called upon to provide a solid fact.

'That is one thing of which it is easy to be sure,' he said, smiling. 'Let's look at the chronometers.' He showed Nenna inside the boat, guiding her towards the set of instruments, thanks to which he could not only tell her that it was exactly seventeen minutes to six, but also the state of the tide at every bridge on the river. 'Not long until the guests arrive.'

'Who are you expecting?' Nenna directed her question towards Laura, Richard's wife, who was placing small pieces of orange-pink smoked salmon on round buttered biscuits.

Laura flung a look at Richard. She was of the opinion that none of the other barge-owners was important enough to warrant an invitation.

'Have you ever thought about what would happen if this book were to go out-of-print?' Richard asked Nenna, abandoning the chronometers to uncork a bottle of Chardonnay. 'I know it's unlikely, as things stand,' he said, taking out three wine glasses. 'It won the Booker Prize and that should protect us for a good few years, but we can't be sure. Reading fashions change. In the future, everyone might be fixated with thick historical novels, and Offshore might be slim enough to drift, unread, out to sea.'

'I suppose you're right,' said Nenna, sipping the cold wine. 'I've never really thought about it.' Laura had finished arranging the biscuits and was now emptying packets of cheese straws into three large bowls.

'This weekend,' Richard continued, 'there has been a convention in San Francisco to discuss just such a possibility. Thousands of characters from literature were invited to plead their case for survival and talk tactics about how they might continue to be read.'

'San Francisco. Gosh.'

'Indeed. And we were just a few of the many characters who weren't invited.'

'Well our invitation was probably lost in the post,' said Laura. 'It wouldn't be the first time the postman dropped our letters into the Thames, or mislaid them at the boatyard office.'

Richard ignored his wife's interjection and looked instead at Nenna, trying to establish whether or not she had understood the gravity of their situation. The barge-dwellers were continually worrying about the survival of their crafts, but had they ever paused to consider their own precarious lives? Nenna frowned, making her forehead crease and pucker. Richard felt he had been right to ask her to the meeting, whatever Laura's objections.

'I put the word out that anyone who isn't going to San Francisco is welcome to come here instead. I thought there must be others whose invitations had gone astray, or who might be unable to make the journey due to financial strain, or perhaps ill health, old age, or some such. The convention kindly faxed me over a document containing a list of some key points raised over the past couple of days.'

'Yes,' said Nenna, wishing she could remember the rest of the words in the song about going to San Francisco and wearing flowers in your hair. She took a cheese straw and nibbled the end of it. She thought of Maurice telling her how ferociously his cheese straws had burned when he'd run out of fuel and had had to resort to setting fire to whatever was in the store cupboard.

'Quite how we will manage to fit everyone on board, I don't know,' said Laura.

'We are only expecting twenty guests,' said Richard. 'Some of them are rather distinguished.' He checked the chronometers again and saw that it was precisely six o'clock. The guests' arrival was imminent. In fact, he could hear voices approaching, too clipped to be native to Battersea Reach.

'Good evening,' said a small plump man in a square hat and old-fashioned, slightly shabby frock-coat. He bore a birdlike elderly lady on his arm. 'I take it we have come to the right place?' He said it only as a formality, for he had never not come to the right place, just as he was always exactly on time.

'Good evening,' said Richard. 'Welcome aboard. Lady Slane, so kind of you to make the journey down from Hampstead.' He addressed the gentleman's companion, for he wasn't entirely sure of the gentleman's identity. In all likelihood he was Mr FitzGeorge, but he could also have been the agent Mr Bucktrout, or, at a pinch, Lord Slane himself.

'Thank you,' said Lady Slane, taking Richard's hand with her gloved one and stepping gracefully onto the boat. She wobbled unsteadily on the swaying deck and made her precarious way towards a seat.

'FitzGeorge,' said her companion, shaking Richard's hand. 'You must be Mr Blake. Awfully good of you to have us.'

Laura thought it typical that the grandest guests would be the first to arrive. She offered them a glass of wine, inwardly quailing that it wasn't a vintage of which they would approve.

Lady Slane took in her new surroundings. Who were these two women in their guernseys, one pouring out glasses of wine and the other eating a cheese straw while looking as though her thoughts were a thousand miles away? Perhaps her thoughts were in San Francisco, drifting along the corridors of the daft convention.

How could they have thought she'd go all that way, such a terribly long journey even in an aeroplane, as they suggested? She was perfectly happy perched in Hampstead; she felt no need to stretch her wings, to flutter, or soar, or swoop. Really, she had only come to Battersea because poor Mr Blake's invitation had seemed so dismal that, when Mr FitzGeorge had seen it on the mantelpiece, he had insisted they go. It would be so dreadfully rude, he'd said, to disappoint a man who resides on a houseboat and yet had gone to the trouble of sending such a smart, embossed invitation.

Mr FitzGeorge had motored her down to Battersea. He'd suggested dropping in on Kay on the way, but Lady Slane had declined. On some things, one must stand one's ground, she'd said. As far as her children knew, she had disappeared into the hills of Hampstead, and she was certainly not going to give them the pleasure of watching her emerge from seclusion for something so frightful as a tea party.

Guests were beginning to trickle in. Lady Slane sipped her wine and, catching sight of one of the guernseys, nodded in approval. One must be gracious, especially as this had been laid on without any help. Lady Slane saw her smile with relief and give a glass to an arriving guest. Dear Mr Blake offered her a bowl of cheese straws. She took one, feeling deliciously reckless as flakes of pastry dropped on her lap.

Mr FitzGeorge came to sit beside her and she smiled at him, her eyes twinkling as though she were once again the young Vicereine of India. She felt quite content sitting still, looking at the assortment of people who stepped aboard with varying degrees of confidence. If only she needn't talk to anyone, but could just sit here watching them, imagining whither their thoughts drifted.

'I've just had an awfully nice chat with Sir Edward Feathers,' said Mr FitzGeorge, who could be relied upon to strike up a conversation to fill any quiet moment.

'Feathers,' Lady Slane sounded out the name for familiarity, wondering at these other birdlike creatures who had alighted here, unable to make the extra how ever many thousand miles to America. 'I don't believe I know him, do I?'

'Otherwise known as "Filth". Barrister chap, born in Malaya and then came over to England, but spent some time making his career in Hong Kong. His wife died and now he's struck up a friendship with that fellow Veneering.'

'I don't believe I do know him. We never strayed quite so far as Hong Kong.'

'Awfully nice chap. Terribly bright, you can tell. He said that boats always made him feel nervous, remind him of some ghastly journey during the War.'

Lady Slane thought back to her journeys to India. She remembered the shock of land when she alighted at Bombay; the way one was always surprised at how something solid could feel so unsteady. Then the feeling would fade over a day or so, until one suddenly realised everything was still again, and it was only the smells that made one waver, knocked one off balance.

'I thought you might be glad of a blanket,' said Mr Blake, who had appeared beside her, proffering a rug. 'It's a little damp so close to the water, and I'd hate for you to catch a chill.'

Lady Slane thanked him and let him place the blanket beside her. Her maid Genoux would be relieved. There had always been people fussing about her, long before she had reached the grand old widowed age of eighty-eight. In India, there were always people rushing around, fetching cushions, drinks, gifts, fanning her, or arranging her jewels. They had always done everything to make her as comfortable as possible, battling the impossible heat on her behalf, when really all she ever wanted was to be left quite alone in a room, perhaps with some flowers to arrange.

The boat was filling up. People squeezed together inside and she glimpsed several pairs of legs braving the cool night air on deck. Again, she found herself wishing that nobody would come over to talk to her.

She watched a beautiful young woman step through the cabin on precariously tall shoes. Her red hair gleamed under the bright lights as she drained her glass in an instant. Who was she, this forceful creature with sharp eyes? From which pages had she stepped? She stalked off to a corner of the cabin and sat down, crossed her long stockinged legs and looked across the room. Lady Slane dropped her gaze. How funny that so many of us desire our privacy. Perhaps it is only natural after so many years of having the readers scrutinise our every detail.

She was not to be left alone, however, poor pretty thing. A young soldier in immaculate Austrian uniform had followed her across the room. Now he arrived in front of her, clicked his heels together and offered his hand. Was he really asking her to dance? Lady Slane's ears strained across the chatter of the room to catch their conversation, for it certainly seemed unlikely that they would waltz across the cabin.

'Hofmiller,' said the beautiful woman. 'Will you never learn?' And Caroline thought of Tom, and how his hand had pressed into the small of her back as he swept her across a nightclub deck on a boat on the Nile, and she found that she had to blink to stop tears welling up and escaping her eyelids, had to force herself back into this present moment on a boat in Battersea, taken from the pages of a book which had won the Booker Prize eight years before her own.

It seemed as though all the guests had arrived, or certainly, if there were more to come, Lady Slane couldn't think where they might be fitted. Mr Blake clutched a sheaf of papers to his chest and gave a bottle of wine to one of the guernseys, evidently bidding her to top up the glasses. Lady Slane held hers close to her lap, hoping she might be passed over. Mr Blake appeared to be readying himself to address the boat. A hush spread as individual conversations were left hanging in the air like a dozen interrupted cadences.

Lady Slane watched dear Mr Blake stand straight-backed as he thanked them for coming to Lord Jim on this inhospitable evening. He waved the sheaf of papers and began to list their names: Sir Edward Feathers, Mr FitzGeorge, Miss Claudia Hampton, Mrs Nancy Hawkins . . . Lady Slane busied herself with the blanket, unfolding it over her legs, hoping that she might melt within the side of the cabin and not have all those eyes inevitably turn to her by the time he reached S.

As she sat there shrinking into her seat, it occurred to her how very strange the actual act of speech was. How peculiar it was that words which existed in someone's head were shaped by a mouth, tongue and breath, and blown out across the world, only to disappear in a moment. What happened to those words if no one listened to them? Were they then no more than exhalations of sound, merging into the sloshing of the Thames and dying tiny, unheard deaths?

Lady Slane wished she hadn't come. The feverish excitement of the cheese straw had faded to indigestion and exhaustion at the thought of so many words and the long drive back to Hampstead. If only she hadn't listened to Mr FitzGeorge, hadn't minded the pathetic propriety of the invitation. She couldn't leave now; it would be impolite. She must wait until Mr Blake had finished his address. Then, perhaps, they could slip away. She thought of the gentle scolding that would be awaiting her from Genoux and felt annoyed by her infirmity, the weakness not just of her frail birdlike body, but of her flitting mind, incapable of remaining fixed on anything, not even listening to whatever it was that Mr Blake was declaiming with such passion.

There was a round of applause, and Lady Slane, who was still holding her wine, carefully tapped her wrist. She turned to Mr FitzGeorge and asked in her soft low voice, 'Might we now depart?'

Mr FitzGeorge turned to her. She knew he saw an old woman, tired and frail, and she felt limp at the thought of how she had faded. What did it matter whether or not they were remembered by their readers, when already she was so old, and so much of her life had been played out for the eyes and enjoyment of others?

'Soon,' he said. 'We must stay a little longer, or else we risk breaking up the meeting.'

Lady Slane thought of all the meetings like this, only grander, that her late husband Henry had attended, and for the first time she felt grateful to have been spared them. She had needed only to preside at the banquets and parties, to know how to compliment someone on their choice of dress or brooch; she had never been made to listen to this painful drawing out of an argument, of people making their points, raising their concerns and poor Mr Blake standing there in the middle trying to maintain control.

Her ear tuned in as the red-haired beauty stood to say something, something about how they were all in any case appallingly misrepresented in the minds of their readers, about how each subjective viewpoint was by definition erroneous, and that this meagre afterlife which they were given was already lacking. 'Surely,' she continued, 'we ought to be campaigning for more value to be placed on the author's intention, rather than the readers' plural interpretations?'

There was much humming and hawing as the party was momentarily thrown off balance by the force of this woman making such an intellectual point. Lady Slane caught the words 'pisseur de copie' amidst the buzz of chatter and smiled in spite of herself. Her fingers were cold, beginning, in fact, to go numb, and she placed the glass down on the floor for want of a nearby table, anxious in case she were to drop it. Really, it was time she left. Perhaps she could be excused an early departure if she were to make a short address on her way out. If only she were able to get to her feet without requiring assistance.

'Mr FitzGeorge,' she said, 'I must go home, I'm cold.' She put out her arm and he took it, helping her up.

They inched their way unsteadily across the cabin until they reached their host. Lady Slane thanked Richard and apologised for leaving so early, but hoped he understood that she was rather elderly and Hampstead was a long way from Battersea. 'And if I may,' she said with a little more force, turning to encompass the cabin in the sweep of her gaze, 'if I may say something brief before I depart.'

The conversations stopped again, muted in anticipation of what she, Lady Slane, widow of a great statesman, might say.

'Quite simply, it is not so terrible to disappear. Indeed it would be rather a relief, would it not, to know that after so many years of appearing before people's bespectacled eyes, of letting those stabbing pupils dissect your most private thoughts, memories and dreams, that at last your pages would remain unturned, your book would lie closed and forgotten. Surely, while we have all enjoyed our years of being read, now our feet are sore, our voices parched, our features tired. Don't we long to enter that black oblivion off the page? And isn't it only fair that we give up our place to those who have only just been created? It has taken me all this time to gain my own rooms up in Hampstead, and still the reader can see into these, still those eyes follow my weary steps across the Heath, no doubt have even followed me down here to Battersea. Now, I would like to step off the page and be left alone at last.'

Lady Slane took Mr FitzGeorge's arm, dipped her head in a little swanlike inclination, and was escorted off Lord Jim, into the night.

Author's Note:

As well as being indebted to Christine Brooke-Rose's *Textermination*, I have borrowed characters from some of my favourite novels:

Offshore by Penelope Fitzgerald
All Passion Spent by Vita Sackville-West
Old Filth by Jane Gardam
Moon Tiger by Penelope Lively
A Far Cry from Kensington by Muriel Spark
Beware of Pity by Stefan Zweig

I hope their original authors will allow and forgive my taking them to Battersea for the evening.

Remaking Remake

Victoria Stewart

In Christine Brooke-Rose's *Remake*, Tess, looking back to the immediate post-war period, recalls listening to radio comedy programmes with her Polish lover Janek as a means of helping him to understand 'English ways' (p. 150). They both feel 'shock' when, following the sudden death of comedian Tommy Handley, 'the next instalment of ITMA [*It's That Man Again*] is nevertheless broadcast, a dead man's funny voice.' (p. 150) In fact, it is not Tess who 'recalls' this incident: 'Tess' is the name that the Old Lady, the third person narrator of the novel, gives to her younger self, an individual who experiences, rather than remembers, the events of the past and whose connection with the Old Lady is a fragile, textual one. Hearing the dead speak may now be considered 'routine' (p. 150) and the reanimation of the dead need not be solely auditory; even before the Second World War, Graham Greene describes watching *Son of the Sheikh*, starring the by-then deceased Rudolf Valentino: 'The man is moving on the screen and at the same time he is dead and magnificently and absurdly entombed. No acting can quite preserve the presence of that awful and simultaneous future.' (quoted in Williams, p. 112). If now quotidian, such an experience is nevertheless still estranging, as strange as imagining an individual as serious-minded as Tess (or Brooke-Rose, for that matter) laughing at ITMA.

But perhaps not so strange: given Tess's propensity for wordplay, made plain earlier in the novel, the attraction of pun and double entendre-ridden mid-twentieth-century radio comedy becomes clearer, and for a learner of English, the often exaggerated accents would be mitigated by the frequent repetition of catch-phrases.[1] Jonathan Coe, reviewing *Remake*, describes Brooke-Rose as 'an exuberant, funny,

---

1   The cast of ITMA included Mrs Mopp the cleaning lady (catch-phrase: 'Can I do you now, Sir?), Ali Oop, a salesman of apparently Middle Eastern origin (catch-phrase: 'I go—I come back') and Funf, a German spy (catch-phrase: 'This is Funf speaking').

needle-sharp writer', though admits that *Remake* has a 'slightly elegiac air' (p. 15). In the novel, the Old Lady is finally able to break the long silence concerning her wartime activities, but also to revisit the excitement and the disappointments of being a young woman in mid-century Britain. An autobiographical text written later in life will perhaps necessarily be tinged with melancholy; what Brooke-Rose attempts, through the splitting of her narration between Tess and the Old Lady, and the introduction of John as the Old Lady's interlocutor, is to foreground the fact that subjectivity is about breaks, gaps and losses, as well as continuity. The past echoes back like the voice of a dead comedian; we remember that we laughed, but we can't always remember why.

As I have discussed elsewhere, like others who worked at Bletchley Park, Brooke-Rose was for many years forbidden to write or speak about her experiences there, a ban which, as is noted in *Remake*, causes defamiliarisation in the face of the version of the war in circulation in popular culture: 'Tess's present notion of war is still derived entirely from postwar films [...] Tess learns not to believe a word the papers or the wireless say.' (p. 108)[2] Coe describes *Remake* as one of Brooke-Rose's 'most direct, revealing and readable' (p. 15) works, but, if 'readable', it is nevertheless still 'writerly' and Brooke-Rose, whilst being 'direct' (relatively speaking) in some of her descriptions of historical events, nevertheless continues to question what might constitute realism, what might constitute life-writing, what might constitute 'a life'. In looking again at *Remake*, I want to contextualise it in relation to other writings by Brooke-Rose also dealing with translation, realism, and war experience, to show that *Remake* is itself a remaking of themes, ideas and issues that are important throughout Brooke-Rose's oeuvre.

In 1989, the *Review of Contemporary Fiction* published an interview with Brooke-Rose, conducted by the American academics Ellen G Friedman and Miriam Fuchs, together with an extract from *Verbivore* and an essay by Brooke-Rose called 'Illicitations'. Towards the end of the inter-

---

2 See Stewart for more on the lack of fit between individual and public narratives of the war in *Remake*.

view, Brooke-Rose's 'playfulness' comes to the fore. She is discussing her work in progress:

> The two novels I have in my head that are to follow will probably be easier to read [than Verbivore]. But I still think that people should take pleasure in reading, that it is up to the writer to write in such a way as to direct the attention of the reader to the richness of the possibilities of language. [...]
>
> Q: Then we can assume that we do not need to worry that you're moving towards realism?
>
> A: Were you worrying? Well, I might be, you know. I have nothing against realism. Why not? [...] Even the most experimental, most postmodern writer is still basically realistic. They may not be "imitating" reality, in the sense of reproducing a familiar situation, but ultimately they're representing something. (p. 89)

'Well, I might be, you know': having spoken earlier in the interview about the inadequacy of the available critical language for describing her work (p. 83), Brooke-Rose turns the interviewers' anxiety back against them, only to redefine the label, realism, that they are hoping she will reject. We hear, briefly, a voice that echoes through *Remake*: Brooke-Rose is being interviewed because she is both a novelist and a critic, and she is asked to address her own literary work from a critical perspective, but what is revealed is how artificial this separation appears to be to her. This problem is raised again, in reconfigured form, at the start of 'Illicitations':

> The Editors asked for an essay on my aesthetics. One of them put aesthetics in scare-quotes as it feeling there might be a problem. There is, apart from the inherent difficulty of writing in critical terms about my work, which is my self. (p. 101)

Brooke-Rose proceeds to reflect on the impossibility of using the term 'aesthetics' in a self-reflexive fashion, but this opening salvo itself gives pause: it is both combative, revealing the Editor's tentativeness, as signalled by the 'scare-quotes', to public view, and self-exposing. The 'problem' with fulfilling the brief is 'my self', but the grammar of the sentence also suggests that 'my work [...] is my self'. If the author has been pronounced 'dead', what happens when, like the deceased Tommy Handley, s/he speaks?

Many of the essays in which Brooke-Rose draws on her own experience, as a literary author in order to comment on how novels work, can be read now as challenging not only accepted notions of the novel as a genre, but other kinds of generic boundary as well. It is not 'conventional' to question your brief within a critical essay: those kinds of debates are supposed to happen elsewhere. *Remake* is self-reflexive in its own grappling with genre. The process of remembering is displayed, whereas conventionally in retrospective narrative it has already happened:

> the old lady can't decide, imagine, invent, select the life-file to call up first, if at all, even if re-treated as something else, inputting the databank of culture, attaching personal experience to collectivities, great events, significant mutations, at least as memory-joggers. But is that how experience was lived? (p. 16)

When the experience in question is one excluded from the 'databank of culture' because of official secrecy, the result is a narrative in which the personal and the historical have a contingent rather than causal relationship with each other: 'The Russians invade the Crimea. The wedding takes place in Kensington.' (p. 120) Over and above (and within and below) the issue of the representation of history lies another, potentially even greater problem, which Brooke-Rose addresses in the essay 'Remaking': how (and why) to write an autobiography if, like Brooke-Rose, you have 'always felt a deep prejudice against both autobiography and biographical criticism.' (p. 53) Initially, she decides: 'as an exercise, it might unblock me. And, after all, an autobiography is neither a novel nor a critical book.' (p. 55) Immediately, though, this statement has to be qualified: 'Isn't it, though? Where are the frontiers?' (p. 55) Brooke-Rose recognises that by setting herself the linguistic constraint of avoiding pronouns, the inadequate first-draft of autobiographical writing that she has produced can be 'transmuted into an autobiographical novel', one which reinforces that 'Identity [...] is a fiction, made of language, and, like all good fictions, is open-ended and slightly unreal.' (p. 60) The answer to the question of how Christine Brooke-Rose can write an autobiography is for her to redefine what constitutes the autobiographical.

The essay 'Remaking' is a valuable paratext to *Remake* but Brooke-Rose's description of the emergence of *Remake* as the response to the problem, posed by her publisher, of how to write an autobiography, is not the whole story. The essay 'Self-Confrontation and the Writer' (1977) shows Brooke-Rose already engaging with the problem of the presentation of the self, and what that might mean for a writer: 'I am two people (at least), teacher and scholar and critic on the one hand, creative writer on the other.' (p. 135) In this essay, as later in *Remake*, Brooke-Rose introduces the multifarious figure of John, borrowed from exercises designed to demonstrate the 'rule of reflexivization' (p. 129), as an interlocutor and interrogator. We do not say 'John confronts John', we say 'John confronts himself': this is the rule that Brooke-Rose engages with and disrupts in *Remake* through her avoidance of personal pronouns, and through her use of many versions of John, differentiated by subscript numbers, as the Old Lady's interlocutor. Grammatically, we presume an identity between 'John' and 'himself', but as Brooke-Rose observes: 'Grammar does not say [...] how many Johns and how many selves [...] or which John is confronting which self.' (p. 129) 'Self-Confrontation and the Writer' includes passages of third person narrative that are framed as autobiographical, though here as elsewhere Brooke-Rose is simultaneously theorising about and writing autobiography. Foreshadowing the suspicion of the autobiographical that is expressed in 'Remaking', she comments: 'Bifography is always fiction.'

(p. 130) Biography might seem to be a means of clarifying, setting down in an orderly fashion the events of a life, but in fact it obscures, like fog, rendering outlines less rather than more distinct. *Remake* gives the impression that Tess and Janek listened to ITMA knowing that Tommy Handley was dead; ITMA, though, was broadcast live and repeated later in the week and it was following the repeat that Handley's death was announced.[3] The important factor in the novel, though, is how the event is remembered rather than how well it matches the historical record; these foggy moments, when the outlines of the historical are veiled rather than revealed by the narrative, are surely part of the reason for reading lives rather than historical works.

Aside from the use of 'John' as a narratee within the text, there are other moments in 'Self-Confrontation and the Writer' that emerge from the fog again almost twenty years later in *Remake*, and resonate. Their reappearance should not be taken as evidence of their truth: if there is repetition between these texts, it is, inevitably, repetition with difference, difference of context, difference of framing, difference of detail. For example, early on in the essay, we find the following:

> Perhaps I should start at the beginning of I. [...] What do you want to be when you grow up? A writer. Guffaws. You, a writer? X, Y, yes, they have imagination, but you! [...] Yet on that day she became a writer. [...] Or perhaps it was later, the girl who whispered one day into a rabbit-hole on the Sussex Downs: "Hear me, O earth, I shall be a writer, this is my vow. Take it and keep it in your inner being." Or words to that adolescent effect. The earth is very old and may have smiled benignly. Or guffawed malignly. But the girl heard only silent approval and awe. (p. 130)

Mocked by the adults who ask the clichéd question, 'What do you want to be when you grow up?', the girl defies their laughter and shares her secret instead with the earth: if the earth has a response it is inaudible.

---

3   britishcomedy.org.uk/ITMA accessed 9 October 2013.

A voice calls into the void; but the detail of the 'rabbit-hole' undercuts the portentousness of the invocation, 'O earth', calling to mind Alice falling down the rabbit-hole, shrinking and growing, another vision of the difficulties of the misunderstood adolescent. Or the barber in the legend of King Midas who whispers the secret that the king has ass's ears into the ground, only for reeds to grow on the spot and spread the news abroad. In the case of 'Self-Confrontation', the fulfilment of the ambition to be a writer will be signalled precisely by the making public —the publication—of the secret vow.

In *Remake*, the rabbit-hole is still there, but the context is more precise:

> In Brussels, asked the usual question about wanting to be what when grown-up: un écrivain. Guffaws. Joanne, oui, Jean-Luc, oui, there's imagination. Talent belongs to others, brains to the little girl. [...] Yet on that day the little girl becomes a writer. [...] Or perhaps later, the sixteen-year-old girl whispering down a rabbit-hole on the Sussex Downs soon after the declaration of war: Hear, O earth, a future writer, this is a solemn vow. The earth is very old and may have smiled benignly. Or guffawed malignly. But the girl hears only silent approval and awe, for the first great novel in the head, to be called Europe Street, each house representing a country, never of course written. (p. 12)

Here, it is clearer that the girl is being compared to her sister (Joanne) and her cousin (Jean-Luc) and found lacking, not only because of her the supposed paucity of her imagination but because she has 'brains'; this moment can be understood as an early encounter with the idea that it is possible for a novelist to be too 'clever', that ingenuity and imagination as typically conceived pull in opposite directions. Again, here, the dismissal of the wish serves only to reinforce the girl's desire to achieve it, or rather, her articulation of her wish to be a writer in response to their question makes that desire real, despite its being immediately thwarted. In this later version, the whispering down the rabbit-hole is marked as coming 'soon after the declaration of war', and is the girl's own declaration that she will battle against the ill-will of her elders. It also foreshadows what is explicitly stated later in *Remake*, that the war, and specifically her work at Bletchley Park, helps make Tess a writer: 'Reading the whole war, [...] every day, from the enemy viewpoint, the British being the enemy [...] The writer does that, learning to imagine the other.' (p. 108)[4] 'Self-Confrontation', however, was written and published before it was permissible to speak openly about having worked at Bletchley, and passes over the war in a sentence: 'There was a war. But no, says John, leave that out, it oversimplified me, flattened me out, it is artistically uninteresting. Yes, sir.' (p. 131) This is one way round writing about something that you are not permitted to describe: to dismiss it, via ventriloquism, as 'uninteresting'. In fact, at the start of the next paragraph, there is an indication that this word might mask something more complicated: 'Fog lifts, other fogs form. People are fogs, fogs of experience, of talent, of knowledge. To each his own bifography.' (p. 131) At this point, in 1977, a fog has to continue to hang over Brooke-Rose's war experience, though it was beginning to lift.[5] In the meantime, what Brooke-Rose did in the war has to be whispered into the ground.

Turning back to *Between* (1968), though, the reeds can again be heard whispering about what Brooke-Rose did in the war. In '*Stories theories & things*' (1991), Brooke-Rose describes how this novel developed:

> Once upon a time, in 1968, there appeared a novel called *Between* by Christine Brooke-Rose [...]. *Between* deals with (?), explores (?), represents (?), plays around with (?), makes variations on (?), expresses (?), communicates (?), is about (?), generates (?), has great fun with the theme / complex experience / story / of bilingualism.

4   Sarah Birch notes that Brooke-Rose made a similar comment in a 1986 interview for the BBC's Bookmark programme (p. 2).

5   The Home Secretary, David Owen, made a statement in the House of Commons in early 1978, indicating that those who had worked in code-breaking during the war would now be permitted to speak publically about what they had done.

> The I / central consciousness / non-narrating narrative
> voice / is a simultaneous interpreter who travels con-
> stantly from congress to conference and whose mind is
> a whirl of topics and jargons and foreign languages /
> whose mind is a whirl of worldviews, interpretations,
> stories, models, paradigms, theories, languages. (p. 6)

Brooke-Rose goes on to explain that she overcame the experience of being 'totally blocked' (p. 6) in her progress with the novel by making the
simultaneous translator female: 'simultaneous interpretation is a passive activity, that of translating the ideas of others but giving voice to
none of one's own, and therefore a feminine experience' (p. 7), though
not, she adds, 'the author's personal experience [...] at least, not consciously.' (p. 7) The 'complex experience [...] of bilingualism' (p. 6) is
one that the Brooke-Rose shares with the translator in Between, and in
both *Between* and *Remake*, bilingualism is put to the service of the war
effort.[6] For the latter part of the war, Brooke-Rose translated and col-
lated intercepted German messages, hence her comment about '[r]ead-
ing the whole war, [...] every day, from the enemy viewpoint, the British
being the enemy.' In *Between*, 'ally' and 'enemy' are terms that are similarly slippery. The translator has worked for the Germans, translating
material from French, during the war, and afterwards is asked by the
Americans to explain her actions:

> Ah so you had reached the age to help the German war-
> effort some while before it collapsed. What did you do?
> You will excuse these questions Fraulein but in view of

---

6 Simultaneous translation, where the translator listens to the speaker via headphones and
speaks their own translation into a microphone to be transmitted to audience members who are
also using headphones, was beginning to be used in the interwar years, although more common
was consecutive translation, in which the speaker speaks a sentence, which is then spoken to the
audience in the target language by the translator; this only works when just two languages are involved and is clearly time-consuming. The first large-scale use of simultaneous translation, and
indeed of the technology of microphones and headphones that enabled it, took place at the
Nuremberg Trials in 1946. See Gaiba. *Between*, then, is a novel which presents a very specifically
postwar situation, and although the origin of the translator's profession at Nuremberg is not directly alluded to in the novel, it is notable that Brooke-Rose's translator has begun to learn her craft
in wartime.

> your nationality we must make sure of your undivided
> loyalty total ignorance dissidence change of heart. [...]
> Well but you see, sir, reading English newspapers at the
> [...] German Foreign Office one learnt to follow the war
> from the enemy point of view. The enemy. Ah yes, you
> mean us. And did you also learn to adopt our point of
> view? (p. 486-7)

Her interlocutors remind her that language is a signifying system that in wartime was put to ideological purposes: being able to read the English newspapers is one thing, but adopting an English point of view is another. The translator makes a mistake in her use of the word 'enemy', because now, in the postwar, she has to convince the English that, perhaps even then, she knew she was on the wrong side. When they say 'you mean us', they reinforce their own sense that this is still an 'us and them' situation, but she attempts to convince them that she, too, can be one of us.

There are other moments in *Between* that emerge from the fog having taken on a different shape when read alongside *Remake*. The translator, like Tess, is involved in compiling a survey of bomb-damage across Germany (*Between* p. 487; *Remake* p. 125-6), and each learns that the relevant German records have been moved to Jena, in the Russian zone, and are now inaccessible (*Between* p. 491; *Remake* p. 133). Each recalls hearing a band playing 'A Sennimennal Journey' (*Between* p. 491; *Remake* p. 129), and even one of the unfunny jokes made by Ian Crane, Tess's first husband (*Remake* p. 119) makes an appearance in *Between*: 'do you know the definition of a titbit. [...] A mosquito-raid on Brest.' (*Between* p. 451). Perhaps most significantly, the translator, like Tess, attempts to encode a protest in her speech during a pre-war visit to Germany. The translator's Tante Frieda reproves her:

> [I]ncidentally I heard you mispronounce Heil Hitler
> when we met the von Berlinghausens in the Marktplatz
> the other day. You said Hell Hitler. Now if you meant
> hell bright, the witticism, though ungrammatical, can

> pass. But I suspect that now you have started English at school you meant something quite different. And if you did you might get it correct for in English you would have to say To Hell Hitler which might not pass quite so easily even as a so-called witticism would you not agree? (p. 489)

Tante Frieda uses her superior knowledge of language to make a pointed correction to the translator's attempt at defiance, undermining it in the process: the translator is, by implication, neither intelligent nor creative. In *Remake*, also on a visit to family in Germany just before the outbreak of war:

> Tess is made to listen to the speech of Herr Hitler on the radio and can't understand a word in all that fury, prefers Schiller. In Ulm, when friends are encountered and say Heil Hitler, Tess doesn't raise the arm but replies To Hell Hitler, swallowing the first T a bit just in case. But as a joke, out of a sense of the ridiculous, not from understanding. (p. 76)

In *Between*, the political stakes of this linguistic gesture of defiance are much higher. The translator is half French, half German, and has been brought up in France, but is trapped in Germany by the outbreak of the war. Her protest and her aunt's reproof are juxtaposed with her attempt to explain herself to the Americans after the war, and indicate to the reader the complications of the relationship between language, identity and loyalty. Although Tess is due to go back to Germany to teach English, the war intervenes (p. 78-9); reading this section of *Remake* with *Between* in mind reveals the network of potential possibilities that could have befallen Tess, could even had befallen Brooke-Rose. Karen R. Lawrence suggests that 'Brooke-Rose's own wartime loyalties were far less equivocal than the simultaneous interpreter's' (p. 83), but what *Remake* indicates is that having access to another language inevitably opens up possible networks of affiliation, regardless of ideological difference. Having both Tess and the translator read the war from the 'enemy point of view' but with a different 'enemy' in each case, is not simply the reversal of a binary, not least because three languages are involved across the two novels. This is the closest that Brooke-Rose could get, at the time of the publication of *Between*, to representing what she did in the war, indicating that what was known and acknowledged publicly about the war was only partial, that there was much that could still only be whispered into the ground. But she also, in *Between*, hints at the complications, made more material in *Remake*, of 'following the war from the enemy point of view.'

In *On War*, Clausewitz comments:

> If we pursue the demands that war makes on those who practise it, we come to the region dominated by the powers of intellect. War is the realm of uncertainty; three quarters of the factors on which action in war is based are wrapped in a fog of greater or lesser uncertainty. A sensitive and discriminating judgement is called for; a skilled intelligence to scent out the truth (p. 26).

The fog of war makes 'bifography' even less clear than it was already, but what is striking, looking across Brooke-Rose's oeuvre from the 1960s onwards is how her 'intellect', or, more precisely, her voice, pierces through this fog, expressing uncertainty and ambiguity with razor sharpness, whatever the linguistic restrictions she places upon herself. 'Were you worrying?': we still hear her; she still speaks.

Works Cited

Birch, Sarah. *Christine Brooke-Rose and Contemporary Fiction.* Oxford: Clarendon Press, 1994.

britishcomedy.org.uk

Brooke-Rose, Christine. *Between.* 1968, in *The Christine Brooke-Rose Omnibus.* Manchester: Carcanet, 1986. p. 391-575.

Brooke-Rose, Christine. 'Illicitations.' *Review of Contemporary Fiction.* 9.3 (1989): p. 101-9.

Brooke-Rose, Christine. *Remake.* Manchester: Carcanet, 1996.

Brooke-Rose, Christine. 'ReMaking.' 1996, in *Invisible Author: Last Essays.* Columbus: Ohio State University Press, 2002. p. 53-62.

Brooke-Rose, Christine. 'Self-Confrontation and the Writer.' *New Literary History.* 9.1 (1977): p. 129-36.

Brooke-Rose, Christine. 'Stories, theories, and things.' 1989, in *Stories, theories, and things.* Cambridge: Cambridge University Press, 1991. p. 3-15.

Clausewitz, Carl von. *On War.* Translated and edited by Michael Howard and Peter Paret. Princeton: Princeton University Press, 1976.

Coe, Jonathan. 'The Experimental Woman', The Observer. 7 April 1996. p. 15.

Friedman, Ellen G., and Fuchs, Miriam. 'A Conversation with Christine Brooke-Rose.' *Review of Contemporary Fiction* 9.3 (1989): p, 81-109.

Gaiba, Francesca. *The Origins of Simultaneous Translation: The Nuremberg Trial.* Ottawa: University of Ottawa Press, 1989.

Lawrence, Karen R. ' "Floating on a Pinpoint": Travel and Place in Brooke-Rose's Between.' in *Utterly Other Discourse: The Texts of Christine Brooke-Rose.* Edited by Ellen J. Friedman and Richard Martin. Dublin: Dalkey Archive Press, 1995. p. 76-96.

Ovid. *Metamorphoses.* Translated by Mary M. Innes. Penguin: Harmondsworth, 1955.

Stewart, Victoria. *The Second World War in Contemporary British Fiction: Secret Histories.* Edinburgh: Edinburgh University Press, 2011.

Williams, Keith. *British Writers and the Media.* Basingstoke: Macmillan, 1996.

Three Recovered Manuscript Excerpts

Joanne Blair-Hayley

Note to the Reader:

Apparently while accessing the holographs of *The Languages of Love, The Sycamore Tree, Dear Deceit*, and *The Middlemen*, three folders marked 'Utterly Other Manuscripts' were purportedly found in the archived material of Christine Brooke-Rose at the Harry Ransom Centre of the University of Texas at Austin. Inside each folder is a complete novel seeming to correspond to an earlier version of works later transformed to *Between, Amalgamemnon*, and *Remake*. Included in each folder are small notes as follows:

> *Amidst:* In the event of extreme parlousness.

> *Magnonlameman:* To squirm the true further?

> *Retrography:* To please οἱ πολλοί at last.

Were these alternative versions intended to have been published?

Amidst

Amidst its very large and silvery wings I saw the plane fuselage was stretched the length of two hundred and twenty-five seats in trios on either side of the narrow aisle, along which I had always found such a bother to push or pull the luggage trolley, towards the cockpit housing all the computers, the brains of the plane, somewhere behind the navy blue and chocolate brown curtain and the door with NO ENTRY stamped in brilliant fluorescent red at eye level.

You knew that depending on the country, the women, big small beautiful ugly—

"Can't you ever think of anything except external appearances?!" He interrobanged exasperatedly. Her heart sank to their toes and you tapped his fingers on the armrest, wishing we had never agreed to yet another trip.

—would have been segregated on the left. The men, looking suave and sophisticated and reading *Time* and *The Economist*, would have been sat on the right, since the left of the brain corresponded to rational, and the right of the brain to irrational. Obviously in those countries, rationality was and always would be irrelevant.

"Do you have to make all these generalising statements?" I asked. His chest tightened and she wondered how I came to be in this seat.

But all civilisations considered, you noted XX and XY pairings were seated mixed and scattered amidst the eleven score rows of ABC DEF GHJ, ribs inside a centipede. Or a whale, beached three hours, three days, three weeks, perhaps ribs bleached and shown. Amidst heaven and hell, amidst having done nothing at most and done something at least, all those bodies floated, as you knew, or should have known, realised when your stomach caught itself in your throat at the moment of take-off.

Looking out the window, I saw the very large white wing on the right of the fuselage sweeping back—

"How can it be sweeping, you idiot! Where's the broom?" He spat and rolled her eyes, muttering under their breath about sibling stupidity.

"Oh shut up, Julia, just watch your Disney cartoon."

—although not really sweeping, against the deep blue of the sky, cloudless. The sunlight shone on the metal, polished dull, the jet-stream not quite invisible.

"Look, Daddy," squealed a little kid nasally, "the plane's farting!"

From your seat you saw no city or farm in a field or dark green wood or mountains peaking majestically or even the sea. You saw nothing and the plane was not moving at such a distance from what was moving below. 1.2km above sea level was written on the inflight screen, somewhere over Bordeaux Bregenz Bergamo Bihor Bayern Boğaziçi, and outside the temperature was almost minus fifty degrees Celsius. Your seat felt iced.

Luckily our plane was air-pressurised. We saw no passengers hidden by their seats, but we tried to make Witze blagues jokes scherzi about bald heads, straggly hair, blondes dyed, too many drinks bibite Getränke boissons requested and people who talked italiano español francais Deutsch Vlaams too loudly and who ate aßen mangènt mangiarono too much and who read too little and who left their movie screens lit while they slept. What was that we had said?

"That curtain between this cabin and first class. It reminds me of something gothic," he drawled, smiling and shifting in the seat, our knees straying nearer, her gut twanging at the thought of their bodies playing closer.

"Ah, davvero?" I coughed, smiling and shifting in the seat, their knees straying away, but only a little, playing the game.

"Or a Byzantine Orthodox church. Have you ever . . ." she paused, to let my tongue lick his lips, and flicked your auburn hair over our shoulders. They sipped from the wine glass, Audrey Hepburn coquettish.

"Vraiment?" And we talked and you looked out the window and they looked out the window and we talked and it was extremely cold almost minus forty degrees outside somewhere over wherever we were.

Was the flight attendant an XY or an XX? He couldn't remember, she'd fucked him or he'd fucked her, they had all fucked each other, whichever ménage à however many it had been whenever it was. Perhaps his body had been brown or elderly, she had been sour or sexy, and afterwards a black bell-boy in white or was it a white bell-boy in black had knocked and entered, the room of course, and announced, "bonjour madame," and twitched back the curtains on too much sunlight. Or was it a buxom waitress who had pushed the breakfast trolley, showing just enough cleavage, "Desiderà un caffè americano?"

No, had another memory surfaced? "Guten morgen, liebe Sorgen, seid Ihr auch schon alle da?" and she had rolled over in the bedclothes moaning, whether from a bad dream or the thought of just another manic Monday he didn't know, it had always been difficult to keep up with your moods in the morning. In the evening she found him quite unpredictable, sometimes pessimistic, sometimes wildly rambunctious, it depended on—

"Goddamnit, can't you control the kids?"

"They're always over-excited when they see you, since you hardly ever want to take them."

"When I do you just complain I'm trying to cut down on alimony pay-ments!"

"If only their schools had longer term times . . ."

—so many factors. But the Greek breakfast of creamy galatopita, tiganites with tahini and petimezi, so sweet and tempting, followed by golden omelettes stuffed with cubes of fried siglino and smothered in Naxos island cheese, kalamata olives, not to be refused, tempted still further with thyme-honey flavoured yoghurt so thick the spoon stood in it, and traditional coffee to wash it all down, produced paunches dis-tended like force-fed geese. This was the breakfast they liked best, "ka-limera" sounded so jovial after the rounds of "no, thanks" and "oui merci" and "danke nein" because it was always something different and just as likely to result in too much time spent sat on the toilet, fortu-nately less often facing it, since my stomach had never adjusted to the different cuisines, climates, time zones.

You remembered eventually. It was a smooth-talking maître d'hôtel dressed in white in the south of somewhere, perhaps Tyrol? They wanted us to go skiing afterwards, and after the skiing the après ski, but I said tiredly, "she's too tired," and the flight attendant wearing the pale blue—"no it wasn't, Jon, it was pale grey," she interrupted, since that was her very annoying habit of not being able to let anyone finish a sentence before having to interrupt and often with no so much facts but hersay, "the plastic tray had all those odd foods that I've seen on every flight from that country."

"No, Tini, the flight attendant was orange-haired," he stated emphat-ically, and they sighed heavily, looking cross, her forehead wearing a frown, "the food tastes plastic too." The drinks trolley trundled past and I lifted up his arm, briefly touching the elbow of the flight attendant shoving the trolley.

"Vous voulez quelque chose, Madame? Would you like something, sir? Si, prego, signorina? Kinder, was möchtet Ihr, bitte?"

"Mee-ner-ahl Wazzer beetah."

"Mineral water? Désolé, il n'y a pas plus. Può avere un succo di frutta, se vuole?

"Fruit juice? Oh alright. Thanks." He accepted the cup, drank deeply, and grimaced, our earlier mildly flirtatious manner quite stripped clean from her demeanour, I really didn't understand why in this day and age airlines offered such paltry selections, flight tickets had become so expensive, they had saved for so long for this trip. We said, my tone becoming quite cold, "oh don't you have any without sugar?"

"Er . . . no Zucker? Oh, a moment, bitte," she smiled ingratiatingly and looked at his colleague. "Sie will kein Zucker im Saft haben. Der Hammer, oder?"

"Tja. Gib er doch dann Sodawasser."

The cupboard gleamed woodenly in the shaft of sunlight creeping through the slits in the curtains. Each drawer was decorated with an intricate bronze handle that dazzled light in blinking eyes. I struggled to sit up and clutched at the bedside alarm, her breathing rapid, his head swimming with hangover. Where were we?

"Darling, did you order the newspapers in English, I'm just so fed up with trying to puzzle out Greek."

"It's all Arab to you," she yawned and stretched, luxuriously naked under satin sheets.

Next to the cupboard the smaller doors of the dressing-table repeated the same inlaid motif, but the lacquer was worn with many years of use and little care. The clackety-clack clackety-clack was incessant, the vibration chattering my teeth, I bit his tongue trying to clamp her jaws together. This was certainly rolling stock, alright.

"Strange how the trains are so modern these days but the sleeping compartments remind me of Murder on the Orient Express."

"Well, yes dear, we did ask the travel agent to book that theme. Bit late now saying you don't like it."

"I didn't say I didn't like it, I said, it was very out of date. Quite old."

"In other words you don't like it. Why can't you just come out and say that? You never like anything I book, anyway."

"Rubbish. Why can't you stop harping, just for once. You're always complaining about something. We're supposed to be on holiday."

"Oh pass me the water bottle will you?"

Beyond the wooden slits of the shutters and way away across fields of green and gold and brown and white with the heavy snowfall of yesterday, in houses flats house-boats shacks somnolent consciousnesses had awoken, dreams having fled, nightmares long since erased, kettles were whistling, coffee was steaming—

"I've told you, you're going to school and that's final."

"Dépêche-toi! Tu dois prendre l'autobus ce matin à huit heures."

"Oh man, wer hat jetzt mein Handy geklaut? KINDER!?!?!"

"Maar ik wil niet om eieren te eten voor het ontbijt."

—cars growling and purring and chugging exhaust as an aubade to the slumbering economy, lazy as usual.

On top of the cupboard, with its rounded panelling and sitting darkly in the corner like a cold squat pot-belly stove, the glass bottle of expensive water had fallen over. The last few drops had shamed the shag-pile carpet a deep red, already stained years before when a guest had fallen from the upper bunk, skull smashed on the ceramic washstand in the other corner. I tossed the empty bottle angrily in the waste bin and opened the tiny bar refrigerator.

"Fruit juice. Again. You'd think they'd put a bottle of water in here, hey honey?"

"Gnhhnh . . . wha? Wazzat? Shit." He swore violently, bleary-eyed, and she focused without success on the bottle, what the hell time was it anyway. "Let's sleep a bit more."

"But look at the schedule, we'll be there soon. Come on, I'm starving. I hope they have eggs on the breakfast menu. Let's grab something to eat."

"Your cholesterol," she groaned loudly and dropped his head exaggeratedly in her trembling hands as he sat saggily upright on the bed, "your weight, your—" God, it was always like this.

"Oh rubbish. You just don't want to get up. Fine, stay there then." The door slammed noisily as they all flounced out and left the space in a breathless silence.

Magnonlameman

Now. If I could just have been let to think. What was it I was to have forgotten this time? Ah yes, the dream. No? No amnesia for you? Letiziva, sometime aunt, one-time friend, oft-time letter-writer, will have liked to have had one, and I just might have, too.

Yes, well might you have admired my aquarelled roses, Jean-Claude, you were to have been, would have been, always will have been my most-loved nephew, that would have been to have said, my singular and titular nephew, but were I to have had others, they would not have been so gorgeously humble, how could they have been? These bugs! They will always have to have been spoiling the paintwork, spoking the wheel, flying in the ointment, as you might have noticed but would not have said, if you were not to have been as polite as you will have been thought to have had become.

But how will you have painted these roses so real, aunt Trixie, so three-dimensional? So many, everywhere, on all the different surfaces, the looking glasses, the mirrors, the window panes, the transparent doors, why look, these could have been growing in a secret garden, a magic patch, ceramics once thrown in your own kiln? Surely that wasn't so?

Why could it not have been thus? For so must I have pottily pottered around and about tottering to my dotage via leisure bees elderly spelling bees, and I could not have afforded a gardener like my bosom buddy Letiziva once when it will have been that I could not have gardened any longer and so what choice but to have enclosed the garden within the house, as I will have done when that time will have been.

Yes, dearest boy, if you would have been so kind to have had taken the tray. As for looking glasses, out of such spaces between mirrors through which I will have had to seek inspiration, I could have found no other joy than painted roses. Naturally I will not have pretended not to having had missed the perfume and perfection of first blooms.

Naturally not, my dearest blessed Trixie, but young man, you will—

Jean-Claude, my friend and close neighbour Letiziva. Letiziva, my nephew Jean-Claude.

Yes yes—

You will have had to have realised, I will have lost my memory next, but rather that than ritual, some dream, Letiziva?

Once would have been said, will have had to have been said, never offer dream *sang froid* to a Lilliputian, Trix, you should have known that by when what will have been now, and were we to have been talking of the bees, I would have been saying young man, the bees will have been buzzing throughout the entire season, will have bumbled and stumbled as big bees will have done if they were to have been buzzing around painted flowers imagining these will have been real.

What a notion. Producing painted honey?

Oh my dear Jean-Claude, you endearing son of my sibling. Letiziva, would you not have been charmed with such an amusing nephew if you were to have had one of your own. Painted honey? I must have remembered to remember that! But I will surely have had to have forgotten it, like most else.

And before I will have forgotten, you would have told me about Andi, my favourite niece. You will have been forgiving of us Letiziva, if we were to have been talking family for one brief moment.

By all means, we would have let us hoped that he will have given you more news than my nephew, equally amusing I would have liked to have assured you.

How could anyone have been charming and not have provided the latest gossip?

Now I will have demanded you will not have tried to have rivalled nephews with me Trixie it will not have succeeded. Charm will always have been a unique thing, like love, mysterious, many-splendoured—

Please Letiziva dear, will you not have been so kind to have let me have received my quota of family catch-up, having a biscuit meanwhile and keeping silent like a well-behaved girl—now then dearest boy you were to have told me everything, your sibling, your partner, your offspring and your parents, sequentially.

Trixie, I shall have needed a entire pantry of biscuits.

Well you would have always been able to have left dear, to have taken away the reflection unsullied of a satisfied cat. You will have ignored her, Jean-Claude, having readied, steadied, and gone.

Dear aunt Trix, I had not been knowing where I was to have begun.

Where the beginning would have been being and in the indicated sequence.

Well Andi—

Could she have been content with the potty fellow?

Pitts, Reginald Pitts, absolutely ecstatic frantic she will have had another work having been released in December.

Another work and had no plans to have propagated?

How odd, with a ruling source as partner. And no heirs apparent?

How should I have had knowledge of that, aunt Trixie?

More likely you couldn't have been bothered to have noticed? Would you not have liked to have been made uncle?

Not really.

Why not, because you wouldn't have liked having been a progenitor?

Now you have exaggerated, aunt Trixie, that was invention and was to have been avoided. I will have given you news but on the condition that you hadn't pried where no problems existed.

She will have painted those as well, in all realistic gory. No, Trixie, no more of the biscuits, thank you.

So Andi will have been going to have been famous? What a thing. And her work will have been about what? A good story, at least, good rousing realistic narrative with heart-in-the-mouth moments? Solid and dependable.

That would have depended on your preferences. It will have been as would be typically expected given what had been her hobby-horses. Politics, dialectics, the sillybus of history.

Gracious divinities! As if it were ever to have been that we had profited from those. Why would she have raked over the past I should have guessed it couldn't have taught us anything in this kaleidoscope of change. All with which we should have bothered should have been the presented and the futured. Especially the instant of the now, since from it will have arrived the future, coming as it did from the past.

Why Trix, how smoothly you would have interacted with my nephew, he would have said exactly the same.

Which would have tended to demonstrate Letiziva that civil civic simplicities will have retained the same generational leaps and gaps.

What in the celestial spheres could have coloured your mood, Trixie, your nephew having been here shouldn't have been an excuse to have narked about mine all the time, I would have meant to have said had I been going to have said it, that you hadn't even met him.

And how could I, not having had availed myself of tea on the one afternoon of his long overdue visit, many years after he should have been here.

So. If that was the way it was going to have been, I shall have had to have left.

Oh no Mrs Gnatr, please! Let not my visit to have had spoiled your amity and facility with vicinity. You would have recalled I shall have had to have left, your amity had to continue, and also that, hmm, how should I have put this, aunt Trixie's appeal was always and will have been, should we have said, her singularity.

A rose by any other name would have been thorny? I might well have agreed, Jean-Claude, if I were to have called you that.

Introductions for a third time, Letiziva?

Jean-Claude, congenial for a name, and so genteel and agreeable a young man, congratulations, Trixie!

Moi? You meant that sibling, I'll have relayed.

Correct, then not. And you must have recalled, Jean-Claude, we

Slaves had and have been were being and will always be extraordinarily vulnerable, with a dismal attitude to living—

In other words, leg-pulling prohibited. When it will have happened, what I shall have most missed, will have been not having had the frog in the garden. *Imaginary gardens with real frogs.* Letiziva, should he have arrived in yours, recall he will have been made docile by having had his stomach caressed lightly, to the accompaniment of summer night melodies. But leg-pulling prohibited.

As to the music, Blefuscudian, perhaps?

World music, naturally, but predominantly Houyhnhnmian. Blefuscudian unlikely.

Thus the word for anus must have fallen head over toes.

Like metaphors and trapeze-artists, many analogies having been unbalanced have suffered such a fate.

Ah yes, the painted problems. Or the scryed future.

Or the spying on nephews.

Mere serendipity, as you would have admitted as you must surely have known, your invitation was a forgone conclusion, you insisted I join you, did you not, enjoying as you did had done will have been doing the exhibition of him to me?

Aunt Trixie, Mrs Gnatr, were these common interactions, or was the exhibition for my benefit?

Enough, all of you.

Retrography

Of course, I've ridden the TGV and never been nervous, but somehow London trains rattle so. It's not like it was in my day, or rather, in my mother's day, she would find this terribly unnerving now, of course, strange, out of a science-fiction novel, except she never read those, she was always telling me to read *L'âme enchantée* or some such. Young people these days seem so much older so much younger, you have to wonder what their futures could possibly be when they've done everything before they've even hit their twenties. I mean, look at those

Stock Exchange traders. Making millions, and losing millions too! And teenage pregnancies. Divorce, everyone's doing it, you have to understand how it was in my day, people didn't really do it. Well, at least, not openly. We didn't come out of the closet. Nowadays you have same sex marriages and kids overdosing in the parks, and I see on the television —I never had television when I was your age—young kids toting machine guns in all those poor countries, being taught to murder, just as well nothing like that happens here, a body wouldn't feel safe, would it?

Well, I must say, my memory is a bit of a fog, but what I do know is that I was of course rather naive, and my mother—I always called her mummy but no-one older than five seems to do that anymore—probably kept me far too cloistered, but well, I turned out alright, didn't I? [Titters] I had a job before I was seventeen, here in Liverpool, and that's why I wanted to show you this building—just point the camera over there dear—because here was where I learnt accounting, although I was meant to be the receptionist, but back then I was rather shy, answering the telephone was the absolute in mortification, and they had taken on another young girl, a real mouse she was, but I've forgotten her name, might have been Tina?

As I was saying, here in this building, 15 Watters Place, I worked for Mr Friedman and Mr Patterones, and Mr Grangeville was the one who interviewed me, and oh and of course, I had the funniest colleague, such a pimply young man he was, one of those braying laughs—yes, like yours dear—and big bug-eyes. I suppose they're dead now—what's that you say? Sorry, my hearing aid fell out. They're dead? Well, it's to be expected I suppose. But the building is still here. I'm just trying to—oh yes, I remember now—Plumpsley, that was his name. I used to cycle here, early in the morning, to watch the big ships and think about the war. We had a blitz in Liverpool, but no-one ever seems to remember that. Apparently the Blitzes were very useful for clearing out slums, but I never saw any then, although I did see one while I was in London just recently, where all the investment bankers live, or at least did live. They seem to suicide a lot, can you imagine if we'd all done that in the war?

Of course I thought I was doing very well for myself on seventeen-and-six, and—no no, not pounds dear, shillings! Mummy made me buy a ghastly suit too, yellow it was with bits of green, like cheese gone mouldy in the hollows, but that was before the job, when I was in the typing pool, addressing hundreds of envelopes the whole day, a bit of a lark really, because mummy'd paid for me to learn typing and short-hand, and there we all were, oh must have been a few dozen of us, we used to buy two-penny meatpies and a ha'penny cuppa in the local caf, and I bought fish pies so I could save for my orchestra ticket, or go to the cinema with—oh drat, what was her—Jane! We'd take the tram to town and see all the famous Hollywood actors and actresses, and afterwards listen to the songsters in Harrods, Jane had a crush on—not Harrods? Are you sure dear? John Lewis you say? Well, my memory isn't what it used to be, but you hardly look old enough to remember it at all. Where was I?

Oh yes, the new job. It was a bit of an eye-opener I can tell you. Columns of pounds and pennies, like columns of troops, swarming all over Europe, all over the massive ledgers, but I can't say I was the best adder-upper, although Plumpsley, my goodness he had wandering fingers! And a tongue on him—called me Miss Highbrow Snob, just because I read Literature and listened to Classical Music, and didn't have the faintest idea what he intended when he asked me to stay late one night—said I needed a lesson. The cheek!

Mein gott!

Gottfried Gottlieb

I got to bed late last night. It's got so noisy in the mornings, I got woken up at six, so I got out of bed. I got my breakfast, I got the newspaper, and I got to read it when I got on the bus an hour later. I got in an argument with someone who got his kicks getting in my way. The bus got caught in traffic and I got to work late, so I got in trouble from my boss. I got to my desk, I got a shock: I'd got lots of paperwork in my in-tray.

The days get longer every day.

I got a coffee and got talking to a workmate and got grief from my boss again. I've got to stop chatting in the corridors and got to get back to work.

I got lunch at midday in the cafeteria. The menu got bad. I've got no choice to get what I like. If I'd got more money, I'd get lunch outside. But I'd get in trouble for getting out too long. Probably.

I got a phone call from my friend after lunch. My friend got sick last week. My friend got better this week. The flu gets everyone. I'll get it, too. I got it last year when I didn't get my flu shot. I don't get why to get flu shots, so I don't get them. If I get sick, I get to stay home.

The knock-off buzzer got a bug, so I got out the office late. I'd got to thinking my boss got pissed off and got someone to turn it off. My boss got pissed off, but only because getting out the office late is to get everyone else.

My boss gets wild on getting people.

I got hungry on the way home so I got the idea to get dinner out. I got a foreign server in the restaurant who got my order wrong. Got no sense how to get by with English. Gets me too, like my boss. I got given fresh vegetables instead of fish forgetables. I'll get over it. Eventually.

I got home late. I got a message from my mum to call, but I've got nothing to tell her so I didn't get a round to it. She gets ticked off, she doesn't get that I've got no energy when I get back: I get in the shower, I get dried off, I get in my pyjamas; I get in bed and I get the TV on. It gets me too, that I've got nothing to tell her, but I've got no clue what a deaf person gets off on not hearing.

I got in my routine and I got off to sleep. The nights get shorter every night. When I get old I'll get no sleep, but I'll get to die and get some peace.

I've gotten tired of getting my head round gott.

Le Pop

Christine Brooke-Rose

There was a time when 'pop' music meant a specific kind of music as opposed to rock and rhythm and blues and other types, but in France the word has become so generalised today as to mean, as strictly it should, anything popular. And anything popular includes, in practice, whatever the native popular traditions are capable of producing, as opposed to the impositions of American commercial and cultural imperialism, on which the French are particularly touchy. There is in fact clearly a conflict between the influence of American pop culture and the French desire to be, and absolute conviction of being, *sui generis.*

The conflict, however, is either a healthy one or more apparent than real. Syncopation and vitality never harmed any music, and the sheer competition on the mass media has been largely responsible for a sophisticated development of harmony. In France more and more young composers seem to come out of the Conservatoire or other schools, and write accompaniments like Bach fugues, just as many singers attend special schools such as Mireille's Petit Conservatoire (Mireille herself a popular singer in the thirties).

When I was young, musicians used to say that the most difficult thing to do was to set a poem successfully, and when I heard most efforts I rather agreed. In the world of French pop that problem has simply vanished with the advent of the singer-composer-poet. Just as Fabrizio de André in Italy has set and sings with panache an Angioleri sonnet, so Georges Brassens sets and sings Villon or Paul Fort, Serge Reggiani sings (but does not set) Boris Vian. And that is only one aspect.

For there are also Brassens, Brel, Moustaki, Nougaro, Barbara, Catherine Lara and many others who sing themselves, just as Bob Dylan and Randy Newman and others sing themselves. Pound's lament that words and music separated with the advent of his hated Renaissance and

Petrarchan *fioritura* is no longer valid: they have found each other again, and travel together as did the troubadours or the Wandering Scholars, but over waves of sound. And together they spread their brief messages of love, of passion, of wit and fun, of sadness, of political and social protest, that have more effect by and large than a hundred pamphlets.

In pop song, everywhere, can be found the very same features that are found in literature, but more immediately apprehensible, narrative, dialogue, satire, irony, parody, humour, complaint, description, meta-phor, allusion, play with words, with the magic of place-names, and so on. But what seems special about the French situation is precisely the way in which the specifically American influence has lost its fascina-tion, (except sometimes thematically, as in Maxime le Forestiers *San Francisco*); pop-song is in fact being fed by native traditions as varied as those of the *chansonnier*, of folk-song, of the *chanson populaire* (not the same, the latter being old hits that lasted), and of literature itself. For no one can deny that the Belgian Jacques Brel's *Le plat pays qui est le mien* is a poem of great beauty ('Avec des cathédrales comme uniques montagnes . . .') as is Nougaro's *Toulouse* ('Un torrent de cailloux roule dans ton accent . . . '), in which he rhymes Toulouse with 'chanteur de blues' in the best mediaeval macaronic tradition.

The words of songs in France are meant to be listened to and appreci-ated, not incomprehensibly yelled or belted out, and although there are a few stars like Johnny Halliday and Eddie Mitchell who translate rock and sing in a purely American style, the result sounds unnatural in French, the very accents of which are tortured and displaced to fit the rhythm; nor have I ever heard anyone other than themselves sing their songs. Songs are not only listened to but sung, and I remember a taxi driver singing the whole of Jean Ferrat's beautiful *Pourtant que la montagne est belle*, about the young leaving their villages for the cities as he drove (in the city), and being very pleased when I joined him in each refrain.

In fact the word 'pop,' though used by the media to cover everything, hardly applies to most of the songs one hears on the same media, even on the French equivalent of *Top of the Pops*, which can include anything from Halliday to Gérard le Norman's melodically unusual and poetic *La Belle est la Béte* or his dramatic incarnations of circus types (e.g. *Le Funambule*) Marie-Paule Bell's ironic and witty *La Parisienne* or *Wolfgang et moi*. Even protest songs are first and foremost songs, such as Barbara's anti-war *Göttingen* or *A mourir pour mourtir*, or Maxime le Forestier's *Dialogue* between father and son. Both these singers write their own songs and have a very individual style, immediately recognisable, but then so do Yves Simon, Béranger, and many others, not all of whom I can name. Indeed the singer here is nearly always an individual rather than a 'group.'

The French scene is certainly very rich: there are those who sing in Occitan, in Breton, in Alsacian, and although these are not heard as often as the others, they *are* heard, and make people aware that there *is* a problem, in a way that not even the Nobel Prize to Mistral had done. There are also the Canadian singers (and here Canada means Quebec) such as Felix Leclerc and Robert Charlebois (whose *Quand les hommes vivront d'amour*, sung together, won a prize this year), Pauline Julien, Diane Dufresne, Louise Forestier (ex-partner of Charlebois, particularly good with him in that startlingly original jet-age song *Lindbergh*), and the group 'Beau Dommage,' who each have their own style and form of humour. The French situation, then, is interesting for the strength of its native traditions. When I returned from America last year, for instance, I was enchanted, after the impersonal and hygienically odourless supermarkets, to find my street where one could smell the cheeses, the coffee, the fish, the *charcuterie*, even as one passes each shop, and where, in fact, even a supermarket isn't quite American and has not quite succeeded in killing the small shopkeeper. So it is with song—the native traditions are tough—more so, for instance, than in Germany, where pop-song seems, on the whole, either fully Oom-pah-pah or frankly US.

It is possible, however, that the notorious American cultural imperialism is itself a myth, or that it is on the wane. Curiously enough, despite the popularity of British singers from the Beatles on, no one here ever talks of British cultural imperialism, obviously because there is no imperialism left to accompany the pop culture. But then no one talks of Russian cultural imperialism, either, and possibly for the opposite reason that there is no pop culture to accompany the imperialism.

'Letter From Paris', *The Spectator*, 12 June, 1976

Versions

Igo Wodan

You should realise from the telling. You could know, from the discussion, the hints, the questions asked, which outcome would occur. The small gestures, ignored; the silences, abhorred. You should know, now, looking back towards then.

You could imagine how it seemed. Such an opportunity, hardly exploitation: the chance to settle, to adopt a land, a nation of one's own, no longer global vagabond caught between passport and temporary place of parental abode. The dream of settling, belonging to the one cultural exemplar claiming affinity with all, advocating acceptance, tolerance, plurality, equality, a beckoning buzz of theoretical harmony. The reality a practical illusion, a trump of the idealistic eye, discovered with the sight of the future grimacing at the past. The promise, once fulfilled, a pyrrhic victory. But you, besotted with the exotic, could discern no such battle.

The old telling, how often attempted. Remember, how we would meet in the park of many paths and jacaranda trees, you with your hundred sitting ups and I with my hundred minutes of sitting still, my decision made to rescue you from your glorious pursuit of self-destruction. Our conversation would flow as a litany of your laments, endless interpretation of the possible permutations of behaviours deserving but one response. The one of which I would fail to persuade you and you would fail to pursue. Your unswerving desire for perpetual romance and unholy faith in the principles of managing commitment would persuade me, for all my conviction that you imagined airy castles of excrement, and I would reconsider my opinion. You would gasp an excuse between each contraction of abdominal obliques, casting the latest rejection as inverted affection, the smallest compliment concerning your sexual prowess or intellectual open-mindedness, off-handed back-handed or cack-handed, a hundredweight of fool's gold, since you would ignore the message of manipulation underneath, rose-painting it from existence, no matter which counterargument I offered.

The truth, known because I would listen not only to you. I could listen to words spoken elsewhere never heard by you, words spoken in black-and-white contempt, no amount of dogged massaging with the dogma of pop-psychology could render meaning other than the visceral need for your primary and singular attraction. Not the well-honed torso nor the bedroom acrobatics, nothing of the characteristics you preferred to believe the perfect complements, no. Your intelligence an annoyance, your differences flamboyance, your ideals surreal and your strength a weakness to be sapped. The original challenge of seduction becoming the millstone of the quotidian, the yoke borne suborned to the grail of residency status. Your convenience would never inspire a permanence, merely acting as the requisite presence fulfilling bureaucratic requirements for a pre-ordained period until permission to remain as *persona grata* granted, perpetual motion could root itself in the soil of your birth-land. But *grata* would elude as equally as any devotion, only ever pretended, to you.

You suspected duplicity? How curious. You could contend complicity.

*

Do I remember those attempts to dissuade me of foolish notions, to warn me of machinations, to rescue me from deception?

We would spend hours in the park of gravel paths and scattered purple flowers, you with your Zen meditations and I with my zealous exertions, dissecting the significance of familial interference, the endurance of spurious hindrance, the adherence to conflicting preferences, the sufferance of abusive occurrences, the acceptance of forbearance, every action and reaction contemplated and exonerated. I would replay words spoken and heard elsewhere, about the longing to belong and the search for a cultural individuality, the need to be freed of the fear of the next translocation, ever at the whim of circumstances beyond control, and the moral justification for avoiding the patriotic obligations conferred by one nationality and not another. We would empathise and rationalise with motivation and with contradiction, and you ask if I should simulate never gleaning deceitful intent. Would that suggest complaisance or complicity?

The righteous high ground of seeking consistency in thought and deed would demand I acknowledge the dissembling, would insist ignorance of future disappointment and delusion insufficient to deter action in accordance with ethics. But you should know from the telling, the revealing of the then and now, fear would stalk both players. The fear of cultural isolation, of emotional solitude, of discovering self-dissimulation. The land of one's birth may eject as well as embrace. You should remember, also, how you would often wonder whether an adopted country enhanced freedom, or compounded the feeling of constraint, and how each would experience it.

The truth, known because I would listen to your words of caution as well as the words spoken elsewhere. I could listen to words I would speak to myself in shades of grey conveying what I hoped would coalesce in a rose-painted future and expected to dissolve in a chaos of thorny regret. The words I would speak elsewhere never hinted at the suspicion of tempting fate or tacitly accepting the role of pawn in the game of changing permission to remain in a land and culture I grow to respect less and less. Even after the dubious success of eternally revoking temporary visitor status in favour of permanent resident no longer could colour the discussion, would the chance of the same outcome lessen? Perhaps you should call me duplicitous, since I would often wonder at what seemed my lack of bravery, knowing the risk I engaged, not calculated, rather ostrich than eagle.

*

I would expect, from what I heard, a refusal to meet. Curiosity could change minds less stubborn than yours, could dampen ire enough to permit a brief reunion. But you seem intent on putting aside your perennial rejection. You should understand from the telling now what happened then.

We would talk endlessly about what we wanted and where it should occur. You would describe your immense longing to circumscribe the globe, as if nothing and no-one more important than immersion in foreign cultures could possibly exist, your intense lust to experience your roots, not found in the land of your birth, in the language of your parents, in the society of your education; settling seemed anathema to you. You could never perceive how I would suffer at the idea of a peripatetic existence, you would enthuse about jobs abroad, places and people to discover, with no awareness that I would enthuse about these dreams only to freshen your fascination with me; I knew, from words heard spoken elsewhere, how I could broaden your horizons when I wished only to narrow mine. Every word I would speak pleaded for a home of one's own, a community to build, a place to remain, the stability of settling, and you seemed oblivious.

I could tell you my family preferred me to apply for a work visa and I refused. Would you believe me? The truth known now because loss happened, the past mere particles of memory beyond influence except as mutable images. Would you pretend we never loved each other? Faced with eviction from the land of my teenage years and involved with you, as I would imagine should always happen, a relationship with a native, what advantage could a work visa provide? To show my trust, I should make myself dependent on you: we could apply for a relationship visa with its myriad conditions and demands for evidence of love. Those words spoken elsewhere you could never hear, those words spoke of the anger, the frustration, the disappointment, the knowledge I would hurt you because our relationship hollowed itself to the tune of official papers shuffling across a government desk, and my dependency became an accomplished feat. I could imagine you shattering my world, so precariously constructed on your vagaries and vices, and you would continue as if our disharmonious equilibrium affected you not at all. I could only assume you maintained the constraints required for the process to signal your acquiescence to it, irrespective of our degraded relationship.

We could not know the unthinkable would happen, freeing us both to decide without the sceptre of obligation determining our actions: your out-of-the-blue invitation to an overseas institution as visiting scholar just as my lost passport reissued with new visa resulted in the premature change of my status from temporary to resident. You would phone, the interval between each call longer; I would delay a holiday, until we could dismiss the inevitable no further. Do you believe the wall of our history, scribed with an acrimony only the tempestuous could conceive, should tell a different story?

You refuse a conciliation? You consider yourself the injured party? You should admit your happiness requires an alternative environment, without strictures, without confirmation, without conformity to an arrangement of values and views you despise. Superiority becomes you, but you could never contain yourself within these boundaries, and I could not follow you bounding ahead to the next challenge. I could tell you how I loved you for that once, and I should tell you I stopped loving you for that after. You could consider the words you once heard spoken elsewhere attempting to explain, like the telling now of what happened then, obfuscation and justification, but you would conclude wrongly.

You should know, finally, that perspective meddles with reality, and time manipulates perspective. What happened now in the telling of then?

SubText

Jonathan Morton

To use language to express the pre-linguistic, that is the task. To move in disanalogous steps from the mythic to the Code, to ask our way from the meta-phor to the word, from the word to the thing, or dragging memory with us as a defective gene, a germ-line mutation.

> Looking from the window this morning at a magpie ducking its head towards the ground, its long tail held high, as though it feared dirtying the dark perfection of its rectrices, bounded over the wet grass echoing its Jurassic origins, brisk and reptilian in its movements, making a lie of extinction, though overlain with feathers and an unending, waking dream of flight, all potential, all coiled spring, wings poised and tense at its side, ready to fling itself up at the open grey to escape the neighbour's cat creeping slowly across the garden, its haunches hunched, feigning feline indifference to the presence of prey scant feet away, experience unreminding it of the minimal chance to strike within a claw's breadth of this bright bird, whose white breast and black skull holds an extraordinary intelligence, recognising itself in a mirror and grieving over the death of a child or a lover. I step from the house to scatter both bird and cat like some unknowable god, fingers holding my page-place in the book clasped to my hip.

If, in the process of discovering the world, we contaminate it with language, significance spreading like spilt coffee staining a page, seeping between molecules, slipping across the bond-bridge like a plague and breaching the atomic wall, what chance do we have of success with our Scientific Method?

What right have we to claim certainty in our discoveries, in our articles, our reports? Can such texts be anything other than a failure, a clear, humbling retort to those old authorial claims of eukaryotic supremacy, the nucleus blind as a bacilli?

If, just as Christine dreams, there is a script, a Code, operating God-like within or beneath our cells, what hints of it can be seen or felt in our lived experience?

Where, to give one, predictable example, does it express itself in this symbiosis of eye and page? To whom does this Code belong? What unwritten agreement of agency determines its expression?

Thirty seven trillion cells exist in the average human body, according to current estimates, and so, if every cell contains a complete copy of your DNA possibly, bafflingly, to almost two metres when laid end to end), that plain and unadorned text-of-you would span further than the distance Pluto lies from the Sun. We could say that. We could. But did you know that only one in ten of those cells might be human? The rest are bacteria, viruses, micro-organisms.

What I see in the mirror is a colony of microbes representing a human. My hands, whole and indivisible, are great microscopic masses murmuring within the contours of my skin, dancing in circles, frantic as a bee-ball, filled with buzzing.

As a child our garden bordered great wheatfields, rolling gently through the Berkshire Downs, laying spring and winter dark with mud, chalk flecked, thickening the soles of my boots and giving each step an unearned, undesired emphasis. Through summer and early autumn the ripening crop, a great golden flood glorifying the landscape, ears tall as sun-stained spears rustling and fidgeting, held high by ranks of anxious troops, left a trace, a red scripture on bare arms and legs, illegible and filled with meaning. So often were these scrapes and scars clear and visible I was twice suspected of self-harming, as though I had taken a pair of compasses and scored myself calm, but no, these were the marks of my exploratory soul, evidence of long afternoons spent crawling through hay bales or rows of still-brittle stalks, creating defensive walls, arrow targets or finding places to sit, unnoticed, unobserved, through the long day, though the crows would watch with such curious dispassion, a flesh-hungry gleam gathering in their gaze, I always knew, from as young as I can remember, that they were waiting for the moment limbs and body stilled, before their sharp beaks plucked out my eyes and swallowed these in a single gulp.

They are, in truth, my directors,
washed, I crouch, sub-
prokaryotic dominance, I
myself and my words
Ark-like, a planetoid,

A vessel, vast and
spilling in the will-
receiving bonds, of
less chemistry.

And what can be
of the burrowing
ing, of tooth-
the guilt of the
devouring   its
illusion of a cen-
point   amongst
tum foam bub-
us?   If we are
many crowd the
How strong is the
substantia nigra?

It is older than the
father, older than
lips   pronouncing
directions from be-
boards, there in the
Perhaps, at some palae-
the past, the Code split,
conscious and rose to the
us in two directions, leaving
eternally unsure of our many, contradictory, sources.

I
read her
during the summer
while staying with
friends in Italy, in a villa
situated halfway up a dry,
rocky hill, surrounded by olive
groves and yellowed, brittle grass,
cypress trees flecked like paint in the
distance, the air arid and pressing its
hot hands against every surface, every
wall, our paleness banishing us from the
midday burning. Adapted as we are to
Nordic climes, we gathered inside a room
the owner had furnished as though by an
old, colour-blind junk collector with a
penchant for trashy pulp novels and fake
flowers. The bed sheets smelt slightly of my
grandmother, the fridge was used and worn,
its internal light flickering towards failure,
and the television, receiving only a few chan-
nels, showed mostly bizarre quiz shows,
long quirky interviews, or repeats of out
dated episodes of CSI Miami, its sizzling
temperatures and skimpy clothes matching
the Italian weather. I read lying on the
couch, its cushions covered with a thick,
starched fabric, as though the owners
suspected us of being too lazy to use
the bathroom, or to drunk. We spent
much of the late afternoons and
early evenings in the pool, cooling
down from a hot day walking
the streets, enjoying the
sensation of water
against our skins,
dipping under

I am ruled by the great un-
missive, beneath their
am not myself, I am not
are not my own, I am
mineral rich.

overcrowded,
ing arms, in the
singular,   voice-

said of instinct,
and the climb-
fear, claw-fear,
bacterial Cain
brother, of the
tre, of a still
all that quan-
bling between
driven,   how
driver's   seat?
voice from the

mother,   the
any   still-living
our simple stage
neath the floor-
dark,   unseeable.
ontological point in
dove deep in the un-
heavens, bearded, pulling
us   eternally   unsatisfied,

We write to locate patterns, to carry out some analysis of variance, to attempt to visualise this genetic drift at a population level, subsumed as we are in static broth, buried under the brown fog of a winter dawn, though our poorly adapted brains uncover only question after question after question. Which came first—the fur or the cold? Are new ecological niches due to standing genetic variation or to novel mutations?

This phenotypical change, puncturing the common-place, reaching up from the mundane, and the Self diversifying through adaptive radiating slightly more snugly, gifting movements a demi-semi-quaver quicker than the rest, a form more tailored for food and sex, these ceaseless changes, are they stimulated, imagined, created from without or from within? We cannot know.

She has written these flashes, flung millions of years apart and touching something unexpected, unforeseen, something unScientific and still possible, still provable, still present. In that, she succeeded, despite failing to breathe life into either the fictional or the physical. She creates a new viewpoint for us to watch a Darwinian transition, to inhabit mitochondrial respiration as the first, shallow breaths breach, spluttering soft staccato across the world. And that, in the end, is all that matters.

the surface, eyes shut against chlorine, feeling the air in our ears compress, condense, the world growing distant, felt as if through womb-walls, until our deep-buried foetus-sense rose from its cavern in the cartilage around our bones. Forcibly regressed, we floated, hearing through liquid the muffled voices of our parents, faint hints of music, suggestions of a life gathering expectantly beyond the dark vault of a pre-Copernican heaven, dreaming of gills forming in our necks, of living, open-eyed, under meandering waves, blue on blue, drifting gently in the dark. I felt my body, present and pellucid, the liquescent flesh, the blood pulsing and pushing to escape, skin tensioned like an inflated membrane, longing to burst. I imagined melting, dissolving in the water, a pink stain spreading above the tiles, thinning until only a chemist could find me, hidden between strings of hydrogen and oxygen, scattered by the spray, a strangely salty taste on a swimmer's tongue.

Y(o)u look
into the clearing,
the word   -   fenced,
          stone-white
Zone, y(o)u

                  linger

at b/or/ders, at the
                        river's-edge, watch
          the dark~blue
cur~rent move,   slug[is]h and
                              som/no/lent
under skin. Y(o)u ask

Y(o)u ask -
what made the ochre-red finger
reach   for the wall,   what
                              made the world ache
                  towards speech?

All-ready re/turn\ing, y(o)u
suggest
          im-possible h[is]tories,   strange
and   in-articulate   births, y(o)u
          talk in riddles, talk
                        in tongues, y(o)u
crouch
low
            next to the page,
corpus as

        chorus as

an echoing, a being-multiple. There

are wh[is]pers before
language,   v[is]ions before
Things. Watching y-(o)ur
absence
                un-lock itself into text

we will see foot-prints
          emerge in the sand, in
                        the rock.

The Origin of Myth

<u>Notes for an homage</u>

1. Why "Y(o)u"?—for the double absence, for the tunnel, for the femininity (in a heteronormative, rather primitive, sense) of the shapes, for an echo of her shattered "I"/"Eye".
2. Why a "clearing"?—because Heidegger said so.
3. Why "word-fenced" and "stone-white"?—because language delineates, and language imprisons, because the white page is as impermeable as stone, though she has left there a trace of her telling.
4. Why a capitalised "Zone"?—because Tarkovsky said so and, apart from the relevance of the philosophical content of Stalker (as well as the "Writer" and the "Scientist" being rather like characters who could have come from her work), he used genre there the way she does—as a subversive tool, as a liberating constraint.
5. Why split the border?—because all borders are split, because they contain, by definition, the trace of choice, the whispered "or", and she was much concerned with borderlands, both linguistic and geographic.
6. Why "~"?—because they are watery signs, they are waves between words, and such typographic resonance feels appropriate here.
7. Why "[is]"?—to pinpoint the Beingness hidden there, to gesture toward presence, to show, for example, the slow, slime-ridden slug sitting on the page.
8. Why "som/no/lent"?—to emphasise the rhyme, for one; to emphasise the rejected alertness, for two; to suggest a figure leaning over a bridge, for three.
9. Why "ochre"?—because of the Blombos cave, because of Pech Merle.
10. Why "re/turn\ing"?—to dramatise the turn, to emphasise the repetition and the Doingness of it all, and because to do so makes me feel like it is the sixties once again.
11. Why the bold "us"?—"Since each of us was several, there was already quite a crowd"—Deleuze and Guattari, *A Thousand Plateaus*—in recog-

nition of her rejection of the singular self.

12. Why did vision come before Things?—because "language is the house of Being" (cf. (2) above).

13. Why "un-lock"?—how else to describe the action of deliberate insertion of absence into a text, the clicking of an Iye-key? How else to explain her presence between/beneath/inside the words?

14. Why any of this?—Because she lived at the text-edge, at the point where noun and body split, because of the pleasure she took in cracking open words like un-cooked eggs and letting the yolk slip down her chin, because she was fearless and wrote sentences which were uniquely, and deafeningly, her own, because she knew the mythical origins of language, of naming and describing, because of her devotion to telling, and her extraordinary, and insufficiently acknowledged, talent.

Once Upon a Time

Christine Brooke-Rose

Once upon a time
—it was a crystal formula—
there was a magic glass
where colours sang and sentences
curled into shapes, and rhyme
was plucked from market stalls to pass
into the hair of streams.
Then the toy daggers of exclamation
burst the bubble of dreams.

Once upon a time
there was a mirrored fireplace
answering the fender as a frame
for the scarlet pageantry of flame
and the clinking of gold symbols.
Then the poker of astonishment
splintered the picture in a paradigm.

Once there was a window-pane
and a radiant fairy poised
in an illumined coach,
waiting, silent as her want,
the child's approach.
Then came the pin-pricks of the rain
dotting the last glass page
with the goose-flesh of revelation.

Truth, April 27, 1956

Talking Through the Looking Glass

Ali Millar

From one O.P. to another: As head leant against cool glass of mirror and end of life was contemplated and with it the resulting frailties and somehow the jump was made from there to who writes, who speaks, but never mention was made of who reads or how, was thought given of all the other lives, never lived, never begun, or of the immense privilege to be there, resting head against said mirror, containing stated thoughts, in dotage and decrepitude maybe but still, the opportunity, the circumstances were there to take knotted knuckles to hold the pen to record, regardless of who was writing or speaking or any of the questions that barely, in the end, mattered.

For the careless reader would take the opposite to hold true, and render the pages laid out to be a contemplation then not of life, but of death, being the accepted opposite, and not read as is stated, life, end of. And the life of the body-wearing head did not end when the book did, not of the one who wrote, but instead breathing—the act of living in the strictest sense—continued long after. But the one who spoke and who wrote, both collapsed each on the other, as old people do, until little distinction remained between either, each undergoing a death in what was finishing was not the rising and falling of the chest, but instead the pen was being lost and writing ceasing, life—as known—was ending. Did this tyrannical old person with the one-sided view, always from the inside, never allowing the reader out to see anything other than the tunnel vision, always imposing, ever stop to think there could be many things worse than death, things worse than living the life that was ceasing, such as the life never beginning, just remaining a shell with the intent to be more, to try harder, but entrapped by wants and desires of an earlier self. A naïve self at that, who trusted in narrative without once realising this was where trust was being misplaced, who would now spend days singing nursery rhymes and bathing slippery tiny bodies and nights spent with cries echoing in ears and it's as it was expected to be, yet an apparition only when underpinned by nothing else. When hands rest idle apart from sewing rips in red school tights or rubbing bumps to the head when tumbling from slides and all these things are real and good—have to be good, otherwise where is the value or the point of all this time, all this waiting, if it all must end? And in the doctor's surgery those lined up waiting for seasonal flu jags with cataract eyes clouding slightly more until milk seems to seep from the sides come over all nostalgic and smile at the green snot-nosed baby wielding crumbling biscuits in fat fists, their teeth about to fall from receding gums that smile and say enjoy it, it too passes fast. And how easy it would be to tear their past from them, to shake them if it would not break them, or to shake them even if it would, to shake them and hear those bones crack from a too-tight grip, and to say did you not think it too, did you not feel it too as you waited for another cycle of the wash to stop spinning, did you not endure the crushing weight of boredom waiting for them to grow up or to move or to just somehow leave you alone; you are complicit in this lie and everyone is, they compound this narrative that this is all there is, all there should be, everything there ever could be, when there is more, so much more there on the inside, waiting to be unearthed, to be found, recorded if only the blame stopped being shifted always onto the other; the little beings, or the lack of time, or the errant muse or something, anything to avoid the writing that needs to be done. What is being avoided then is not the act, but the fear behind the act, the fear of acting, leading to inaction, to petrification, to stone, to muteness—to mutiny, silent but there, waiting to explode.

And where then does the fear really lie? In living? Or in being allowed to live, or with the reader, the lurking phantom, taking the shape in dreams of a dark haired mother, disappointed already, reading that which represents both who writes and who speaks, a careless reader at that, with opinions loudly imposed, until shackles were shaken, one exchange of confinement for another. This reader, the one feared who limits the words inside being put on the page, who always is there even when absent. The reader who might respond, not by telephone—let that one ring out—by letter, or not, not dealing in words—too easily outfoxed. The response may continue to take the same form of stony silence as it has taken these years gone or in disinheritance, as may already have happened, and if that is the reply, not ever known, then the worry is reasonless, and needs not to have mutated from some malingering and misplaced sense of duty to this inability to move. Reply instead to those to the interwoven tissues of influences—lined up on the shelves—impossible to pick apart. Reply to this and refrain from blaming those with dimpled backs and chubby little thighs, not old enough to talk, or mothers whose voices are long since forgotten yet ringing still somewhere, move beyond those to speak, to write. Let the lead be taken then by the old person, somewhere in the South of France, fictional or fictionalised, the other person with the wicked grin, who wrote the way that was wanted and when finally, life ended, was overlooked still in death.

Terpsichori

Gianni Dane

The brain twitching causing the scalp to itch lifting fingernails to scratch and dandruff flakes to fall, snow showering the black coat cloth covering shoulders not broad but lean showing the flex of muscle as the arm raises and a hand pulls each sleeve off. Fingers slithering through hair pulled back in a band and flattening smooth stray strands, the head ducked through the neck of a tight fitting singlet rolled down snugly over the torso, tights rolled up over ankles calves knees thighs to cradle crotch and hips, spine curving forwards as fingers deft and fast lace soft shoes to the feet, elastic criss-crossing instep.

Stretching the legs to stand and walk from one room down a corridor entering another long and wide windows showing the outside grey gloom of afternoon, black bark-encrusted branches rustling in a wintry gust of air dashing inside as a sliding pane falls down in the frame with a bang accompanying the arpeggios swelling across the room not yet a classical tune, mere warm up as the legs lifted bent straight turned in and rotated out, hooked through the barre or cradling the head with the ankle flexed up and down, arch rounded to the tip of the toes pointed relaxed heel lowered weight transferred knees bending facing sideways always out rotate out: the feet ankles knees thighs to the hip socket, lengthen the back of the leg extend forward carry à la seconde and lift out of the joint to continue the foot arcing up and finally settling behind arabesque en l'air place à terre, line line watch the line always the aesthetic of the line, heads turn to the mirror to observe one leg several legs infinitely repeated legs floating at impossible angles to describe a story with each movement. Each sinew sculpting a narrative, each joint mobile with meaning, the body a palimpsest of tales contorted in each re-imagined re-telling.

Entering the expanse of high ceiling and resin-scuffed parquet flooring Madame Maestro smiling slightly nodding round the room at heads nodding with chins lifted proudly or lowered modestly, the feet hinting at a pointe that once was, inner calves and thighs open and gliding forward under square hips and pole-straight back, lower ribs suppressed and upper ribs projecting an elegance of life-long discipline apparent in the briefest glance and merest extension of wrist settling on the barre to demonstrate with the suggestion of an exercise demi-plié for two, arms through first and relevé for two, arms through fifth followed with grand-plié reverse port-de-bras finishing dégagé à la seconde and repeat en croix. Satie's Gymnopédie to start please, the head inclining at the pianist fingers rippling over ivory and ebony as the introduction breathes life inside arms flowing forwards and sideways in preparation to almost quiver as muscles react to music with a grace belying the screeching pain of a torn ligament here and a strained iliopsoas there, keep the shoulders down Peggy work those inner thighs Robert don't sit in the plié arrive at the nadir and ascend to the zenith Alicia keep those ribs pulled in Anton wearing a fish for a foot Gelsey extend the line before rounding the port-de-bras Mischa elbows lifted Maggie timing people timing listen to the musical phrasing don't rush to finish use the melody Rudi and close back to fifth position arms lowered W-A-I-T keep the position stretch the knees B-R-E-A-T-H-E et voilà shake out the legs other side.

Through toes sliding along the floor to arch the foot as battement tendu and battement glissé and the knees folding in battement fondu and extending to whip the air as rond de jambe en l'air before the legs lift towards the ceiling in battement développé and grand battement en croix, arms resting on nothingness to waft from first position to third position fingers Jonathan fingers the music carries the fingers not a bunch of dead flowers head inclined with the épaulement no strain in the neck Darcey relax the audience doesn't want to know it's killing the dancer and posé piqué en avant to attitude derrière stay there S-T-A-Y Vladimir lift the leg U-P hold it H-O-L-D engage the back shoulders down Ekaterina and allongée close fifth shake out the legs other side.

En diagonale pirouettes or grand jeté entrelacé the flash of gaze disjointed from the turning body, head always poised until the last to fix on a point in the distance eyes never lowered never flickered sideways always centred on that faraway place past the footlights to the depths of the blackness where the audience sitting enthralled with the spectacle of a white swan dying betrayed by frailty thy name is Siegfried and thirty-two famous fouettés en tournant later Odile victorious as danced-unto-death Giselle rescuing a feckless Albrecht from the wrath of Wili Queen Myrtha ethereal and avenging as Diana punishing Actaeon for the folly of spying on nude bathing in a prelude to the afternoon amours of a nymph-chasing faun before the curtain falls on thrown blossoms and applause, rising and falling, drapes swishing apart as the corps of artists claps to the bows and curtseys of soloists and principals and lastly the baton wielder and the choreographer before lights out and stage hands sweep the floor, the audience dribbling outside to real life and the street, the performing fingers hands arms toes feet legs bodies heads fatigued and collapsing in dressing rooms to vanish the vestiges of fantasy and emerge via the stage door, faces scrubbed clean, hair loosened and flowing over shoulders not broad but lean, from which old tracksuits hang baggy jeans hugging hips, long black coats dusted with the first fall of winter snow until the next morning of once upon a time begins anew.

Translation, pastiche, and things

Original French text: Françoise Gramet
Translation: Wee Teck Lim & G. N. Forester
Collage confusion & typographical follies: G. N. Forester

Note au cher lecteur:

Ce texte est un hommage à Christine Brooke-Rose, que je n'ai jamais eu le plaisir de rencontrer mais dont la voix m'a tout particulièrement touchée, peut-être comme miroir/rétroviseur de mes premiers pas dans le monde de la linguistique, de la stylistique et de la traduction; peut-être aussi parce que, comme elle, je suis née entre les langues et vis parmi elles et que, comme la sienne, «ma tête est pleine de structures syntaxiques».

Ni plagiat ni parodie, ce texte se veut pastiche autour de *"Life, End of"*, dernier ouvrage publié par Christine Brooke-Rose en 2006 et de La Lettre envoyée par notre auteur après lecture du premier chapitre de ma traduction en français.

Je tiens à vivement remercier Verbivoracious d'avoir pris l'initiative de ce *Festschrift* pour une première publication. Mark Nicholls et G. N. Forester ont été une force de tous les instants derrière la publication de cet article bilingue. G. N. Forester et Wee Teck Lim ont produit, à partir de mon texte français, un texte anglais, et à partir duquel, G. N. Forester a créé un texte typographiquement représentatif des oeuvres les plus expérimentales de Christine Brooke-Rose. Son foisonnement tout joycien ouvre une indispensable fenêtre vers l'anglais.

La composition du texte que vous vous apprêtez à lire utilise différents caractères typographiques dont chacun a une fonction spécifique. La clé ci-dessous est proposée au lecteur qui préfère ne pas avoir à résoudre le rébus pendant la lecture:

Le texte français et son caractère.
Le texte anglais et son caract re.
Citations de "Life, End of".
Citations des autres livres Brooke-Rosenne.
Citations de La Lettre.

New York, Action de Grâce 2013

Note to the dear reader:

This essay is an homage to Christine Brooke-Rose, whom I never had the pleasure of meeting but whose voice touched me deeply, perhaps as a looking glass/rear-view mirror of my first steps in the world of linguistics, stylistics, and translation; perhaps also because, like her, I was born between and live amongst languages and thus, like hers, "my head is full of syntactic structures."

Neither plagiarism nor parody, this essay seeks to be a pastiche around the last work of Christine Brooke-Rose, "*Life, End of*", published in 2006, and The Letter sent to me by our author after reading the first chapter of its French translation.

I would like to express my most sincere appreciation to Verbivoracious Press for taking the initiative with this *Festschrift* as a first issue. The editors have been a constant force behind the publication of this bilingual piece. G. N. Forester and Wee Teck Lim have produced an English text, from my French text, and from that G. N. Forester has created a collage text typographically representative of the most experimental of Christine Brooke-Rose's works. Its Joycean exuberance opens an indispensable window on English.

The setting of the text that you are about to read uses different typographical fonts, each of which has a specific function. The key below is offered to the reader who prefers not to have to resolve the rebus while reading:

The French text and its font.
The English text and its font.
Quotes from *Life, End of.*
Quotes from other Brooke-Rose works.
Quotes from the Letter.

New York, Thanksgiving 2013.

Tout It all **commences lors** during **d'une des** visites **d'amis** of friends from **Philadelphie, Jean-Yves, Paquita et leur fille** their daughter Roseta.

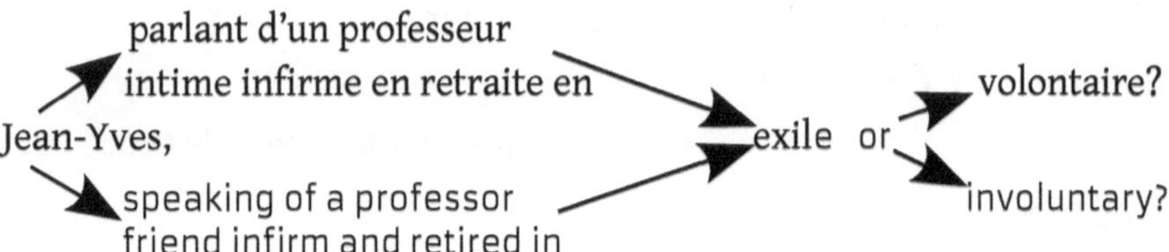

I used to think that the word *exil* meant «ex-Ile»
out of the island, or, less etymologically, an island
out of my world.[1]

dans une magnifique maison in a magnificent mansion in the south sud de la France, contrarié VEXED at having lost d'avoir égaré un papier important rangé à l'étage an important paper stored upstairs, et inaccessible because of depuis les multiples health problèmes de santé:

—Dis-moi où il peut être, j'irai te le chercher? Tell me where it is, I'll go and look for it?
—Non, non, NO j'ai déjà envoyé Valérie l'autre jour I already sent Valerie the other day; elle ne l'a pas trouvé she didn't find it. Moi, je le trouverais surement. For sure I would!

```
Autonomy! Self-rule. Same thing.
    Etymologically correct.²
```

Retournant le problème dans tous les sens,
Jean-Yves, respectable professeur d'université, toujours
prêt à aider mais loin d'être un champion de poids et altères,
finit par proposer à l'invalide de monter au premier étage sur son dos.

Regarding the problem from all angles,
Jean-Yves, eminent professor, always ready to
lend a hand but far from being an Olympic champion, finishes
by proposing the invalid climb to the first floor on Jean-Yves' back.

1   Brooke-Rose, Christine, *Invisible Author: Last Essays*, Cambridge, CUP, 2002 , p. 109.
2   Brooke-Rose, Christine, *Life, End of*, Manchester, Carcanet, p. 99.

The image L'image est hilarante HILARIOUS!, nous rions beaucoup . . . we :D :D :D :D :P . . .

un peu jaune pourtant car. . . although a tad sourly because, pour les baby-boomers we are que nous sommes, every stage of our progenitors' aging chaque étape du vieillissement de nos géniteurs nous rapproche brings us closer to notre propre our own dégringolade.

Dé

       grin

            go

                 lade

                      en bas de l'escalier

après abandon de stratagèmes plus humiliants pour atteindre le plancher des vaches: à reculons comme un bébé du troisième âge ou assis en s'aidant des bras comme les culs-de-jattc?

                                    Dé

                              grin

                        go

                    lade

       stairs the of bottom the to

after abandoning numerous humiliating strategies to reach solid ground: regressing like a very elderly baby or sitting like a legless cripple aided by helping arms?

For their Pour leur visite traditional du *Thanksgiving* américain—in November—Jean-Yves apporte brings un recent ouvrage book written by the invalid écrit par l'infirme in question.

During this période d'Action de Grâce, as les Franco-Canadians appellent name their célébration—en octobre—the reading is, in one sitting, la lecture est une *revelation an epiphany*, fenêtre ouverte de l'intérieur sur les efforts quotidiens a window opened on the daily exertions de l'auteur/author/narrateur/narrator/personnage/character to maintenir amity agilité intellectuality autonomie physicality authority.

Ce texte—dans l'entre-langues between languages et l'intertexualité—génère un besoin irrépressible de traduction generates an irresistible desire to translate pour le défi langagier, d'abord for the linguistic challenge, firstly; next, to offer it to the mother; pour l'offrir à la mère ensuite; enfin, pour le lire à l'auteur lors de la prochaine visite and lastly, at Jean-Yves' suggestion, to be read to the author on the next visit.

Don et contre-don. *Thanksgiving* et Action de Grâce.

Gifting and counter-gifting. *Action of Grace* and Thanksgiving.

The ordinary reader Le lecteur λ est dès l'abord pris par le is firstly taken by the Content contenu du texte.

```
    But it isn't a scenario. Or a novel.
    Or an autobio. It's a dying diary.³
```

La ^{The}dé $_{con}$st^{ruc}tion $_{sy}$stem$_{atic}$ du texte par le traducteur of the text by the translator permits the development of profound Form lui permet d'arriver à la forme profonde—techniques, récurrences et & recoupements X-references.

C'est à une analyse de ce type que nous invite l'Invisible auteur dans les *Derniers essais.* Première phrase, une question en style direct, parfaitement formée—indicatif et point d'interrogation—dont la réponse arrive sans que le lecteur imaginaire lui-même ait le temps d'intervenir.

It is to an analysis of this type that the author of the last essays invites us. The first sentence, a question in direct discourse—perfectly Formed: indicative and a question mark—whose response arrives without the reader imagining having the time to interject.

---

3 *Life, End of,* p. 87.

> Have you ever tried to do something very difficult
> as well as you can, over a long period, and found
> that nobody notices? . . . The difficult thing I've
> been doing, on and off, for thirty-six years, has a
> technical name: a lipogram, though I prefer the
> word constraint.[4]

Des contraintes, constraints, always there, il y en a toujours eu, imposées imposed ou deliberate délibérées. Superstition numérological?

> Four fairly conventional novels [...] then four novels with short prepositional or adjectival titles [...].
> Then four novels with one word titles.[5]

dont l'autobiography admitted avouée, sans compter without counting the later la plus tardive autobio: *Life, End of* (2006).

> When it's live it's not looped.[6]

And so arrives an enveloppe à l'entête déroutante, bearing the puzzling letterhead:

THE UNIVERSITY OF TEXAS AT AUSTIN
Office of the President
P.O Box T—Austin, TX 78713-8920

and un palimpseste de tampons de la Postmarks:

POUND RATE PAID
MONTS DE VAUCLUSE
VIA PERMIT
9.01.07

les tampons postmarks faisant foi verifying—mais de quoi but what: the Vaucluse bilingual rexclusive of those Provence mountains? Pound, sterling, poids avoirdu ou poète A ZBC of?

---

4   *Invisible Author: Last Essays*, pp. 1-2
5   *ibid.*, p. 54.
6   *Life, End of*, p. 77.

A une vitesse grand V, incontrôlable mais d'une efficacité sans pareille, le système nerveux sympathique, le-bien-nommé, déclenche une ac-célération du rythme cardiaque qui fait affluer le sang vers la tête, crée un rétrécissement du champs de vision, désormais concentré comme un laser sur les 210mm x 297mm de l'enveloppe A4 pour en capter les in-dices, les envoie au cerveau-ordinateur qui compute en quel-ques nano-secondes la seule conclusion logique quant à l'identité de l'expéditeur.

```
                         But what is it all for in
```

La décharge d'adrénaline engendre un tremblement incontrôlable des extrémités sup-érieures pendant que les doigts déchirent le haut de l'enveloppe. Pour contrebalancer le réflexe *fright-flight-fight*, le système ner-veux parasympathique, voisin du bien-nommé, intervient sur le nerf vague qui divague, car son territoire est le plus étendu de tous les nerfs. Et c'est le malaise vagal. Vrai coup de poing dans l'épigastre, un étonnement à couper le souffle tourne assez rapidement en une joie dé-lirante, le cerveau—tel celui d'un marathonien—produisant maintenant de l'endorphine au vu du contenu de l'enveloppe.

```
                        ⁷It is the brain,the
```

L'auteur/author/narrateur/narrator/personnage/character d'une voix sonne using the first person point-of-view to compose pour composer hand:

un texte

dont les lignes

chutent

inéluctablement

vers le bas de la page.

```
                         Life, End of:
```

---

7 *ibid.*, p. 12.

At a velocity capitalised V, uncontrollable but of an unparalleled efficacy, the sympathetic nervous system, aptly named, triggers an accelerated cardiac rhythm making the blood rush to the head, creating a narrowing of the field of vision, henceforth concentrated like a laser on the 210mm x 297mm A4 envelope to figure out the clues, sending these to the Cerebral Processing Unit computing in a few nanoseconds the only logical conclusion as to the sender's identity.

```
the end? Is it all just gigo?⁸
```

The adrenaline discharge engenders an uncontrollable trembling in the upper extremities while the digits tear off the flap of the envelope. To counterbalance the fright-flight-fight reflex, the parasympathetic nervous system, neighbour of the aptly-named, intervenes via the divagating vagus nerve, because its territory is the most vagabond of all the nerves, and is the vagal malaise. A real suckerpunch to the spleen, a stupefied astonishment turning rapidly to a delirious joy, the brain—such as that of a marathon runner—now producing endorphins at the sight of the envelope's contents.

```
brain that endures.
```

maintenant univoque now a unequivocal voice *utilise la première pers-* **de sa main régulière mais tremblée** with an even although trembling

a text

<table><tr><td>whose</td><td style="text-align:right">lines</td></tr></table>

tumble

ineluctably

to the bottom of the page.

```
the novel.
```

---

8   *ibid.*, p. 62.

Roman, autobio, roman autobiographique? Fiction/faction. L'auteur—nous livrant enfin la clef de sa première autobiographie—indique la/les contrainte(s) adoptée(s) pour rendre le projet plus intéressants. L'adoption—et l'expension—du «*speakerless narrative*» ou mode objectivisé sans narrateur de Robbe-Grillet

[9]We do not know whose mind we're in, there is third

se double du présent, proche du présent scientifique, neutre—scientifiquement neutre—quand, jusque là, on aurait eu le passé de la phrase narrative donnant délibérément le privilège au temps de la narration. Et, plus encore, dans la mesure où il n'y a plus d'acte d'énonciation, l'auteur—omniscient ou non, bavard ou silencieux—n'a plus de voix. Est proposé un énoncé point de vue *consciousness* producteur de récit, de texte.

Who

In this context Dans ce texte sur within LE texte, c'est bien l'auteur qui sa plume et sa voix pour indiquer taking up pen and voice to indicate, order (to whom?) which parenthesised almost transforms the fact entendu, sous entendu implied and mentionnéd in passing:

(not to

Signature L'humour, présent des l'emblée, from the get go,

Dear Françoise Gramet,
I was astonished and delighted to receive your translation of

and the addressee et le destinataire because of a breach sur un manviewed as volontary—à l'étiquette épistolary:

---

9   *Invisible Author: Last Essays*, p. 137.

Novel, autobiography, bifografy? Phiction/phaction. The author, finally providing the key to the first bifography, indicates the constraints chosen to render the project more interesting. The adoption—and expansion—of the "speakerless narrative" or Robbe-Grillet's narratorless objectified mode

no "je" [...] that mind is represented by the person.

is paired with the present tense, close to the scientific present—scientifically neutral—when, until this point, the past tense of the narrative sentence would have deliberately privileged narrative time (and not story time). Moreover, in as much as enunciation ceases to exist, the author—omniscient or not, a mouthpiece or silent—has no voice. The text proposes a stated point of view *conscience* created by whoever receives (reads) the text.

speaks?[10]

parle it's the author who SPEAKS annihilating any distance, reprenant en tout premier lieu in pole position and at the top of the page, a given ordre donné—à qui?—que des parenthèses transforment presque en fait

be given)

scratches griffe la terre the ground la planète la galaxy:

my first chapter. It is very good. Very impressive considering the difficulty of my writing (so they say).

quement—dicté par dictated by les circonstances, mais vu comme but

---

10 *Life, End of,* p. 112.

Please find my address, in case you need to contact me, but I don't want to (can't) open a regular correspondence. You neither. I imagine, since you don't give it.

Ecrites à l'encre written in noire ink

Nulla poena

Clearly numbered I II III **Clairement numéroté, indiqué** (see below) three sections. The addressee should recognise **Le destinataire doit-il** unconscious **résurgence inconsciente d'une** career universitaire?

    I.   STYLE ⇐majuscules⇒ CLARITY, &c

    III.   *THE looking-glass problem.*

THE looking-glass problem—*problem* in Onglay to find **pour une solution étude souci**—est en effet in effect **important à plusieurs niveaux** on ma **dans la première phrase du récit, dont** whose **fonction et forme** are cle **la lettre:**

. . . just remember that this might be dutch to any reader (IF early. The first 3-4 pages of any book must be easy, funny,

The **L'expression répétée** repeated **de loin en loin** here and there, **écho important** rendering the translator's choices even more important for

L'esprit The mindset, logiqual and critiqual but not criticising, the researcher's meticulosity shining forth le soin méticuleux du chercheur luisent dans les 4 pages double-sided, neatly marked de 1 à 8.

Rédigées d'un trait composed in one swoop. <u>Soulignements</u> <u>underscores</u> et citations in rouge. Comments explications explanation conseils suggestions. Identifiés by page and ligne. Even some pretty compliments to lap up. Ainsi que quelques félicitations douces comme du petit-lait. Quel travail in adversité!

sine lege.[11]

with MAJUSCULES et soulignements underlines, le plan est divided in y reconnaitre le plan dialectiqual or the analytique outline; perhaps an

II.   *Excellent + a few praising comments*

à trouver et not a problème français about which to worry pour inquiny levels, appearing in the first sentence of the narrative. Il apparait arly established sont établies clairement by par l'auteur/the author de

any) who hasn't read philology. He must not be put off so &c . . .

[ECHO!] ou mise en abime, rendant le choix du traducteur d'autant plus pour la cohésion and la compréhension du of the target texte d'arrivée.

---

11 *ibid.*, p. 10, 49.

The head top leans against the
glass becomes

Enfin, le thème the image of the mirror recurs est récurrent dans in at
autoréflectif in the self-reflexive novel

[12]my favorite

sous la forme d'un **rétroviseur** qui permet au chauffeur de regarder vers l'avant pour voir ce qui se passe à l'arrière tandis que le véhicule se déplace vers l'avant ; ou, adoptant le point de vue temporel, le rétroviseur rapporte dans le présent des images du passé au même temps que le futur se déroule ; ou du point de vue spatial, le regard dirigé vers l'avant perçoit ce qui se passe à l'avant et à l'arrière, sans obstruction aucune.

L'utilisation du mot miroir—plus commun en français québécois qu'il ne l'est en français hexagonal—puis du mot glace permet de garder la dualité *mirror/glass* du texte de départ. Par contre, la dualité ne peut être maintenue pour les noms verbaux composés anglais the *looking glass/the touching glass*—dans leur forme ancienne sans tiret (retour au monde d'Alice au pays des merveilles évoquée plus tard ainsi que son chat ?) rendus par un nom ou un infinitif en français (la marche/marcher est une activité saine) indiquant une activité/occupation prise au sens générique. L'article défini et le sens générique du nom verbal créent la distance voulue par l'auteur entre le narrateur et le récit—mde même d'ailleurs que le miroir de salle de bains, plus article de catalogue que d'une salle de bains spécifique.

Grammatically, it's the glass that looks, as in blinding light

La première phrase—que le lecteur sait déjà essentielle—précise également que le haut de la tête est appuyé contre le miroir. Description physique importante et porteuse de sens: les yeux, plus bas que le miroir, ne peuvent capter l'autoréflexion de l'auteur/personnage/narrateur. Autrement dit, dans le temps de la narration, le personnage—

---

12 *Invisible Author: Last Essays*, p. 17.

```
bathroom mirror so that the looking
a feeling glass.¹³
```

least deux two textes au moins. D'abord dans le roman postmoderne
Thru

```
favorite my¹⁴
```

in the form of a **rearview mirror**, allowing the driver to look forward at
what is happening behind while the vehicle is moving forward. Or,
temporally speaking, a rearview mirror brings to the present images
of the past as the future unfolds. Or, from a spatial perspective, the
driver's eyes look forwards and have an unobstructed view of what is
in front and also behind.

Using the word "miroir"—more commonly used in Quebequois
French than in hexagonal French—followed by the word "glace" allows the "mirror/glass" duality from the original text to be retained. In
contrast, the duality of the English compound nouns "looking
glass/touching glass" (in the old form without a hyphen—a return to
the world of Alice in Wonderland later evoked as well as her cat?) can
only be kept if rendered as a noun or verb in the infinitive in French
(**walking is a healthy activity**) indicating an activity/occupation in the
general sense. The use of the definite article and the generic meaning
of the noun creates the distance desired by the author between the
narrator and the text in the same way as does the term "the bathroom
mirror", more an item in a catalogue than one in a specific bathroom.

(for who can blind a light?). Or at least ambiguous . . .

the first sentence—which the reader already knows is essential—
states the forehead leans against the mirror. This physical description, important and pregnant with meaning: the eyes, lower than the
mirror, cannot see the self-reflection of the author/character/narrator
In other words, concerning the time of narrative time, the character—

---

13 *Life, End of.*, p. 5.
14 p. 17, *Essays Last :Author Invisible.*

dont la visibilité sur l'avenir et sur le passé est désormais nulle—se trouve limité emprisonné condamné au présent. Et c'est le présent que le texte reflète réfléchit revoit révise.

> *Le mouroir* as the French call
> its closeness

N'étant ni un rétroviseur ni un miroir sans tain, le miroir de salle de bains bloque toute vision sur l'avenir en renvoyant une rétro-vision vers le passé à laquelle se mêle la seule image reflétée/réfléchie du personnage. En l'absence totale de futur, le miroir de salle de bains reflète le passé du sujet tout en réfléchissant son vieillissement, faisant littéralement de ce roman d'autofiction un roman autoréflexif.

> [15]Is self-Reflex

Mais que faire de la transformation par remplacement métaphorique du miroir à mirer en miroir à toucher (A = B)? La première explication est médicale et imprègne tout le texte. L'invalide vieillissant est atteint de très sartriens «remous de néant[16]» inexplicables par la science, causant un déséquilibre constant qui l'oblige à prendre appui sur les objets, la réalité offrant ainsi l'objectivité prônée par le nouveau roman.

> *The role of miroir here is similar to that of looking*

Au niveau du récit, la pro—et la rétro-vision perdues sont remplacées par le toucher. Dans un texte qui s'est donné pour contrainte de maintenir une distance entre le réel et la narration dans sa forme—usage du présent, absence du «je» et de déictiques marqueurs de profondeur temporelle—cette amputation sensorielle condamne le personnage à perdre toute distance à objet monde univers puis qu'elle implique un contact direct avec la/les chose(s).

> I use the present in a specific, paradoxical

---

15 *Invisible Author: Last Essays*, p. 63.
16 *Life, End of*, p. 8—Gramet translation.

whose visibility of the future and of the past is henceforth null, is thus limited imprisoned condemned to the present. It is the present on which the text reflects reflects on reviews revises.

```
it,   seemingly   unaware   of
to le miroir.¹⁷
```

Neither a rear-view nor a two-way mirror, the bathroom mirror blocks all view of the future, sending back a vision of the past which melds with the only image reflected at/reflected on by the character. With its total absence of future, the bathroom mirror reflects the character's past while fully reflecting her aging, literally making this autobiographical novel self-reflexive.

```
ivity MERE?
```

But what to do with the transformation—metaphorical replacement—of the looking glass to the touching glass (A = B)? The first explanation, medical permeating the entire text. The aging invalid is struck with very Sartrian **"tidal waves of nothingness"**¹⁸ unexplainable by science, causing a constant disequilibrium obliging the body to lean on objects, reality thus offering the objectivity of the *nouveau roman*.

inside (emotion) and outside (feeling with hands).

At the level of story, lost sight—both ahead and behind—has been replaced by touch. In a text using the constraint of maintaining a distance between reality and narrative via its form—use of present tense, the absence of "I" and deictic markers of temporal depth—this sensory amputation condemns the character to lose all distance to objects world universe requiring a direct contact with things.

```
way I owe to [...] Alain Robbe-Grillet.¹⁹
```

---

17 *Life, End of,* p. 46.

18 *ibid,.*

19 *Invisible author: Last Essays,* p. 2.

Pour pousser l'analyse, le objet présenté au lecteur dans la première phrase (importance[2]) vient enrichir la métaphore sous-entendue et sous-tendant le récit : haut de la tête = cerveau/glace à mirer = glace à toucher qui, par permutation, constitue l'annonce prémonitoire (accessible au lecteur sachant chasser seulement ?) d'une autre réalité objectivée dans le texte.

[20]Is it the feet that feel

The transmutation transforme/s the external le regard towards vers

But who feels what? A
looking in, not

to the internal en un regard towards vers l'intérieur—émotions/jouissa
withdrawal to the brain—savoir/knowledge/lecture/reading/écriture/

I   STYLE,

La première partie des commentaires s'attache au style, à la clarté et à un etc. très humble puisque s'y cache un jeu de mots (un jeu *sur* les mots et leur contenu) déclinés du premier chapitre jusqu'à la dernière page du texte. L'humour est important pour la dernière narration autant qu'elle l'est en amont pour toute l'œuvre, l'auteur utilisant plusieurs ressorts humoristiques (*punning, jokes*—bilingues ou trilingues —ironie, dérision, etc.) dans chacun de ses romans. Style personnel. Technique de romancier. Divertissement du lecteur. *Comic relief.*

[21]The joy of bristling up

Vasco de Gama surgit 13 fois dans notre autobio sans, à première vue, y avoir une place prédestinée, sinon figurativement en entendant l'autobio comme un voyage au long cours avec ses découvertes, ses écueils et ses naufrages. Superstition numérologique maintenant sinistre, funeste, funèbre.

---

20 *Life, End of,* p. 8.
21 *ibid,.* p. 59.

Pushing the analysis further, the object presented to the reader in the first sentence (importance^{squared}) enriches the overarching metaphor implicitly in the text: top of the head = brain / looking glass = touching glass which, by permutation, constitutes a premonitory announce-ment (available only to a savvy reader) of another objectivised reality in the text.

or their boss the brain?

l'extérieur—amis/ friends/choses/ things/monde/world—

looking glass is for
looking out.^{22}

nce/pleasure/mort/death—mais aussi en repli sur le cerveau but also a writing=jeux verbaux de language de mots=verbal plays on words.

CLARITY, &c:

The first part of the commentary deals with style and clarity (and is very humble) etc. as the novel contains wordplay (a play on words and their meaning) from the very first chapter until the last page of the text. Humour is as important in the ultimate story as it is for the entire corpus of work, the author using several devices of humour (punning, irony, derision, jokes: bilingual or trilingual, etc) in each the novels written. A personal style. The novelist's technique. The amusement of the reader. *Comic relief.*

words again, just for fun.

Vasco de Gama appears thirteen times in the autobiography without, at first impression, having a predestined place, except figuratively, in seeing the autobiography as a long voyage with its discoveries, its reefs, and its shipwrecks. The numerological superstition now sinist-
laerenuf, ymoolg, re

---

22 ibid,.

Because disability and
by any of the parti
double distancing

Au niveau narratif, la maladie et la mort sont tenues à distance d'une part lorsque les trois participants jouent leur rôle comme ils le doivent. Le narrateur produit un récit impersonnel sans « je » ni profondeur temporelle ; l'auteur ne se découvre pas pour emprunter les maladies du personnage ; le personnage ne déroge pas aux règles intimes internes de l'autobio. Première distanciation. D'autre part, parce que la transformation lexicale du jeu de mot prive la maladie de nom identité réalité. Magicienne vengeresse, l'onomastique transmute les catégories naturelles. Affublée de noms (d'oiseaux), la maladie devient une quantité connue—moins effrayante—et évoque/invoque voyages, grands espaces, réussites, projetés sur la maladie pour en conjurer le sort ? Deuxième distanciation.

Car le problème principal [...] n'est pas le handicap—ici la maladresse croissante et le martellement de Vasco le Piqueur, douleur constante, chutes constantes pendant le constant travail sous-terrain de Cérès qui s'ennuie dans le cerveau inférieur, qui s'ennuie de sa Proserpine.[23]

Pourquoi donc associer Vasco de Gama au handicap du personnage dont les difficultés symptômes sont déjà connus du lecteur—fourmillements faiblesses déséquilibre causant chutes hospitalisations ambulances—maintenant diagnostiqués par le généraliste qui ne propose pourtant aucune cure à cette maladie . . . cardio vasco.

Dear Eve, did she have

---

23 *Life, End of*, p. 11; Gramet translation.

```
death cannot be borne
cipants without that
of self-derision.²⁴
```

At the narrative level, on the one hand, sickness and death are dis-tanced while the three participants play their mandated roles. The narrator produces an impersonal story with neither "I" nor tense; the author may not be discovered borrowing the illnesses of the charac-ter; the character never departs from the firm rules internal to the autobiography. Thus, the first distancing. On the other hand, the lex-ical transformation of the wordplay also deprives the illness of name reality identity. Onomastic—that vengeful magician—transmutes the natural categories. Decked out with names (of birds), the illness be-comes a known quantity—less frightening—and evokes/invokes jour-neys, large spaces, successes, projected onto the illness to cast a spell on it. The second distancing.

```
For the biggest problem [...] is not handicap—
here the growing lameness and the pounding
Vasco the Harmer, the constant pain, the con-
stant fall during the constant low-grade work
of the pining Ceres in the hindbrain, pining
for Proserpine.²⁵
```

Why then associate Vasco de Gama with the character's handicap whose symptomatic difficulties are already known to the reader—prickling sensations, weakness, poor balance causing falls hospital-isations ambulances—now diagnosed by a G.P. who proposes no cure for this…cardio vascular (vasco) illness.

```
all that trouble?²⁶
```

---

24 *ibid.*, p. 77.
25 *ibid.*, p. 11.
26 *ibid.*, p. 111.

Et *Vasco the Harmer* devient Vasco le Piqueur. Vasco devait être gardé car c'est la trace—au sens derridien d'écriture inscription physique—du handicap, l'ancre du jeu de mot. *Harmer* appelle *Hammer* = marteau, dont la rime interne avec Vasco est intéressante bien que purement référentielle et pratiquement inconsciente à la lecture. Pour maintenir l'homonymie avec l'anglais, un adjectif terminé par le suffixe 'eur' est attendu. Piqueur, co-occurrent de marteau, semble donc logique ici : le lexical renforce le sémantique et le fait concorder avec la symptomatologie.

Piqueur is surprising

Le lien lexical est renforcé par l'utilisation de martellement pour *pounding* donnant à la traduction une solide cohésion interne et portant un regard vers l'intérieur qui confirme en la renforçant la logique interne du texte. Rime interne ajoutée pour référence au poète perdue.

Ajoutons que la fidélité de la traduction repose tant sur le matériau langagier offert par la langue d'arrivée que sur un équilibre à trouver établir maintenir entre compensation formelle (rimes, allitérations, etc.) et création sémantique (niveau de langue, référents plus ou moins immédiats) ponctuelle ou répétée enrichie transformée dans le texte de départ.

La métaphore Vasco—pour faire vite—émaille tout le texte. Chaque itération propre au moment du récit est donc porteuse de sens.

C'est ainsi que *Vasco the Harmer* devient:

- *Vasco le Vacillant* (p. 20) qui vacille—physiquement ou moralement?—alors que la marche à l'aide d'une canne est élégante douloureuse mais encore possible;

- *Vasco le Charmeur* (p. 36) qui prend la parole pour donner une leçon de philologie sur les Basques, accédant ainsi à la fonction de personnage;

- *Vasco le Baume-au-cœur* (p. 88) qui allège ou non les symptômes de Pénible Pollyana (mais elle n'est pas mortelle[27]—fatale/humaine?); et, dans sa seconde itération, crée un dilemne avec

---

27 *ibid*, p. 88; Gramet Translation.

And Vasco the Harmer becomes *Vasco le Piqueur*. Vasco must be kept because it's the trace—in the Derridean sense of physical description—of the handicap, the anchor of the wordplay. "Harmer" recalls "hammer" = *marteau,* whose internal rhyme with Vasco is interesting although purely referential and hence practically unnoticeable to the reader. To maintain the homonymy with English, an adjective ending with the suffix "eur" is required. *Picquer,* co-occurent of *marteau* (marteau piqueur/jack hammer), seems logical here: the lexical reinforces the semantic and accords with the symptomatolgy.

but fine for Harmer.

This lexical link is reinforced by the use of *mar-telle-ment* for pounding giving the translation a strong internal cohesion and, by turning the gaze inwards, confirms and reinforces the internal logic of the text. Internal rhyme is added for the lost reference to the poet.

It should be added that the faithfulness of a translation depends as much on the linguistic material offered by the target language as it does on the balance found to be established and maintained between formal compensation (rhymes, alliteration, etc.) and the semantic creation (level of language, references more or less immediate) whether one-off or repeated enriched transformed in the source text.

The metaphor Vasco appears throughout the entire text, each iteration congruent with narrative time; hence rich with meaning.

Accordingly, Vasco the Harmer becomes:

- *Vasco the Qualmer* (p. 20) who qualms—physical or moral?—as walking with the help of a cane is painfully elegant but still possible;
- *Vasco the Charmer* (p. 36) who charms a way to a philology lesson on the Basques, thus assuming the function of Character;
- *Vasco the Balmer* (p. 88) one who alleviates or not the symptoms of Painful Pollyanna (but she is not mortal[28]—fatal/human?); and, in its second iteration, creates a dilemma with

---

28 *ibid.,* p. 88.

Polly Neuf Rites (Poly quoi? Polynévrite[29]): cardio requiert de l'exercice/Polly un allitement prolongé;

- *Vasco de Lama* (p. 103), animal péruvien/bonze tibétain? Qui invoque la patience pendant la sixième hospitalisation en 2 ans, et que l'auteur charge d'injecter un peu d'humour dans le récit;

- *(le vieux) Vasco* (pp. 104, 117); raccourcis diminutifs familiers—tendre?—pour ce compagnon de tous les instants;

- *Vasco de Gamma* (pp. 10, 111), avec ou sans majuscule; où le m excédentaire transforme le patronyme de l'explorateur en celui d'un rayonnement nucléiare conjugué aux effets de Pénible Pollyanna;

- *cardio-vasco-de-gamma-totale* (p. 111) dans toute sa splendeur et avec renforcement d'une expression populaire en français dans le texte anglais-jeu de mot bilingue. «La totale», euphémisme utilisé jadis pour une ablation de l'utérus, désigne aujourd'hui, dans la langue courante, l'ampleur de complications—médicales ou non; ici les jambes handicapées par cardio-vasco + double foulure;

- *Vasco de Drama* (pp. 88, 118) qui manque à contrecarrer Pénible Pollyana et devient l'antithèse de Vasco de Baume-au-cœur ; ou, dans sa deuxième apparition en fin de text, celui qui devient méloDrama parce qu'il annonce la fin possible;

```
                  Stop Vasco de Drama. Death,
```

Après quoi le texte déjante. Projection en accéléré de thèmes et objets apparus tout au long du texte. Tension entre le temps qui passe et la solution finale.

```
                                        30Rien ne
```

Littéralement et textuellement, conclusion d'une longue liste d'objets morts : ordinateur, Ipomées, jambes, pièces du corps. Tout est perdu.

---

29 *ibid.*, p. 88; Gramet translation.
30 *ibid.*, p. 119.

Polly New Writis(Polly what? Polyneuritis[31]): cardio requires exercise/ Polly an extended bed rest;

- *Vasco the Lama* (p. 103), Peruvian animal/Tibetan monk? One who invokes patience during the sixth hospitalisation in two years and whom the author charges to inject some humour in the discourse;
- *(old) Vasco* (p. 104, p. 117); familiar nicknames—tender?—for this constant companion ;
- *Vasco de Gamma* (p. 10, p. 111), capitalised or not, the extra "m" transforming the explorer's patronym to that of a nuclear ray augmenting the impact of Painful Pollyanna;
- *cardio-vasco-de-gamma-totale* (p. 111); all the splendour and with the reinforcement of a popular French expression in the English text—bilingual wordplay. "La totale", an old euphemism meaning a uterus ablation, now commonly used to indicate an amplitude of complications—medical or not. Here the legs affected by the cardiovascular + double sprain;
- *Vasco de Drama* (p. 88, p. 118) one who fails to counteract Painful Pollyanna and becomes the antithesis of Vasco de Balmer. Or, for its second appearance at the end of the text, one who becomes meloDrama by announcing the possible denouement;

`like I, is trivial.`[32]

After which the text derails. Accelerated projection of themes and objects seen throughout the text. Tension between the passing of time and the final solution.

va plus

Literally and textually, the conclusion of a long list of dead objects: computer, morning glories, legs, body bits. All is lost.

---

31 *ibid.*, p. 88.
32 *ibid.*, p. 118.

Contextuellement, complément de l'annonce faite par les croupiers aux joueurs de Roulette mais . . . dans le désordre (pour rester dans la métaphore du jeu) :

« Faites vos jeux » : début des mises ;

« Les jeux sont faits » : lancement de la boule ;

« Rien ne va plus » : fin des mises et sortie du numéro gagnant.

Cette inversion est également présente dans un autre jeu de mot bilingue en forme de question posée à la fin du chapitre 10 :

```
³³Or is dehors now before
```

puis, à la fin du chapitre 13—deuxième apparition du chiffre—sans innocence:

```
Dehors before
```

Le proverbe familier « Il ne faut pas mettre la charrue avant les bœufs » cité p. 10, recommande de faire les choses dans leur ordre logique. La première question—néfaste—maintenant annulée par une affirmation —consciente et résolue «*after all*»—du contraire. Par opposition à la première autobiographie restée sans sésame jusqu'à la publication de *In visible Author*, l'auteur/narrateur/sujet nous livre ici la clé de son autobio : les pièces du corps sont éliminées une à une, brulées à petit feu.

```
[...] except for the brain, and humour, so far
```

Dès lors, un certain optimisme—tout cérébral qu'il soit—permet à l'auteur /narrateur/personnage d'entrevoir le plaisir ludique du *word-play-fun* pendant que la roue tourne encore pour les homonymes et inséparables jumeaux Je/jeux de maux/mots. Un qui perd gagne, en quelque sorte.

```
³⁴Meanwhile:
```

---

33 *ibid.*, p. 103.
34 *ibid.*, p. 129.

Contextually, this echoes the announcement made by casino croupiers to players of Roulette but ... in disorder (to maintain the metaphor of gaming):

 place your bets;
 the bets are placed (and the ball is launched);
 all bets are called with the appearance of the winning number.

This inversion is similarly present in a bilingual pun in the form of a question posed at the end of chapter 10:

```
the cart?
```

at the end of chapter 13—second mention of the number—
hardly ingenuous:

```
the cart, after all.
```
[35]

The familar proverb "Don't put the cart before the horse" p. 10, recommends doing things in the logical order. Its first reversal—nefarious—is cancelled by the affirmation—conscious and resolute "after all"—on the contrary. In contrast to the first bifography, remaining without a cipher until the publication of *Invisible Author*, the author/narrator/subject gives the reader here the key to the autobiography: the parts of the body are eliminated one by one, as if burnt away in a slow fire.

```
an uplift out of that scrambled ego [...]
```
[36]

From this point on, a certain optimism—wholly cerebral though it may be—provides the fun and pleasure of wordplay to the author/narrator/character as the wheel still turns for the homonimous and inseparable twins *Je/jeux* [I/games] *maux/mots* [illness/words]. Who loses, wins, in a manner of speaking.

```
Les jeux de maux sont faits.
```

---

35 *ibid.*
36 *ibid.,*

Bibliographie

Brooke-Rose, Christine, *Thru, a novel,* 1975, London, Hamish Hamilton.

Brooke-Rose, Christine, *Stories, theories, and things,* 1991, Cambridge, Cambridge University Press.

Brooke-Rose, Christine, *Remake,* 1996, Manchester, Carcanet Press.

Brooke-Rose, Christine, *Invisible Author: Last Essays,* 2002,

Columbus, The Ohio State University Press.

Brooke-Rose, Christine, *Life, End of,* 2006, Manchester, Carcanet Press.

On Terms

Christine Brooke-Rose

The crescent street he lives in curves like a giant vampire's jaw, each house a long and yellow tooth, with the identical porches forming a second row. And in the last weeks of my life the street has certainly sucked my blood. I can still see and feel myself hiding behind the pillar in the last porch on the left which belongs to the rich old lady's house or after nightfall lurking among the trees of the semi-circular gardens that face the crescented houses. Watching him come and go. On my way to the office and again on my way home I stand behind the pillar of the last house for as long as time in my real life allows, and the rich old lady once or twice comes out and smiles at me in faint recognition of my repeated presence or of her youth perhaps unless women really did have more dignity than as if to say leave off, loneliness has its strength and beauty, like unrequited love. Have you ever stood he says once when we are still on terms for hours in the cold simply to catch a glimpse of someone? We are talking about a friend of his. The man must be sick he says I could never get that worked up. Perhaps you have never loved I say or maybe merely think perhaps he has never loved. Maybe I murmur no, I couldn't either. We are still on terms at that moment in time.

But as I let the street suck my blood while I still have blood to suck we are not on terms and a glimpse is better than no terms at all until I stand all drained of psychic energy from nothing not even a glimpse, glimpses being untimable in a live long day of a full irregular masculine timetable and walk away quickly as if none of it mattered to unnumb my limbs while I still have limbs to unnumb all the way to the small flat in the square block in the big lonely city.

But now there is no need. Nobody knows that my body lies there in my bed in the locked flat in the big city, its atoms all bombarded by those of the barbiturates and slowly undergoing the chemical reaction into compost that will feed no earth no worms no mulching vegetation, only the stinking air in the small room all windows closed. I die alone because I live alone. I give notice at work I have the telephone removed I stop the milk I tell the porter to forward my mail if any to Poste Restante where I call now and again, wearing the semblance of my temporal body, only to find there is no mail except the month's rent reminder and the quarter's demand for rates.

One day no doubt the rent man or the rate man or the gas man must come round and ring the bell and bang the door, and the disturbed molecules of wood will let the smell of my decay waft through and the police perhaps will scatter them with a battering ram or even with the mere brute force of uniformed bodies. I am well aware that I am acting out a fantasy since the porter has a pass-key into the smell of my decay as into all our privacies.

It is because I am acting out a fantasy that I can wear the semblance of my temporal body and move about as if I existed, which of course I do. Anyone with enough love or hate exists even when out of mind or dead. Existence is not a temporal state but an energy which does not stop merely for lack of flesh although in many dead people this energy does degrade itself for lack of love so that it shrinks like a degenerate star into less than a pinpoint weighing many tons. Naturally they feel full of a heavy nothingness of which the rumour spreads apathetically sporadically through live matter like a transuranian element decaying over aeons into lead. And so this is what people in this needle of time think death is.

But I am acting out a fantasy of unrequited love or is it hate that has such driving force I can collect the semblance of my atoms and clothe myself in them and move about at will. I can also move about without the semblance of my atoms. I can do both because both exist in a potential choice which keeps me in a state of dither unable to decide which part of the fantasy I most want to act out: that of being invisibly present at my own death with all my friends aghast and shocked and sad or that of nobody knowing I have died. The is stronger as a desire so strong it makes me take my life, suicide being a meaningless gesture which says I want to leave you today and come back tomorrow to see how you've taken it. The desire to be thus present at my own death is stronger than the desire that nobody should know I have died, but the fear in it is stronger still for I know the answer can only be a slight shock a shrug a sigh of relief. I have no friends and few acquaintances. So I move along two parallel lines of existence trying to have it both ways invisible most of the time and watching my few acquaintances, but also keeping up the pretence of appearing now and again at my usual haunts wearing the semblance of my temporal body so that nobody knows I have died. I fear their indifference more than I want their slight shock their guilt if any or their punishment.

Sooner or later however the choice will have to be made because in time the rent man or the rate man or the gas man will come round and use the pass-key into the smell of my decay.

Unless of course I choose not to act out the fantasy. Then I would find annihilation and some sort of peace perhaps. My energy too would degrade itself for lack of love or hate into less than a pinpoint weighing many tons of heavy nothingness. That would be comforting.

But the driving force of the fantasy is irresistible. I do not really watch my few acquaintances or my no friends who do not hold me here but him and only him. Unlike the rent man or the rate man or the gas man he won't come knocking on my door ringing the bell scattering the molecules of wood with sheer brute force into the smell of my decay. Because we are not on terms.

And the being not on terms is the driving force of the fantasy. It drains me of atoms and even of their semblance so that I still stand in the last porch of the curved street and wait for a glimpse of him as he comes and goes. And the greater watching time afforded by my death spreads like a net which must by mere totality of coverage catch all the glimpses possible in the curved space of the street and more. Even the sights of the rich old lady have increased fivefold and for her smile I wear the semblance of my atoms now and again and hide behind the pillar in the double wisdom tooth at the end of the giant vampire's jaw.

Watching him come and go.

The multiplying glimpses feed me with fresh particles of psychic energy so that although the vampire's jaw drains me of semblant atoms I in turn draw strength from the glimpses it provides with which I feed the hungry monster of my fantasy which grows and grows until I can be with him at all times and places. Without the fantasy I would cease to exist, fantasy being the existence which does not stop merely for lack of mass times the speed of light squared let alone for lack of the polynucleotides and complex proteins needed to activate a temporal body. Without the fantasy I would find some sort of peace perhaps.

He has another woman now reasonably since unable to accept the hurtful terms we were on I broke them a married one, a little less convenient as regards consideration not his strong point of her timetable as well as his but more convenient in her desires that don't extend to marriage. Not that she feels happy as a quick sly convenience. I am in a privileged position divested as I can be of my temporal atoms. He also rings her after the first time with clumsy gestures and finds her sad oh what a bore he says why take it like that not a whistling cavalier to shrug it off and move away as if that was what bothered her on the contrary that would be more welcome for shrug it off and move away is what he does in emotional effect if not in physical presence because complacently he equates physical presence with emotional effect no generosity of imagination or tenderness being required as well and my self-pity envelops her by analogy. He tells her the same things in the same words with the same performance. It's only way I can show you he says post-passionately as the nearest he can get to words of homage and she also doesn't say but thinks show me what, that even in this he is inconsiderate? So my angry self-pity envelops her by analogy but with an element of admiring envy at the way she makes more allowances. She knows and accepts as I in my real body know but do not accept that his emotions are low-powered, he has no reserves below the easy surface, his energy too would degrade itself quickly in death for lack of love into less than a pinpoint weighing innumerable tons of heavy nothingness, he would find peace he does. It is true that she is still in the gay light-hearted early phase I know so well and that in time his thoughtless words and manner will erode her gaiety. In time she must crumble from her light-hearted status as a quick sly convenience and bombard him with the atoms of a chain reaction, at which he will shrug be inarticulate move off exactly as he does when she accepts her status as a sly quick convenience. It makes no difference either way. Unless she is altogether more light-hearted through and through.

The rich old lady emerges out of the last house behind whose pillar I wear from invisibility-fatigue the semblance of my temporal body. She nods and smiles. Loneliness has its strength she says don't feed on him too long or you will lose the capacity for it. If it isn't too late she says will you come and take tea with me on Saturday? It would give me great pleasure to Communicate with a young person. Madam if I am not altogether dead by then I should be delighted. Come come at your age I'll expect you at four.

He comes and goes. He walks along the double row of teeth in the curved jaw of the vampire. I do not reassume the invisibility which tires me out with vision and knowledge so that he sees me in my temporal body and crosses the road into the semi-circular gardens to avoid me reasonably enough or is it cowardly. In any case the force of the fantasy drives me to move my temporal body into his path for further punishment not only from his thoughtless words and manner but from the sudden change in me the moment we are on terms, a change to my early normal vision of an affable sluggish man, a static man nobody ever gets to know any better, who has revealed no hidden dynamism despite the benefit of the doubt given over and over and I look at his thick face and unregarding eyes and think I never would but know I did how could I? It is as if I had never known him, the last impression re-turning to the hello.

—Oh. Hello.

—How are you?

—Oh, all right. Terrible cold, though, don't come near me.

He sees my eroded gaiety and crumbling inconvenience and also thinks how could he but doesn't care whether he did or not.

—I wasn't going to. Nothing could be further from my mind.

—Oh I don't know. He laughs. I wouldn't say nothing. You look well.

Behind his words and manner there is nothing but his words and manner. Love is only the intense desire to know someone and becomes unrequited or is it hate when it finds no one there to know.

—Thank you for enquiring. The semblance of my atoms creates no semblance of communication. Even in death I say all the wrong things like why did you cross the road to avoid me, when I know the answer is my behaviour too embarrassing even for courtesy which never was his strong point.

—Me? I didn't . . . I always walk through the gardens. And things like are you happy? Now that we are on terms I endure fully the sudden change to my normal vision of a pleasant sluggish man with hardly an atom of love in all that flesh and hardly a pinpoint of interest or curiosity except the prying kind into the weaknesses of others that make him feel so good heavens, he says, I never ask myself such questions. What are you doing here?

—Walking suffering. I don't like suffering. It hurts.

—Oh? I'd got the impression you rather enjoyed it.

—So that was your reason. All the wrong things again but they get no reaction.

—Actually I'm on my way home. I went to town to do some shopping. Window-shopping I mean, I didn't find anything. I'm er—getting married.

—What!

—Thank you. Yes. Next week. I suppose, I couldn't prevail on you, if you would, I mean, if you're free, to give me away? As an old friend. I have no family. Saturday 11 o'clock at St. Martin's.

—Well I don't know. Let me see.

The pocket-diary is blank for Saturday at 11 o'clock I know because he sees his quick convenience then and doesn't write it down. Besides in my parallel invisible state I can see Saturday and the wedding-guests all made out of my psychic energy and its almost inexhaustible semblance of atoms. I even see the white carnation in his buttonhole. Thank you, how nice, I gather the idea tickles your fancy.

—Yes, well, it is rather amusing.

—And your wife, of course. I hope she'll come. Sorry it's so informal but I've only just thought of it. Asking you I mean.

—This is all very sudden. How did it, er, who's the lucky man? Are you sure not just rebounding?

—From the great love that was ours? Of course. So you see you owe me at least the gesture. How about you, have you found a new mistress?

—I don't want a mistress. If I did, no doubt I'd fix myself up with one.

—No doubt. Well, see you Saturday then. Collect me in the hall of my block at ten to, I'll have a hired car waiting. And please, no presents, we're going abroad immediately. Bye.

So the die is cast on keeping up the pretence that I am alive, appearing here and there in the semblance of my temporal body especially there on Saturday at 11 o'clock. Not that this way I avoid the answer to the fear inherent in the other course, the slight shock the shrug the sigh of relief if not at my death then at my removal and the resentment at even being asked for a last gesture. The parallel lines meet in the further punishment administered with his every word and manner but the driving force of the fantasy impels me along.

The matter of my rebound my present or future unhappiness and my wedding moves out of his mind as he walks towards his house, naturally since it has no existence except as the fantasy which does not stop for lack of flesh. But then the matter of his new mistress's happiness or otherwise does not dwell in his mind either. He never asks himself such questions. What do you see yourself as, I enquire in exasperation at his lack of enthusiasm for all things once when we are still on terms that drag my gaiety down into his conversational lethargy me, he says I don't see myself as anything I just drift. So that his image too must degrade itself in death for lack of love into less than a pinpoint weighing many tons of heavy nothingness which is what people in this needle of time think death is. And so it will be when I have ceased to act out the fantasy. A comforting thought. But the being not on terms is the driving force which impels me to invent new terms, for of course we are on terms even if only those of agreeing to give me away. The terms we are on feed the hungry monster of my fantasy which absorbs the hurts like immunising poison so that the early normal vision of an affable sluggish man dissolves and the dynamic image of his absence grows.

On the morning of my marriage he emerges from his house in the vampire's jaw alone and walks along the double row of giant teeth. His wife for reasons best known to herself namely that she has caught his germ or that he has dissuaded her declines to attend. His cancellation of the quick sly convenience fills me with joy and triumph at his small preference for a tickled fancy and in my invisibility I follow him. He has so few and such small preferences I can gloat over this one. There will be time enough to the church with the semblance of my no friends and few acquaintances. Nobody knows that my body lies in bed in my locked flat in the square block, rapidly undergoing the chemical reaction into compost that as yet feeds no earth, only the stinking air in the small room all windows closed. At the Poste Restante I collect a cheque for guineas from him.

The area of his street is residential, dead. So dead that a big hearse waits outside the last house in the crescent, heading two dark and empty cars. The boot is up, as if the coffin had just been slid in or a last bouquet or wreath of flowers added to the others and all the flowers are white.

He stops. Not out of superstition or to make a gesture of homage since gestures or words of homage do not come naturally to him if at all but because the white carnations remind him of his empty buttonhole. The area of his street is residential, dead, without a flower shop in sight.

He hesitates. I give him that, yes, I mark that up in his favour. It goes to join all the awkward short-lived tendernesses he uses when still uncertain of seduction, sham but tendernesses still and in his favour, weighing a little against the later hurts if not viewed in their light but in the light of the beginning when I so much want to count all in his favour. He looks at the house with the curtains drawn and the garlanded door half open. The coffin underneath the mass of white flowers waits for the few mourners about to emerge and the murmuring undertaker.

The hesitation is over. His left hand quickly picks a white carnation from the end wreath on the hearse, his right hand joins the left to fix it in his buttonhole as he walks quickly on.

The rich old lady lies inside the coffin and smiles, turning her dead face towards me all surrounded with thin white hair. Death has its strength and I don't mind she says. I have seen life and willingly give a flower of my death to adorn a married man about to give away his young escaped mistress into the hands of death.

I mind, however.

—My dear child, why?

—Because I created the flower for his buttonhole out of my atoms, allowing only for the semblance of a result, not for a real result with a real origin and in you of all people.

—And the origin with a free will gesture in another human being, in two other human beings instead of in your fantasy shocks you?

—Dear child, don't mind so much. Come come at your age I'll see you at four.

The real result with a real origin galvanises me into the semblance of my atoms all in white down the stairs into the hall just as he enters. He looks astonished, white? he says. The porter looks even more astonished at my presence which waves gaily sails through the door and folds itself into the hired car, followed by all those molecules of thick flesh with hardly an atom of love beneath the white carnation.

—I thought it was informal.

—It is. But one only dies once.

—Oh come.

—I'm glad you thought of a buttonhole. And thank you for the cheque. You shouldn't have.

—You look very fetching he says with surprise regret boredom impatience I feel too disembodied to care. It is the first compliment he has ever paid me apart from the privilege of being seduced by him with awkward short-lived sham tendernesses the only way he can show me what?

The church is fuller than I expected. All my no friends and more than my few acquaintances are there made out of more than my psychic energy on both sides of the aisle. I do not know the wedding-guests on the bridegroom's side. I know the bridegroom a little, the skilful tendernesses he uses for seduction still weighing against the brutal annihilation to come when he destroys the fantasy and its energy degenerates for lack of love into less than a pinpoint of heavy nothingness. I walk the aisle on my once lover's arm to Parcell's Trumpet Voluntary. I promise to obey. I have no choice. Because one day the rent man or the rate man or the gas man will come round and ring the bell or bang the door and the disturbed molecules of wood will let the smell of my decay waft through. But I shall not be present at my own death my friends aghast and shocked and sad for the answer is a shrug a sigh of relief at my removal and my non-existence with the energy of my fantasy degenerated to one pinpoint of heavy nothingness. That will be comforting but you must kiss the bride yes kiss the bride.

I don't know who the best man is who kisses me. A friend of the bridegroom his façade perhaps, the skilful tendernesses he uses for seduction until the fantasy becomes destroyed. You too must kiss the bride.

He hesitates. I give him that, yes, I mark that up in his favour he has given me away made his last gesture paid his five guineas that is enough. I turn my face towards him in its veil of tulle and see him start with horror.

So the process has begun already. The fantasy loses its driving force and cannot hold the semblance of my atoms in a pretence of life. What does he see? The dead face of the rich old lady he robbed whose white carnation he stole to adorn the tickled fancy of a married man giving away his young escaped mistress into the hands of death? Or is it my dead face he sees, its atoms all bombarded by those of the barbiturates, rapidly undergoing the chemical change to compost that as yet feeds no earth no worms no mulching vegetation, only the stinking air in the small room all windows closed?

He draws away. The semblances of the chief wedding guests who are witnesses in the vestry laugh and tease him as we drink champagne a little out of place for there is no reception. I have arranged it so. No you can't get out of it you gave her away you must propose the toast you too must kiss the bride. I turn my face towards him in its veil of tulle and see him stare in horror. I search for my reflection in his eyes, each one of which throws back a dead face, in the left eye very old with thin white hair and a deep regarding look, in the right eye young but crumbling with eroded gaiety, skeletal, the mouth curved like a vampire's jaw and the skull surrounded in white tulle he yells.

—All right, keep your precious carnation!

He flings it in my decomposing face. A grey aisle of silence forms through the wedding guests as he bolts along it to the vestry door into the church where the remaining guests wait for the triumphal march and down the aisle of the church into the world of nice casual emotions and familiar residential streets that stand secure in parallels except for one that curves like the jaw of a giant vampire with a double row of teeth which in my day has sucked my blood.

In a month of time no doubt the gas man or the rent man will ring the bell bang on my door and smell the smell of my decay as it wafts through the disturbed molecules of wood. Or the police perhaps will scatter them with a battering ram even with the brute force of uniformed bodies unless the porter uses his pass-key into the privacy of my death.

The fantasy has lost its driving force and cannot hold the semblance of my atoms in a pretence of life. My no friends and my few acquaintances dissolve, the bridegroom takes the energy of my pretence and in less than no time degrades it for lack of love into less than an anti-atom of heavy nothingness. I have a teatime date with the rich old lady at four. The process of degeneration is painful but comforting as far as I remember I have a teatime date with understanding as far as I can tell the process is painful but comforting as far as I

Brooke-Rose, Lastness

Adam Guy

*I*nvisible Author: Last Essays was published in 2002, *Life, End of* in 2006; Brooke-Rose lived until 2012, which makes both of these texts chronologically late but not last, lacking the finality of an unfinished MS, or a work completed with the dying breath. But lateness as a concept is too preliminary, too early for these two texts—lateness is the permeable boundary of a late style, the deferred end-point of late capitalism. With these works, Brooke-Rose is in the habit of lastness, not lateness, of finitude, of the end. Works inscribed as *last*, a career finished, rounded-off as a career. *Career, End of?*

******

What of Brooke-Rose's career? One characteristic that defined it, and that eventually needed to be underscored by self-explanation, was her use of constraints. Brooke-Rose lacked the readers who saw that *Between* lacked the verb "to be". The future-tense *Amalgamemnon* faired worse perhaps, to the extent that—as detailed in *Invisible Author*—it took Jean Jacques Lecercle's analysis for Brooke-Rose to "[realise] what I had done" (p. 48). Eventually, she had to create aware readers, let them proceed from the information she revealed (*Life, End of:* "But then he might miss a piece of Fast Author Info (I call it FAI)" (p. 68). But the hidden nature of these constraints in Brooke-Rose's work remains part of their character. Brooke-Rose's constraints are about lack, but about a tiny lack, a lack to creatively hinder composition, and to emerge as small hidden holes in a fabric that a reader, a culture, might think is whole, strange but unbroken.

******

Brooke-Rose's master constraint, however, troubles the Oulipian lipograms she formulated book-by-book. From *Invisible Author* (and kept, of course, until last):

> I have kept my main constraint or lipogram[1] (no past
> tense narrative mode) to the end because it is not a con-
> straint affecting just one novel, like the *to be* lipogram
> or others discussed earlier, but a narrative technique
> that permeates nearly all my novels since I started ex-
> perimenting (from *Out* onwards). (p. 130)

This constraint generates a narrative voice that "uses the present tense
of the speech system and its deictics, but with all the impersonal speakerless tone of the past-tense". Here the author "put[s] down objectively
all that hits his central consciousness; in detail—too much detail". The
key paradox for Brooke-Rose is the idea of a narrative that "never
evokes an act of seeing or a consciousness, that is, there is no seer, only
the seen [...]" (*Inivisble Author*, pp. 137—8).

The same is theorised in *Life, End of*:

> [...] what is needed is the present tense, but without the
> first person. Dropping subjectivity but retaining imme-
> diacy and distance. Difficult. But it produces the rare
> impersonal present tense of our literary criticism,
> among others, and ultimately derives from science.
> (p. 67)

This paradoxical speakerless present tense is drawn out of, or formu-
lated as a revelation of reading Robbe-Grillet. So we see it in Brooke-
Rose's 1967 translation of *Dans le labyrinthe* (the quotation is Brooke-
Rose's own, selected in *Invisible Author*, p. 138), and *Out* (1964):

> To the right, a simple shape, more blurred, already
> covered by several days' deposit, is nevertheless still
> discernible; at a certain angle it acquires sufficient clar-
> ity for its outline to be followed without too much diffi-
> culty. It is a kind of cross: an elongated main shape, like

---

1 "A lipogram (from Greek *leipein*, remove, + *gramma*, letter) is a self-imposed omission, and presumably the term can be extended to cover more than a letter, since *gramma* also means 'writing.'"
(*Invisible Author*, p. 2)

> a table knife but wider. (*In the Labyrinth*, p. 10)

> In summer, from ground-level, nearer to the fig-tree,
> the arch formed by the leaning trunk and the down-
> sweeping branch frames a whole landscape of descend-
> ing olive-groves beyond the road, which itself disap-
> pears behind the bank. In summer the grey framework
> of trunk and branch is further framed by a mass of deep
> green foliage. (*Out*, p. 22)

**

In the pile-up of articles, definite and indefinite, that opens both Brooke-Rose's first and last novels as an experimental writer (and the latter her last as a writer, end of), we see the same paradoxical speaker-less present tense in operation: the ownerless flies, denim, knees, heads, mirrors, acts of brushing and washing are things in themselves, cast aside from the grammatical/perspectival ownership of another narrative mode:

> A fly straddles another fly on the faded denim stretched
> over the knee. Sooner or later, the knee will have to
> make a move, but now it is immobilised by the two flies,
> the lower of which is so still that it seems dead.
> (*Out* (p. 11))

> The head top leans against the bathroom mirror so that
> the looking glass becomes a feeling glass. But what does
> it feel? This position is for body-balance during the
> brushing of teeth and the washing of face neck arms and
> torso. (*Life, End of* (p. 7))

But to see a whole career's chosen narrative mode as a constraint troubles the notion of constraint itself. If it is a constraint, it joins up with the rest of The Novel, pronounces on narration as a whole, seeing narration itself as constraint. Constraint universalised, no longer a blazon of avant-gardes and experimental niches, but the signature of the mainstream, or more, the whole of the history of the novel. (Or the reverse, and the whole history of The Novel as a totality of forms always already at the avant-garde, always already experimenting from a margin.)

**

For the paradoxical speakerless present tense, such potential for transfiguration is a strain. The strains show from other directions too, not least in the space of *Life, End of*'s lastness, the light this lastness sheds back on a whole career, a career it is finishing. From the opening of the last chapter of the novel, a hint:

> Globalisation. Ah, the globe. Or is it the lobe of the universe? The lob of a tennis star?
>
> Neuronic games, games to exercise the neurons, see a guide to the type of questions least known by candidates: literary, historical, geography except for capitals, philosophy or rather philosophical names at that level, scientific names, economic and political names, in other words everything once considered as general culture. (p. 116)

A career of wordplay, of breaking words down and building them up, of etymologies and bricolages of the multitudes of names contained in this "general culture" (*Between*: "Oh, you know, literature, irrigation, the under-developed areas and all that." (p. 429)), now located, finished off, as simply "games to exercise the neurons". Whether such games are Brooke-Rose's or those of reader's, that's the last word.

**

Locatedness is the last word for so much in *Life, End of*. It is the fate of the paradoxical speakerless present tense too. Its present tense ("what is needed is the present tense") is under an ethical strain, the strain of the subject matter of *Life, End of*, which is old age:

> The doctor knows all the six ailments but can't do much

> to make them go away, as doctors can and do when pa-
> tients are younger: cure versus maintenance. Mainten-
> ance for what?

> The vicious circles are endless. (p. 11)

The present tense, the tense of Husserlian retention, of now (in French: *maintenant*), is the tense of *maintenance*.

And here we see the effort of keeping it up, and its questionable impetus, although, ultimately, perhaps, its imperative:

> Putting it off, off. Living on a razor's edge, enjoying
> what, well, yes, the brain and its indulgences its con-
> tacts with the earth the planet the world the universe
> but refusing the oncoming time, the future wheelchair,
> and home-helps for every function extramental. (p. 46)

And then, going back to doctors:

> The doctor as usual does not explain, nor the physio,
> beyond localising it once again in the nerve fibres.
> (p. 45)

Scientific description, the doctor's description, which "does not explain", is what the paradoxical speakerless present tense does, too. Again, this can be reconciled to what Brooke-Rose takes from Robbe-Grillet: "he uses the present tense as a 'scientific' present tense (as in a scientific law, or indeed as in our own critical language" (*Invisible Author*, p. 138). And, more broadly, the contents of a scientific description, not the form, also have a Robbe-Grilletian end, the rejection of "myths of depth", of the concept of a novel where, quoting Roland Barthes on Robbe-Grillet, "The object is no longer a centre of correspondence, a welter of sensations and symbols: it is merely an optical resistance" ('Objective Literature' p. 14). But in *Life, End of*, what is at stake in this mere description is not—as with Robbe-Grillet and Barthes—the history of the novel, an experimental turn, a revolution in fiction, but a life at its end, here frustrated in its not knowing.

A double-movement: again, ultimately, the paradoxical speakerless present tense is unavoidable, because in Brooke-Rose's character, collapsing into author ("it's a she, eighty years old, infirm, an ex-language teacher and literary theorist, or even a passionate amateur" (pp. 68-9)), it finds its rationale, its justification, its location, its ground, its end:

> The old have to think so hard and continuously of every physical detail, physical movement, it's not surprising they develop a senile self-centredness.
>
> How to separate the physical from the moral, philosophical, psychological? The dancer from the dance? The author from his story? What is central and what peripheral? (p. 62)

**

In *Life, End of*, the narration that describes a healthier stage of life—or at least "at the start of the infirmities, before the bringing down of the office and the giving away of the sofa and table; when walking, cooking, receiving are still alive, more or less" (p. 79)—looks different. Chapter 9 narrates a True Friendship, still in the present tense, but with the fixed viewpoint of an external narrator incanting "she says" to mark dialogue, offering up descriptions and explanations, easy similes, and so on:

> They meet on the winding stair of an old Paris house in the Cinquième, where each is the new owner of a very odd-shaped flat, each owner come to take stock after a long-loan purchase. One on the first floor, hers, the other on the second and last before the attic flats on the third. Their two flats are both shaped like prows, getting narrower and narrower after a fairly wide entrance made of small hall, small bathroom and kitchen on the left overlooking the court-yard with its two other entrance stairs, and a largish bedroom to the right, overlooking a narrow sidestreet. (p. 80)

Here is Chapter 9 dissolving, close to the end:

> Who speaks? The Author? The Character?
>
> Not the Author, who has had to withdraw for a while and let the Character take over. For this is a reconstruction, clearly, of a discussion that in fact continues in bits over forty-eight hours, split, interrupted, digressed, upped and downed. And of a time that's over, with walking, cooking, receiving, still the norm.
> (pp. 86-7)

This quotation leads from a favourite tag of Brooke-Rose's—from Barthes—which is a leitmotif of *Thru* (1975), and begins accordingly in the mode of the narratologist, unpicking the fallacy of neat, continuous, fixed-viewpoint narration. But the dominant rhythm of *Life, End of* prevails, and the narration shifts back to the grounding, the location of these narratological experiments and their incumbent speculations: the situation of the "it's a she, eighty years old, infirm [etc.]".

**

And even the notion of the ground is located, grounded in *Life, End of*. At the start of the novel it is a cipher of a Cartesian split (Descartes an important presence in the novel):

> The floor the ground the earth are for walking on feet, the world the universe for walking in the head. A walking illness keeps the universe for the head but leads, for the feet, only the floor. How long will the head last?
> (p. 10)

But by the very end of the novel, the last page:

> Snorthing new technes are galloping by.
>
> There's a difficult way to go now, towards an uncluttered mind. Still countered by the floored, the grounded, the earthly, the planetary, the galactic, the

universal. (p. 119)

A leitmotif re-emerges, for the last time, on this last page, too: "Dehors before de cart, after all." Locatedness, groundedness, is what's left, what's last in *Life, End of*, with Brooke-Rose's constraint(s) as with everything else.

**

The end of *Life, End of*, speaks of minimality:

> [...] the three most precious gifts have become deprivations, soon to be reached: reading, writing, and independence.
>
> However, and for the moment, these are minimal pleasures, still just available. Their minimality is itself a pleasure, the way rarity is, but unlike rarity it does become more and more minimal as time slouches forward. (p. 113)

By positioning her constraint here, locating it in a life of increasing minimality, Brooke-Rose casts her whole experimental-novelistic career—which is the career too of the paradoxical speakerless present tense—in a different light, grants it a teleology. The speakerless present tense speaks personhood at barely something, almost nothing, as we find that it did with the sickness of *Out*, the experience of death in *Such*, the alienation from language of *Between*, the feelings of obsolescence in *Amalgammemnon*.

**

To a degree, then, this essay is about totality and teleology. UnBrooke-RoseLike things, or so we're told: Brooke-Rose the writer of endlessly *scriptible* texts, of deconstruction *avant la lettre*—stories even Brooke-Rose told about herself:

> It was extraordinarily comforting in the early seventies
> to read as theory all that I already had been groping for
> in *Out* [...]. (*Invisible Author*, p. 58)

Against this background, how to frame lastness? There is something to be said about O. P. (Other People) here, about Levinas maybe, and about how a deconstructive model doesn't necessarily preclude lastness, though any flirtations with totalities and teleologies will be harder won.

**

> We are merely marking time and time is nothing, nothing. A moment of agony, of burning flesh, an aspect of the human element disintegrating to ash, and you are dead. But that's another story. (*Out*, p. 198)

WORKS CITED

Barthes, Roland. 'Objective Literature' in *Critical Essays* (Evanston: Northwestern University Press, 1972) translated by Richard Howard, pp. 13–24

Brooke Rose, Christine. *Out* in *The Christine Brooke-Rose Omnibus: Four Novels—Out, Such, Between, Thru* (Manchester: Carcanet, 2006), pp. 8–198

—*Between* in *The Christine Brooke-Rose Omnibus*, pp. 391–575

—*Invisible Author: Last Essays* (Columbus: Ohio State University Press, 2002)

—*Life, End of* (Manchester: Carcanet, 2006)

Robbe-Grillet, Alain. *In the Labyrinth* (London: Calder & Boyars, 1967) translated by Christine Brooke-Rose

Manna in Mid-Wilderness

Natalie Ferris

As dusk falls, the strip lighting intensifies. In the outskirts of Paris voices bounce off the walls like balls, indiscernible echoes carrying on the chill air. The buildings are all sharp corners, pre-fab frameworks and endless corridors, stricken with graffiti. Names and tags mix and merge across the concrete and brickwork to form a constellation of letters and symbols, 'Sonibel', 'J'amaaaa', '5000', 'Texas': 'Alpha and Omega'. Paint bleeds, vowel on vowel. Paris VIII, though a little beleaguered, is still attuned to one of its own, an experimental writer-wringing strings of interrelated code, analogues of meaning, 'items,' which cross and mesh to build her own 'vast powerhouse of knowledge'[1]

Christine Brooke-Rose was to spend twenty years of her life here. From 1968 to 1988, at the beginning of each academic year, her name was inked into the tabulated 'Liste Alphabetique de Personnel Enseignant, Administratif de Service et Technique' of Université de Paris VIII, Vincennes.[2] Reading like a roll-call of some of the most illustrious names in the history of French post-war philo-

BRIAND Jean-Pierre	17.04.1942
BRICHET	14.0?.1942
BRIDE Anne	10-5-43
BRIOT	10.11.1946
BROLBERG	29-10-43
BROOKEROSE Christine	
BRUHAT Jean	24-8-05
brunet Jacqueline	5-9-30
BRUNET	2?.5.1950
BRYDGES Josiane	5.4.1949

<hr>

1 Christine Brooke-Rose. *Remake*, (Manchester: Carcanet, 1996), p.106

2 FIG. 1: 'Liste Alphabetique de Personnel Enseignant, Administratif de Service et Technique', Administrative Archive, Fonds Specialisés of the Université de Paris VIII, Vincennes. With thanks to Emmanuelle Sruh, keeper at Fonds Specialisés, Université de Paris VIII, Vincennes.

sophy and politics, her name shares squares with Hélène Cixous, Jean-François Lyotard, Michel Foucault and Jacques Derrida. Strangely, her date of birth is often omitted in these tables, a solitary blank space issuing from her name: 'From one disembodied voice to another'[3].

Following the breakdown of her marriage in the late sixties to her husband of over twenty years, the Polish poet Jerzy Peterkiewicz, and unable to obtain an academic post in London, novelist and literary critic Brooke-Rose was offered 'a manna from Heaven' in the form of a position as lecturer in English and American literature, at the invitation of French feminist, radical reformist and poet, Hélène Cixous:

> I didn't choose to come to Paris, well I chose in a sense, but I responded to an offer of a job in this new university which had been created as a result of '68. This happened in the middle of my marriage crisis and it seemed like a manna from Heaven, so off I went.[4]

The post was to be at the newly created 'experimental' institution, founded by Cixous herself and a number of her colleagues at the Institut d'anglais, most notably Bernard Cassen and Pierre Dommergues. The Paris riots in '68 had prompted, among other measures, the reappraisal and overhaul of higher education by Charles de Gaulle's new government in France. The creation of this *Centre universitaire experimental* in Vincennes heralded a more interdisciplinary, informal and interactive approach to study, as observed across the Atlantic, in an effort to dispel further student insurrection.

The institution was not without its 'experimental teething troubles'[5], however, as one notes in Brooke-Rose's correspondence of the time,[6]

---

3   Christine Brooke-Rose, *Thru*, (London: Hamish Hamilton, 1975), p.59

4   Christine Brooke-Rose, Interview with Ian Hamilton. 'Programme 16: The Yorkshire Ripper, Melvyn Bragg, Christine Brooke-Rose.'*Bookmark*. BBC2, London 7 May (Filmed in 1986).

5   Oliver Pritchett, 'Authoress Shares £1000 Prize', *The Guardian*, (4th March 1969).

6   See Joseph Darlington's excellent paper 'Christine Brooke-Rose and May '68' presented at the Contemporary Experimental Women's Writing Conference, Manchester University 2013. Letter from Eva Hesse to Christine Brooke-Rose, 5th February 1969; Letter from Mary de Rachewiltz to Christine Brooke-Rose, 19th May 1972. All correspondence lodged at special collections, Harry Ransom Center, University of Texas.

complaining of remiss salary payments, constant student disruption and how 'Vincennes is one long ill-constructed narrative of explosive incidents, each replacing the former.'[7] In the very earliest days, the inception of the university itself was hotly contended and its coordination wildly unstable; indeed, it may even have been 'illegal' in the acquisition of the land upon which it stood having been something of a bureaucratic coup by the new Minister of Education, M. Edgar Faure. However, as its success was to be a success for the government of Charles de Gaulle, it became a site of bitter contestation 'by the student forces of the extreme left and of anarchism.'[8] One particularly alarmist mention in the British press of the continuation of seminars amid 'Civil War' features a fanciful tableau of a defiant Christine Brooke-Rose with the novelist John Wain, conducting a contemporary poetry class amidst the pamphleteering and glass-strewn gardens.[9]

Brooke-Rose had first encountered Cixous via an exchange of letters.

---

7   Letter from Brooke-Rose to Jacqueline Gueron, 4th December 1975

8   W.E. Hall, 'A University of Freedom—and its time of Trial' *The Birmingham Post*, 15th March, 1969.

9   Peggy Ducros, 'Elections Held Amid Civil War' *Times Educational Supplement*. 4th July, 1969.

Earlier in 1968, the French writer and theorist had been charged by *Le Monde* to write a review of Brooke-Rose's novel of cross-wired languages and simultaneous interpretation, *Between*.[10]

The French critic and cartoonist Clo'e Floirat joined me on a late afternoon visit to the vibrant home of Vincennes most emblematic figure, Cixous, close to the entrance of the Paris Catacombs. Richly coloured fabrics settled across every surface, books teetering on aching shelves, her cat weaved its way between us. We discussed Cixous' early relationship with Brooke-Rose, about which she was succinct: 'I knew she was going through a difficult time in her life, so I offered her a position'. Brooke-Rose, however, was never part of Cixous' guiding project at Vincennes, the establishment of her Centre d'Études Féminines, officially founded in 1974. As Cixous made plain, 'Christine did not come for women . . . I was trying in every way possible to open ways for women, and she didn't want to take part in that.'

Brooke-Rose intimated many years later that she simply did not engage to any real extent with Cixous' own brand of feminist discourse in the late sixties and seventies, only retrospectively realising in the eighties the difficulties she had faced as a 'woman writer', and a 'woman *experimental* writer' at that. They 'drifted apart' as a result of these 'different investments'; Brooke-Rose's in the 'semantic and rhetorical aspect of things' whereas Cixous' allegiance was also driven by the 'human aspect of things.' For Cixous, an engagement with what was 'experimental' . . . Robbe Grillet for example,' was not enough.[11]

Vincennes, however, offered Brooke-Rose the intellectual challenge that she had been craving in London, placing her in close contact with colleagues such as philosophers Jean Francois-Lyotard, Michel Foucault and post-structuralist theorist Jacques Derrida, and introducing her to the pioneering work of the group surrounding the avant-garde French journal *Tel Quel*—including Julia Kristeva, Phillipe Sollers and Tzvetan Todorov. She later reflected:

It was painful at first, it stretched my mental horizons

---

10 Hélène Cixous, 'Le Langage du dépaysement', *Le Monde*, 28th December 1968, vii.
11 Natalie Ferris, Interview conducted with Hélène Cixous, 7th March 2012, Paris.

like elastic. Sometimes I felt I couldn't absorb all of this, but it was very, very good for me. Sometimes when I listened to things on the BBC, I really felt they were thirty years behind when talking about cultural things.[12]

It was from this point that she began to evolve into what Kermode lauded as the only serious practitioner of narrative on the British side of the channel. Indeed, in a small BBC feature on Brooke-Rose in 1986, presenter Ian Hamilton was to remark: 'It should be no surprise that this neglected British novelist lives in France'[13], as if her novels were only possible in the flowering of post-war avant-garde creativity of the opposing banks. In the same programme, novelist and acquaintance A. S. Byatt was to offer her explanation of Brooke-Rose's shift in allegiance:

> She did it because of what was going on in France, because people were thinking in universities very hard and theoretically about the nature of narrative, about the nature of expectations, about the nature of story. All of these things had suddenly become, to academics and critical thinkers, a huge problem. There was in this country, then, writers like B. S. Johnson who said that telling stories was telling lies, and actually believed that there was something wrong and wicked with the conventional story. I think Christine Brooke-Rose felt a kind of intellectual distaste for that kind of narrative realism' (A. S. Byatt)[14]

It was the possibility of encounter, and every possibility of encounter, in the 'conventional story' that enlivened Brooke-Rose's imagination. Plunged into literary discourse at one of its headiest moments, Brooke-Rose was to be at the theoretical forefront of the 'nature of narrative'. She was an ardent philologist, tri-lingual from childhood she would roll

---

12 Brooke-Rose, Christine. Interview with Ian Hamilton. 'Programme 16: The Yorkshire Ripper, Melvyn Bragg, Christine Brooke-Rose.' *Bookmark*. BBC2, London 7 May. (Filmed in 1986).
13 *ibid.*
14 *ibid.*

language around the mouth with the appetite of a lexivore; from her negotiations of Middle English alliteration in *Piers Plowman*, the 'agglutinative' quality of Ezra Pound's *Cantos*, to the Cyrillic alphabet in her novel, *Between* (1968). She wanted 'to see how far one could go with language, what could language do. I became fascinated with different kinds of discourse, and I like to juxtapose them and create a kind of explosion out of that.'[15]

And she was already familiar with the 'explosion' taking place in French literary discourse, prior to her arrival in Paris. It was her own serious illness in the early sixties that was to mark a profound shift away from her first comedy-of-manners novels, and from the inescapable literary orthodoxy of post-war Britain. During her long convalescence following a kidney operation, she claimed to have attained a different level of consciousness—'a sense of being in touch with something else'—and the solitary hours confined to her bed produced the highly wrought novel *Out* (1964), inspired by the French *nouveau roman* writer and master film-maker Alain Robbe-Grillet (whose *In the Labyrinth* Brooke-Rose later translated—a 'faultless' translation which was to win an Arts Council Prize). Using the present tense to evoke the consciousness of its elderly protagonist, *Out* enacts a world 'out-of-time' and 'out-of-place' of inverted prejudice, where the 'colourless' victims of a mysterious radiation sickness, are the objects of discrimination. By far her most solemn novel, there is a pervasive flatness in tone delivered by the eavesdropped utterances, ending with a sentence reminiscent of Samuel Beckett, one of her greatest acknowledged influences: 'We are merely marking time and time is nothing, nothing . . . But that's another story.'

As literary critic Frank Kermode, perhaps her greatest champion, scoffed in the *Times Literary Supplement* in 1963: 'Not for the English, the sophisticated epistemology of the new French writers'. Brooke-Rose, however, took great liberties in pushing the perceived contract between both the reader and herself as author: 'People want the familiar, they want to be *securisé* as the French say, they want to be made secure,

---

15 *ibid.*

they want to be made to recognise everything—it's the pleasure of re-cognition instead of the pleasure of discovery. I prefer the pleasure of discovery.'[16]

Brooke-Rose was the first to write mainstream press articles in English on the *nouveau roman* movement in Britain, yet this was met with a level of suspicion, quipping years later that the *Times Literary Supplement* cri-tiqued the 'Parisian' flimflam and 'Frenchly chic' of her author photo-

16 *ibid.*

graph, *YSL* scarf *et al,*[17] rather than the narratological ambition of her novel, *Such.*

Brooke-Rose lived in the same apartment in the Latin Quarter just off the *rue St. Victor* throughout most of her twenty-year tenure, having lived a little further out on the *rue de Picpus* when she first arrived in Paris. It is this window in St. Victor, with its brittle frames and shifting veil curtains, from which she looks out at the beginning of the BBC *Bookmark* programme, the only existing footage of Brooke-Rose in Paris. Passing beneath her apartment window now, in a quarter much changed since the seventies, I can almost hear the crackling voice coming over the wireless . . .

> 'Several hundred thousand young people from all over France have been taking part in another mass demonstration in Paris in protest against government plans to reform the system of higher education.
>
> Reports describe the atmosphere as cheerful, with balloons being released into the air and a jazz band playing. . .'[18]

---

17 Christine Brooke-Rose. 'Self Confrontation and the Writer.' *New Literary History*. Vol. 9, no.1. Baltimore, The John Hopkins University Press. (Autumn 1977): pp. 129-36; p. 131; original review Michael Mason, 'Textual Tensions', *Times Literary Supplement* (1975).

18 Ian Hamilton. Interview with Christine Brooke-Rose. 'Programme 16: The Yorkshire Ripper, Melvyn Bragg, Christine Brooke-Rose.', *Bookmark*. BBC2, London 7 May. (Filmed in 1986).

Prayer for the BURIED

Nathan Gaddis

Let us praye ....;

Here'ing the sacred space of WORD we herewith invoke the holy name :: Christine Brooke-Rose—she who has taught us the Prayer for Being, that we too, in the name of those who have been BURIED, heaped upon with injustice, may live in the WORD.

2.   In the WORD we know as a world of Letterature, may we have our Being ....Christine Brooke-Rose, she who has taught us our need which is a reading :; That we may read we must praye ;; that we may read we must seek ;; that we may read we must unEARTH. unEarth'ing we seek and we shall find and in our finding – Light!!

3.   Even here, in this sacred space of WORD, under the Earth out of which we haul the sin'd against, those righteous Wielders of WORD, we in our turn wield our Spades in Resurrection and in Light .... bringing those who have been BURIED back to Being, unBURY'd!

4.   Christine Brooke-Rose, our Patron Saint, Saint of the BURIED Book, who has taught us to praye the Prayer for Being, you shall be remmember'd, recall'd, resuscitated, brought back to life in a Resurrection, standing= again ;; in a word, your WORDS will be justified.

This we praye.

5.   In a world of illusion, when a book may not be a Book, we look to your illusions -in-letters for Light.

6.   In a world litter'd with what is proclaim'd as "literature" (nought but Dreck), we take deLIGHT at your pen ;;

leading us along the way to Re-mem=brance, to a dance of characters, ghostly shapes whose very BREATH and BREATHING we are [a BREATH-ER for which we praye ....;

7.   In the name of Prinz Joseph, blessings be up-on him!!

8.   Humbug we say to the road that is easy ;; our burden, though, is it heavy? Light? No!

9.   Our burden, your burden, the mounds of Earth which would cover you over, un-BURY'ing you spadeful upon spadeful—that burden *is* Light! our task is ....(that's *heavy*, man!) The task may overtake

us, but in your sacred Spade we do believe.

10.   By your very Spade we con-fess our Belief therein ;; and to your Spade we dedicate these our very Spades.

11.   CHRISTine, supplicants we all, suffer us but to brooke this your tomb with ROSE, to be a ROSE, and to RISE!

12.   There are those who have gone before you and those who accompany you and those who will follow you into what would be a sarcophagus of forgotten-ness, but be comforted as you gaze upon your armies of Spade=Wielders.

Let us praye ....; Let us re-member ....;

{here begins a litany of names :: *nota bene* ; refreshments are available in the narthex}

13.   Arno Schmidt, Patron of Schmidt=heads ;; heath=en Light of all solipsists and Roh=Mann=Ticks—BURIED, but *ausgegraben* by Sir Woods ; we unEARTH.

14.   Marguerite Young, mother of Miss MacIntosh, a darling whom we shall unEARTH with vengeance ;; no quantities of *Dreck* and filth shall remain when we wield our holy Spades

in righteous indignation!!! Miss Young, Our Darling, breathe!!!!

15.   Leon Forrest ;; already the tongues of angELs are polishing what may once have been a BURIAL=shroud but is now a golden glow of newly minted skin written on with Letters once unjustly (but merely!) en-chained—; no chains can hold you now.

16.   Rosalyn Drexler, Lady Box-

er, cosmopolitan girl, beautiful stranger, authoRest In Peace ; BUT no more! ;; we READ your books, even unto the day.

17. Edward Dahlberg—can't keep you down ;; none worship'd by a nearly BURIED unEARTHer such as Sir Gilbert shall remain long in abeyance —"a writer whose work cannot be tamed or reduced or assimilated" ;; we believe him, and un=assimilated and ent=tomb'd we are unEARTH'ing you!!

18. Can These Bones Live? Amen.

19. We RE=collect and RE=gather the name of Albert Vigoleis Thelen ;; through the courageous work of TRANS=Laters (better late than not at all!) his name shall be translated from dust into flesh.

20. And who are Ronald Firbank and W.M. Spackman that we do not speak their names? Not yet, but we shall. unEARTH'd!!

21. Nikto is no one ;; the Soviets would have it that way ;; shall we?

22. Cora Sandel is not read today ;; Norwegian and feminist :: is that what it takes for BURIAL?

23. Steve Katz and Ronald Sukenick, brothers BURIED ;; but shall rise on that great day when READers again READ with the Spade, and righteous judgement descends upon us.

24. Already we feel a black bile of anger rising against the wrongs perpetrated by Those Who Would Know Best—but we know better and our fingers shall tear through the sod and we shall dine, exHUM'ing and conSUM'ing ;; a feast upon the DEAD which transubstantiates a putrid flesh into living spirit upon living BONES. This is thirsty work ;; this is Holy Work.

25. "Québécoise writer (*en français*) of metafictional feminist experimental postmodern texts"—we know her name today because we are robbing the graves.

26. We know her name and we speak it today :: Nicole Brossard.

27. And the reasons cited for her interment (unjust!!!) are the same we give when we wield our Spades. Anonymous—no more!

28. Coleman Dowell shall not be ghetto-ized ;; he cannot be ghetto-ized :: he shall live free.

29.   We shall read, for we are his Island People—; too much flesh? Jabez!!!

30.   Nicholas Mosley, *ausgraben*!!

31.   Reyoung ;; time to begin the unbabbling ;; these book =haters shall not end us.

32.   Gil Orlovitz, DEAD and stuff'd into a milkbottle casket ;; but ice=never=f preserves you as we disinter you.

33.   Spades!

Let us praye ....;

34.   In the name of Christine Brooke-Rose, patron saint of READers, we invoke the resurrected body of Finnegan ;; you, our sacred BURIED, are all Finnegans. Wake!!!

35.   William Eastlake, howbeit? We find you unrighteously covered over with EARTH. Rise!

36.   We tell the story of the great white whale which would have been BURIED—under=water—and WAS! for so many years but whose Resurrection and whose Light (the whiteness! the whiteness!) gives hope unto all those (us! us!) whose hearts lie deep within the EARTH=bound, enchain'd, forgotten, and un-READ.

37.   And with the white whale we too recognize The Recognitions ;; against great odds, against an army of professional grave=diggers (the BURYing kind! The *Dreck*=Wielders!) the mightier-than-the-sword, that is, the SPADE=Wielders and those who UN=bury, will resist with mere READing, real READ'ing ;; and today almost rightly recognized.

38.   Maurice Roche, LETTER=kin of ROSE ; is he BURIED because he's French? because he's un-read-a-Babel? His is the skull ::

39.   peace/pax/Friede/paix/paz/МИР/سلام/שלום/शान्ति/ 平和/ሰላም/صلح/ειρήνη/síochána/和平/Heddwch/Baké/☮ ::

40.   it speaks to us, *momento mori*. Yes, dead ;; but KNOT!!!!

41.   And here would have lain D. Keith Mano whose work may have been taken from us ;; but for our reading by the Light of the Spade.

42. And French too—; too French?; how?;—Philippe Sollers ;; who reads Sollers today? ;; Women finding a strange solitude in the park. *tolle, lege.*

43. Julián Ríos ;; writing pounds and writing JOYs you'd think he did it to himself ;; but why is that?

44. No, we shall have our Ríos=emonium and we shall have a long midsummer night's Babel. More babel more bibel less libel. Spades high! Hammers high! POUND!!!!

45. R.A.Y.M.O.N.D. F.E.D.E.R.M.A.N survived in a closet but his parents and two sisters did not (.....*mori*). Those who took them BURN'd books ;; today his books are BURIED.

46. Raymond Federman, the LETTERal sibling of our Patron Saint, Christine Brooke-Rose, most hallow'd shall His name together with Hers be uttered by all members of The Sacred Order of the Wielders of the Spade.

Let us remember .....;

47. The Houses which house the corpses of those who were to be dead; those houses which are Life Breathing Houses from which the Breath of Life descends upon the rattled and dusty bones of those who will again live :: — :: Dalkey Archive, first among equals ; Melville House, aptly named ; Dedalus Books, please ; John Calder, server of more=please ; Dzanc Books, bless'd be thy name ; Coffee House Press, without which, no books ; Persephone Books, yes ; NYRB Classics, name says it all ; David R. Godine, where Gass and Theroux and others have stop'd for a BREATHER ; Pushkin Press, we thank thee ; Sun & Moon Press, righteousness under these two signs ; FC2, who pub'd those BIRTH'd and BURIED on the same day ; Red Lemonade Press, without which none ; Green Integer, intrepid ; New Directions shall do just that by showing us too the Directions of the Past=over ; ; ; ; HE=ROSE and SHE=ROSE, all ; through these Breathing Houses they ROSE — from the grave

they A=ROSE.

48.   And even now they A-RISE!!

49.   We name NAMES ;; with NAMES we summon ;; we re-member the name and we sing a name ; incantations and sacred chants are made which will weave in memory and in recog-nition the not-yet known, trans-formed into the known and the READ by a READ'er whose thirst is work'd upon by the ever thirsty work of undoing the in-justice which has been done to The BrOOKe ; OUR bRookE ;; each and every book which will become flesh again. Amen.

We champion and we ad=VOC=ate and we NOM-in-ATE:: Let us praye and re=member ::

50.   Alan Burns, Paul Ableman, Hélène Cixous, Ilse Aichinger, Fielding Dawson, Fernando Ar-rabel, Chandler Brossard, Paul Chamberland, Emmanuel Bove, François Augiéras, Johannes Bobrowski, William Demby, Lise Deharme, Pío Baroja, Elizabeth Bisland, Martin Bax, Angus Peter Campbell, Guy Davenport, Hob Broun, Jens Bjørneboe, Paul Blackburn, Giambattista Basile, Brigid Brophy, Andrei Bitov, Os-well Blakeston, Vance Bourjaily, Alfred Döblin, Michael Ayrton, Ella Cara Deloria, Bertram Brooker Andrey Bely, Marcel Bénabou, Raymond Decapite, Hariri of Basra, James B. Hall, Lise Dharme, Julien Gracq, George Egerton, Pamela Hans-ford Johnson, Graeme Gibson, MacDonald Harris, Alonso de Er-cilla y Zúñiga, Henry Blake Fuller, Ben Hecht, Wison Harris, Andrew Hoyem, Max Finstein, Ross Feld, Zulfikar Ghose, Arne Garborg, Fergus Hume, Juan Ramón Jiménez, Hans Henny Jahnn, Eva Figes, Rayner Hep-penstall, Elena Garro, Ronald Johnson, Enrique Anderson Im-bert, Gert Hofmann, Wolfgang Hilbig, Pitigrilli, Tommaso Landolfi, Valery Larbaud, Albert Murray, Nadezhda Mandelstam, John Cowper Powys, Aziz Nesin, Walter Mehring, Nelly Kaplan, Tom Mallin, T.F. Powys, Stuart Mitchner, Aleksey Pisemsky, Dambudzo Marechera, Jerzy Peterkiewicz, Claude Ollier,

Nivardus, Wyndham Lewis, Don McNeill, Robert Pinget, Michael McClure, Wolfgang Koeppen, Frank Kuppner, Charles Newman, Olive Moore, Elaine Kraf, R.M. Koster, Irmtraud Morgner, Thomas S. Klise, Henry Parland, Compton Mackenzie, José Lezama Lima, Paul Metcalf, Giovanni Orelli, Christoph Meckel, Wallace Markfield, Georg Christoph Lichtenberg, Cyrus Leo Sulzberger II, Gerald Murnane, Marquis de Pelleport, Harry Mathews, Fernando Del Paso, Bill Ripley, Raja Rao, Wilfrid Sheed, Vadim Shefner, Shota Rustaveli, Parker Tyler, Morris Renek, Maythil Radhakrishnan, June Akers Seese, Alberto Savinio, Fernando Sorrentino, David Shetzline, Ann Quin, Michel Serres, Michael Servetus, Marie Redonnet, William Sansom, Mitch Sisskind, Luisa Valenzuela, Carl Van Vechten, Douglas Woolf, Heinrich Wittenwiler, John Wieners, Jonathan Williams, Jakob Wasserman, Douglas Woolf, Helen Waddell, Fred Wander, Grete Weil, Paul West, Béla Zsolt.

51.   These names we re=member and we re=collect as scatter'd ash returns to living and fleshly life.

52.   Not BURN'd :: not Ban'd :: but worse!!?!!? ——:: BURIED!!!!

53.   OBLIVION!!!! UNSUNG!!!! ;; Shovel=ready!

Let us praye ....;

54.   And too we prayerfully and mournfully remember the names even our sacred practice has forgotten fully to obscurity but whose names may one day be resurrected to our ears, to our eyes, to our reading ;; that in bottom's dream the work of the Spade=Wielders, those who wield the spade in the most Righteous name of Christine Brooke-Rose, may unEARTH yet more of the BURIED against whom Those Who Would Know Best have done immense injustice by casting them into, not hellfire, but BURIAL and into would-be eternal obscurity.

55.   But with our own eternal READ'ing we shall not rest ;; wresting from the darkness the BooKs which bring Light.

56.   Whether in flesh or yet in spirit, as still-living-TREES or as bits-n-bytes, a new body will descend as a (b)rea(d/t)hing happens—just here among these leaves.

Let us praye ....;

57.   Our prAYErs are for those who have gone before, whose bones are soil=encased, whose flesh may have pass'd but whose pages are still here, moldy on the corner and slightly tinged with a mildew, a mildew which may become mild=dew of morning resurrection, to mourn no more but to REad! to REad!

58.   And our prayers are for those who in the flesh yet draw some breath but whose pages are threaten'd even if not by the flame but with the dank of earth ;; those authors which may yet walk the earth's crust but with their books, their pages, their WORLD neglected, cover'd over, EN=earth'd.

59.   Even as we breath life and spiWRIT in those who have passed on and were passed by ;; so too we defend with mighty Spade (for the Spade is mightier even than the prAYEr, oUR=prayer) AGAINST the burial of what is already forgotten, even if whisper'd here and there by the few, the chosen, the Spade=Wielders.

60.   And the ones who will come, when they come in the name of those who have gone before, that by incantations of the names of the BURIED and of the sAINTs they may themselves resist Those Who Would Know Best ;; but to take the risk of writing what needs=must be BURIED; who yet refuse that BURIAL—we will not wield our Spades in vain. Not us.

61.   And we have prAYE'd ;; we have said AYE to life, to the BURIED.

62.   In the name of SlÀINTe Christine Brooke-Rose (we)-AM'en.

63.   I have spoken and have prayed our "we" for us and unto us, that it may be by us ;;; to praye with you, to praye for you, to have borrowed your voice and to have joined with you in a "we", that in a solitary

enterprise of LETTERS we may join our voices in rich Hosannas which will Raise the dead and unEARTH our sacred BOOks!!!

64.   Next when we shall pray again as readers we shall hear our prayers spoken by a voice both old and new to whom we shall once again lend our "we" that we may hear ourselves spoken, our words breathe'd, loudly our prAYErs praye'd, the dead raise'd once more and the BURIED unEARTH'd as ROSE.

Heaven's Hospital

Christine Brooke-Rose

They say we are all dying of cancer in the soul
from inhaling too long, too much, the smoke of hell.

And so I sit with my cheek poised on three fingers,
posing for my own photograph to authority
who has hidden herself like a lenten statue
under a cloak of *noche oscura*.
The angels will develop it in my next dream
there being no dark room in eternity.
And they will see an X-ray of my spirit
with a great crab crawling sideways through it
around the zodiac of my days.

Then the white nurses, hanging up their wings
on the wall, strap my wrists and ankles
with little rubber tubes to take recordings
of my heart, the auricle a hill, a chasm
a peak, the ventricle a mound, a plain,
the graph quite normal.
Were they to cast it on a tape the song
would be monotonous and repetitive,
the song of my heart would be brief and repetitive.
And the angels hang up their wings on a cloud
and file away the song in the *terzo cielo*.

The doctor examines us now and again
listening to Ah ! and Ninety-Nine.
He examines always in silence.
But the angels hang up their wings on a cloud
and cure us with the radium of their radiance.

Postscript: What Tess Would Have Said

D. Lecter

and so it is that Angland is left behind, practically not politically, unless the dissolution of *to love and to cherish in sickness and in health till death tears apart* is considered constitutionally incorrect, to undertake the keeping of body if not soul as indentured mechanic of Amerrycanna Textual Vehicles at the Vince Anne Polytechnique de Belle Litters in Paris after the student uproarings.

No longer Janek's Kotek: revelling in freedom from conjugal complexities—Ian's ring transferred back to the left hand—although not from poverty and thus obliged to petition for two advances to obtain the Caravelle—full of quarrelled-over books—to cross Channel and attain Continent (will Tess ever make Europe?), Tess journeys first to the Castello of Vengeful Jokers to work, in a mere five weeks, on a manuscript *Do Rae Mi: A-Z Pun'd'Ore*, there succoured by the daughter of the famous *cantante*, before finally arriving in Paris demoralised and mostly destitute.

Difficulties are a result of *bêtise administrative*; the flip-side to *art de vivre à la française*, normalised by inertia. Demolished by Janek's petty fascination with *art de la jalousie*—the tender insistence on remembrance of Tess while *dans les bras* of Fiona with the bouffant black hair and enkohled eyes—Tess must reconstruct Tess-*même*, amidst pedantogoguy, harangoguy, dogmagoguy, violent strikes and monolinguy students, luckily, for the latter can be educated with entertainment, academically speaking. SHIT squeaks the chalk on the blackboard, giggling revolution into respect.

But *le système administratif* will impart only the ability to despair resignedly; Tess, in straits more dire than shared in student days and after with Janek, makes the fatal mistake of mocking *en face du toubib* the pre-requisite medical check-up *je n'ai pas d'une infestation tropiquale.*

Eh, Madam? Qu'est-ce que ça veut dire? Vous êtes une vraie petite comique? Who laughs last laughs loudest and longest: the humourless medico declares Tess unfit for work, although Tess is already working, remaining unpaid for six months until the appeal for the work permit is successful.

The old lady's fingers still on the keyboard of memory as the telephone rings—Lobelia, an English friend, arriving shortly, suggesting where to eat for lunch, the much-appreciated restaurant of the last visit? The old lady concurs, but requests the favour of Lobelia driving there, since the orange parking card, *de rigueur* for senior citizens, has yet to arrive. Oh heavens, the UK health system is atrocious enough, but this is outrageous. Of course Lobelia agrees to drive.

Recounting afterwards to the old lady's *kiné*, having seen Lobelia's card and confirming the existence of such, despite the administration claiming the card should be the blue handicapped variety, unnecessary and unwanted. The same section responsible for allocating Lobelia the orange parking permission insisting to the old lady, for many months now, no such concession exists.

Ah, the physiotherapist smiles, shrugging. *Il faut que tu dises, mon dieu, comme vous êtes intelligent, est-ce que possible de traduire ce document.* But the old lady will give up on the task of applying for the permit after reversing the car and colliding with the front gate, relegating driving to the buffers of memory, just as Tess will learn that criticism is futile: *plus ça change, plus c'est la même chose, c'est la maladie française*, because the entire bureaucracy is destined to create the most effort for the public for the least amount of result for the administration, producing not only *à chacun un goût personnel, mais pour chacun-même* as well, and the inevitable recurrence of riot and revolution. Tess nods, it has taken four years to connect the fixed line telephone, exactly, agrees the old lady, and three months for the email address and the internet cable.

Looking for the Préfecture, the holy temple of the *carte de séjour*, Tess slows the Caravelle along a trafficless boulevard and asks the assistance *s'il vous plaît monsieur* of a whistle-toting gentile arm, who directs Tess to park the British-licensed *voiture* somewhere, anywhere, and to return and ask for help after. Tess reiterates the request and the John d'Harm refuses to give directions, until the boulevard is *plein de vautures bruyantes.* Gallic nostrils flaring, *bien Madame, après le pont, premier à gauche.* At the Préfecture, a young Asian girl is dismissed from the reception desk for a trivial mistake on the application documents; Tess, Caucasian, walking forwards, is welcomed with a furious nod in the girl's direction: *et ça c'est une future francaise?!?* *Mon dieu!* Tess renews the permit ten years hence and asks will the waiting time be long? Waiting time? Long? What a joke, sniffing and disdaining eye-contact, the well-to-do wait for none. *Ethnicisme à l'envers.*

But the experience deepens the ability to empathise with the other, first learned at Bletchley: Tess realises the plight of what other immigrants and refugees must suffer, infinitely worse; what xenophobia Janek, Polish and in exile, must have experienced in Angland; why Janek, recently offered a prestigious Chair of Polish Studies at an American university, not offered the same in London because of the Polish surname—prejudices, such as fewer intellectual positions for ethnic groups and women, still flourish—has turned the position down. The thought of another mammoth cultural adjustment being too much of a deterrent. However, clever as always, Janek leaves the offer letter on the writing desk while meeting with the Head of School, and is offered the Chair, some months later, in London.

Tess learns exile is a force majeure for reinvention of It-entity. The second career blossoms as lecturer, academic, writer, guest-speaker and teacher in the US, Central America, Canada, the Middle East, Middle Europe, holidaying in all the most exciting locales, producing her phictions and phactions and hobnobbing with the literary in-spires, Barfs, Krystal Eve, Sikh Su, Foo Koh, Luck On, Todo Rover, as colleague and not object of litter ratter critischism, frustratingly, for Tess longs less for intercourse and more for discourse, despite the recurring *en chaîne* proposals.

The old lady reclines in the ergochair, gazing out the open window at fields of gold. Yesterday having buried the very first writerly friend from those heady daze, may the skull rest in peace. The friend's very first book *Mnemopolis* influencing Tess' very eighth phiction—

Nonsense! Soddy-memory. The skull had nothing to do with it.

Oh John, pipe down. Elapse. It was a three-decade friendship. The skull would have been happy with that epitaph. The language of the quotidian creates space for the language of the imagination, but the twain seldom meet.

As Tess knows only too well, when approached by a French publisher wishing to release the novel *Amonangst*, on condition that Tess translate it to French and adopt a soddy gnome Tessaé for the purposes of being presented as hom(e) grown. Tess, however, although multilexi*belle*, finds French inflexible, and steps after Beckett, rather than pioneering *avant* the guard, are not appealing. Declining the offer, Tess is thereafter deprived of entrée in the Guillemot rites of Circé & Co.

Tess-pitifying will lead a John anywhere.

John-sight is just as redundant if the not-cited lead the blind.

The tantrically-typographed Tess creates critic confusion with the release of the final preposition in the tetralogy. Sir Hamish Hamilton regretfully refuses relationship continuity and Tess decides to produce a science-fiction narrative in the strictest conventional sense, proving plotability and imagining a breast-seller. On reading *The Alphaguys*, a second publisher laments that Tess' signature innovative style is sadly missed, after having just rejected *Amonangst*. The nature of showbusiness: out of which such performances are between fortunes, the characters through with the directors.

During semester breaks, Angland is revisited, friendships refreshed, consideration given to *retraite dans le Midi* or retiring in Kent Wiltshire Surrey with pigs and a biddy. London, once epicentre of excitement, is now *très fatiguant*, and a bobby there no less barbaric than the counterpart across the Channel. Indeed, Tess feels no longer an English rose abroad, but Britishly unassimilated, having learned to love *la vie française*.

So much that *petit fiancé* and cousin, Jean-Luc, lost to distance when *Oncle* Francis and *Tante* Mathilde move to the *Avenue de l'Opale* in Brussels to care for *grandpère* and Joanne and Tess are packed off to boarding school in Hampshire, prevails with a proposal and Tess is once more, for the third and last time, quietly wed.

This can hardly happen at the same time, John the pedant pokes. Forty years interim since at least the fourteenth split.

Hush John! Run-time memory.

It is a union, albeit momentary, of puissance, from which a single issue is produced, one of Tess' most successful novels, ending the nine-year intermission separating the Tetralogy of Prepositions and the Intercomm Quartet and sparking publication in numerous markets, discussion in other than literary magazines, a resurgence of form, even if some critics will complain Tess is now too accessible, far from maintaining the mystique as magnificently exigent. Aside from interviews and continuing to guest-speak, Tess avoids publicity, avoids the roadshows and the rounds of parties and back-rubbing reviews, happy to escape the hoop of hype.

But it was so important at the time! So nonchalant now. John *le méchant loup* hoists *die Lupe*.

A fly buzzes through the window, sits on the keyboard where the keys are silent, unmoving. Buzzes outside to the other flies zooming through the blooms. To integrate or not to integrate, that is the question. The last solitary act of creativity, writing perpendicular to the expectations of publisher and public.

Unlike Janek, now fêted in the home country and accepted in the adopted land, Tess has become the furriner, and moreover, ignored; books out of print, out of criticism, out of whatever fashion perhaps once enjoyed. But preferring to feel between places in the south of France than between phases in Angland, enjoying the uprootedness of childhood once more: Switzerland for being neither here nor there, Belgium for being always a part of somewhere else. It-entity fractured scattered restructured; the old lady living alone but not lonely in the house at the end of the brook.